Collateral Damages

CALIFORNIA SERIES IN PUBLIC ANTHROPOLOGY

The California Series in Public Anthropology emphasizes the anthropologist's role as an engaged intellectual. It continues anthropology's commitment to being an ethnographic witness, to describing, in human terms, how life is lived beyond the borders of many readers' experiences. But it also adds a commitment, through ethnography, to reframing the terms of public debate—transforming received, accepted understandings of social issues with new insights, new framings.

Series Editor: Ieva Jusionyte (Brown University)

Founding Editor: Robert Borofsky (Hawaii Pacific University)

Advisory Board: Catherine Besteman (Colby College), Philippe Bourgois (UCLA), Jason De León (UCLA), Laurence Ralph (Princeton University), and Nancy Scheper-Hughes (UC Berkeley)

Collateral Damages

TRACING THE DEBTS AND
DISPLACEMENTS OF THE IRAQ WAR

Nadia El-Shaarawi

UNIVERSITY OF CALIFORNIA PRESS

University of California Press
Oakland, California

© 2025 by Nadia El-Shaarawi

All rights reserved.

Library of Congress Cataloging-in-Publication Data

Names: El-Shaarawi, Nadia, author.
Title: Collateral damages : tracing the debts and displacements of the
    Iraq War / Nadia El-Shaarawi.
Other titles: California series in public anthropology ; 60.
Description: First edition. | Oakland, California : University of
    California Press, [2025] | Series: California series in public
    anthropology ; 60 | Includes bibliographical references and index.
Identifiers: LCCN 2024042512 (print) | LCCN 2024042513 (ebook) |
    ISBN 9780520392120 (cloth) | ISBN 9780520392137 (paperback) |
    ISBN 9780520392144 (ebook)
Subjects: LCSH: Refugees—Iraq—21st century. | Iraq War,
    2003-2011—Refugees.
Classification: LCC HV640.5.I76 E48 2025 (print) | LCC HV640.5.I76
    (ebook) | DDC 362.8709567—dc23/eng/20250207
LC record available at https://lccn.loc.gov/2024042512
LC ebook record available at https://lccn.loc.gov/2024042513

GPSR Authorized Representative: Easy Access System Europe,
Mustamäe tee 50, 10621 Tallinn, Estonia, gpsr.requests@easproject.com

34 33 32 31 30 29 28 27 26 25
10 9 8 7 6 5 4 3 2 1

Contents

	Acknowledgments	vii
	Note on Transliteration	xi
	Introduction: Departure	1
1.	"Bad History": Imperial Unknowing and the Iraq War	31
2.	War Archive: Telling and Listening to War Stories	61
3.	Living in the Transit City: Seeking Refuge, Refusing Refugeeness	89
4.	Negotiating Humanitarian "Solutions" to Displacement: Iraqis' Experiences of the Refugee Resettlement Process in Cairo	123
5.	Allies and Enemies: Resettlement and the Conditionality of Iraqis' Relations with US Empire	153
	Conclusion: Arrival	184
	Notes	193
	References	213
	Index	235

Acknowledgments

The process of writing this book has been an exercise in some of its main themes: an undertaking of many years only made possible through supportive webs of relation and debts that will always remain unpayable. The people to whom I owe the most gratitude are the Iraqis who not only made this work possible at every stage but who have marked my life indelibly. I want to thank the many people who welcomed me into their homes, shared daily life with me, and so patiently and generously narrated their experiences, stories, struggles, and triumphs during a challenging time in their lives. In moments of uncertainty and hardship, I recall your grace, dignity, and steadfastness and try to achieve some poor approximation of it. I am committed to an ethnography that regards the theorizations of its interlocutors as coequal to those of the ethnographer. To protect their privacy, I am unable to name them, but any bits of truth or wisdom in these pages are not mine alone. I hope this book does justice to the narratives and experiences with which you generously entrusted me.

Also in Cairo, I am grateful to the late Barbara Harrell-Bond for first inviting me into the work that would turn into this book and for encouraging me to continue. The Center for Migration and Refugee Studies at the American University of Cairo, long a hub for important work on displacement in Egypt

viii   ACKNOWLEDGMENTS

and the region, was also a space of learning, support, and academic fellowship. I am especially grateful to the humanitarian workers and volunteers whom I worked alongside and whom I also cannot name but who have also contributed significantly to this work as well as to RLAP, which continues to offer refugees access to legal support in a context where they would otherwise not have access to representation.

This project began when I was a graduate student in anthropology and public health at Case Western Reserve University. I received much valuable guidance and advice as well as unconditional encouragement from professors, staff, and fellow students in the Department of Anthropology and the Master of Public Health program. Thanks are especially due to Eileen Anderson-Fye, Atwood Gaines, Janis Jenkins, Jill Korbin, Janet McGrath, and Scott Frank. The project has shifted a lot over the years, but your support has been unwavering throughout. Bridget Haas has read probably every word of this book twice and is an indefatigably kind interlocutor; thank you for your friendship and your companionship throughout the long and daunting task of book writing.

In North Carolina, I found a home and supportive friends in the Kenan Institute for Ethics and Duke Islamic Studies Center at Duke University as well as in the Department of Anthropology and especially the Moral Economies of Medicine working group at the University of North Carolina, Chapel Hill. The members throughout the years of our long-standing writing group have sat with this project for as long as it has taken, and I am grateful for their generative comments on many drafts of this book: thanks are due to Doerte Bemme, Mara Buchbinder, Jocelyn Chua, Lauren Fordyce, Tomas Matza, stef shuster, Harris Solomon, and Saiba Varma.

In Maine, I am grateful for the encouragement of my colleagues in Global Studies and Anthropology as well as to the Provost's Office and the College for funding and time to complete this manuscript. I am also indebted to capable and adept research assistants, each of whom has left their mark on this project in some way: Conall Butchart, Maimouna Cherif, Charles Gauvin, Pheobe Sander, and Ira Mukherjee, who made it possible to finally get this book across the finish line. Chandra Bhimull, Audrey Bruneteaux, Laura Fujikawa, Britt Halvorson, Annie Hikido, Mary Beth Mills, Gwynn Shanks, and Winifred Tate read drafts and offered constructive ideas. The Vulnerable Bodies Collective read early versions of part of the book and has remained a source of strength and softness throughout this process and everything—Alicia Ellis, Rebeca Hey-Colón, and Jay Sibara: our friendship is one of the great gifts of this profession.

In Montreal, I was lucky to have space to think and be in generative and creative academic community in the Division of Social and Transcultural Psychiatry, the Department of Anthropology, and the Refugee Research Group at McGill University. Laurence Kirmayer offered an intellectual home during a sabbatical spent at the Culture and Mental Health research unit. I am especially grateful to Diana Allan for ongoing support and inspiration. Diana and Megan Bradley graciously made possible a book workshop where I was able to share parts of this manuscript; it made a transformative difference for me, not least because of their organizing work and brilliant feedback from discussants Carole McGranahan, who graciously read and offered comments on the entire book, Lama Mahrous and Nayrouz Abou Hatoum, all of whom offered comments and suggestions that have improved the work tremendously. And of course Deniz Duruiz—my partner in book workshopping—as well as Neha Vora, Lisa Stevenson, Natasha Bissonauth, Anna Shah Hoque, and the other generous and thoughtful attendees. In the time of COVID and beyond, I am held by the scholarly and supportive friendship of Kiran Sunar, Doerte, Nayrouz, Anna, Natalie Kouri-Towe, Sarah Berry and others who were such good company during that challenging time. The brilliant Megha Sharma Sehdev shared many early book writing sessions with me and her passing is a tremendous loss to anthropology but more so to the world.

I would like to express my gratitude to the series editor of the California Series in Public Anthropology, Ieva Jusionyte, who was an inspiration even before she took on my project but is even more so now. Her encouragement and feedback have improved this work so much. I am also appreciative of the capable editing and thoughtful insights of Kate Marshall and Chad Attenborough at UC Press. I could not have been in better hands. Thanks also go to the anonymous reviewers for their constructive and generative comments and suggestions. The brilliant Sundus Abdul Hadi (www.sundusabdulhadi.com) graciously allowed her work to be reproduced on the book cover. I feel so lucky to have the book adorned with the work of an artist who I have long admired.

Parts of chapters 3 and 4 are excerpts from articles previously published in *Social Analysis* and *American Ethnologist*. I have presented parts of this research at Brown University, Duke University, Harvard University, King's College, McGill University, the University of Maine, and the University of North Carolina, among other places, and I am grateful for the opportunity to think through my work and to audiences for thoughtful questions and comments that have helped me to refine the ideas presented here. The research for this project was funded by the Canadian Institutes of Health Research, the National Science Foundation, Case Western Reserve University, Duke University, and Colby College.

To my aunts, uncles, and cousins, thank you for taking such good care of me and enveloping me in the warmth of family during my time in Cairo. Getting to spend time with you all was the biggest gift of my fieldwork and I will cherish it always. To my beloved Tant who housed me and fed me and nurtured me when I was ill or just stressed—you may have teased me for always working but you made the space around all that work one of home. My mother and father show me every day me what can grow out of curiosity, a desire to have scholarship intersect with lived concerns, and collaboration. I will never live up to what you two have accomplished and I admire who you are so much. None of this would be possible or worth doing without my younger but wiser sister Sarah. Maple Razsa has been such a generous and challenging interlocutor and a supportive presence when I needed it most. Thank you for reading every page, for talking through every idea, for pushing me to keep going, and for being my best friend in Maine (and everywhere).

There are many others to whom I am indebted in ways close and distant. To all those whose traces are in my life or on these pages in some way: Thank you.

Note on Transliteration

I have transliterated the Arabic terms in this book using a modification of the simplified system of the *International Journal of Middle East Studies*. I have elected to forgo most diacritics, especially in names, for simplicity and accessibility to non-Arabic speakers. If the name of a place or a person has a common rendering in English, I have used it. Occasionally I have adjusted some transliterations to reflect either Iraqi or Egyptian dialects, as appropriate. When applicable, I have used alternative spellings to be faithful to the transliteration used by people themselves.

Introduction

DEPARTURE

We stood in Cairo Airport's old terminal, scanning the crush of people, bags, and luggage carts for Um Muhammad and her family.[1] It was the spring of 2010 and my friend Haydar and I had come to say goodbye. After four years of exile in Egypt, Um Muhammad and her family were finally leaving to begin a new life in Oklahoma, in a state and a country where they had never been and where they knew no one.

I was feeling a bit breathless, partly out of jumbled feelings of nervousness and excitement for my friends as they embarked on this long-awaited journey and partly because we had rushed to the airport and then rushed through the terminal, afraid we would arrive too late. Um Muhammad had initially told us that the flight would leave at 1:00 a.m. But earlier that day she had called us from the Cairo office of the International Organization for Migration (IOM), where she had been called in to finish some last-minute paperwork. She sounded harried. "They changed the flight. It's at 8:30 p.m. now. Can you still make it?" Um Muhammad and her family had spent years navigating the resettlement process. Its interlocking bureaucracies seemed to move at a snail's pace, with no regard for the temporal strictures and milestones of the human lifespan. Birthdays, graduations, engagements, illnesses, holidays all passed as the process

2   INTRODUCTION

inched forward. Then for eleven agonizing months it ceased moving entirely when Um Muhammad's final security clearance did not appear alongside the rest of the family's, raising the fear that she had been flagged as a threat and would not be permitted to travel with them. Now, after so much waiting, the end was in sight, and it was suddenly accelerating. I thought about how out of control it all felt, both the months of painful, slow waiting and then, in the final hours, the lost moments for preparations and goodbyes when their flight was moved up on the very day of travel.

But Um Muhammad didn't complain about the change, at least not to me. She had become used to creating pockets of control even when things felt uncontrollable. In an earlier life in Baghdad, she had been active in the Women's Union while working full time as an accountant, raising a family, and managing a household. Um Muhammad loved meeting people, socializing, organizing things, working. As the violence escalated in the years following the US-led invasion and occupation of Iraq, she was the one who reluctantly decided that their Sunni-majority neighborhood had become too dangerous for their mixed-sect family. She was also the one who had selected Egypt as their place of escape partly because of the educational opportunities Cairo offered for her two youngest children, still in the midst of their studies.

At times she regretted that decision. Once in Egypt, Um Muhammad found a life more constricted and less temporary than she had hoped. The lack of resources reminded her of the years of the US-backed sanctions when Iraqi women, including herself, learned to make things at home that they could no longer procure because of the blockade.[2] But the waiting was the hardest to endure. In the months before her resettlement, Um Muhammad and I had become friends while working long days together at the legal aid clinic where I was conducting ethnographic research and where Um Muhammad worked as a peer psychosocial counselor. We had many discussions about the violence of the imposed uncertainties of the resettlement process and how she and other Iraqis sought to cultivate patience (*sabr*) in the face of it. In an earlier conversation, she had explained the source of her fortitude to me: "What we faced in Iraq was really difficult. What we have here in Egypt is not more difficult than what we dealt with in Iraq from the 1980s until now. The thing that helps me is that I know that this is what God wants. We have to stay strong. At least in front of our children. We cannot be weak in front of them." Now after four years of testing this strength in exile in Cairo, she was on the threshold of a new and unknown future in the United States.

Haydar and I spotted the family across the departure hall and hurried to join them. As we approached, I saw that Um Muhammad, Abu Muhammad, their daughter Zahra, and their son Abdallah stood in a loose group with five other Iraqi families who were also traveling that evening. Everyone was dressed formally. Many of the women wore pendants in the shape of the map of Iraq around their necks, the gold glinting as it caught the harsh overhead light.

A bit removed from the group, standing under fake palm trees that offered little shade from the glare of perpetual airport daytime, stood two employees of the IOM, one Egyptian and one American, each holding clipboards and wearing ID badges. A small and solemn ritual of departure was occurring as each traveling family handed over their United Nations High Commissioner for Refugees (UNHCR)–issued yellow asylum cards to receive large white plastic bags emblazoned in the center with a conspicuous blue IOM logo and their name and case number written in thick marker along the top. The documentation that had marked them as refugees in Egypt was exchanged for the bags, which visibly signaled their impending resettlement. Unlike the yellow card, which could be stuffed in a purse or a pocket until needed, the bags were to be carried, stapled closed with their contents undisturbed, for the duration of the trip, making the purpose of their travel easily identifiable to case workers on the other side as well as to airport and airline personnel and any travelers who might happen to recognize the iconography of refugee resettlement.

While he waited to receive his IOM bag, Abu Muhammad worried aloud about how he was going to pay the US government back for the airplane tickets. Resettlement is often described as a humanitarian program, but the flight that refugees take to actually come to the United States is not offered as aid but is instead a loan that they are expected to repay. Before being allowed to travel, Abu Muhammad had to sign a promissory note stating that he would begin making payments for the family's four tickets just six months after arriving in the United States. "The US Government pays people to go back to Iraq," he mused, citing

4   INTRODUCTION

recent US and UN efforts to incentivize some of the then nearly three million Iraqi refugees to return, "but when it brings us to the United States, we have to pay our own travel." Although addressed to me, Abu Muhammad's words were spoken just loudly enough to cut through loud-speaker flight announcements and the ambient din of the terminal. The IOM employees made no sign that they had heard.

A large and boisterous crowd of young men, Abdallah's friends from university, arrived en masse to say their goodbyes. Um Muhammad took us aside and told us that many of them, like Abdallah, had just graduated. They were unsure what their future would hold since they could not return to Iraq and were not permitted to work legally in Egypt. Unlike Abdallah, few of them were likely to be resettled to another country. Tonight, they celebrated and grieved as they saw their friend off, hugging him tightly one by one. Each goodbye was more tearful than the last. In their midst, I noticed Abdallah was quiet and looked uneasy.

The young men moved from Abdallah to say goodbye to the whole family, calling Um Muhammad *khala* and Abu Muhammad *'amu*, terms of respect and affection. The flight's departure time drew nearer and it was soon time for us to say goodbye too. We embraced and Um Muhammad squeezed my hand and held it. "How are you feeling?" I asked, feeling the warmth of her hand around mine. "Scared!" Um Muhammad and Zahra answered almost in unison before breaking into nervous laughter. We hugged once more and then Haydar and I watched them walk through the metal detectors towards the departure gate, our eyes following them until they receded from view.

COLLATERAL DAMAGES

Um Muhammad and her family's journey from Cairo to Oklahoma took place almost exactly seven years from the day that the United States and the United Kingdom had led the invasion and occupation of Iraq. It was an improbable odyssey and certainly one that Um Muhammad had not imagined when the bombardment of Baghdad began in the spring of 2003 nor when she had moved to Cairo in 2006, thinking and hoping that it might be safe to return to Iraq in a matter of months, if not sooner.

Instead, after years spent in Egypt, the family was relocating to the United States, first as refugees but eventually, perhaps, as citizens.

How are we to make sense of the subjective experience of being on the cusp of resettlement, especially for an Iraqi family about to move, perhaps permanently, to the country responsible for their displacement in the first place? It might be tempting to think of Um Muhammad and her family's departure from Cairo as the beginning of a new story—a humanitarian rescue—and indeed, most of the literature on refugee resettlement and asylum begins either at the terrestrial borders of or within countries of the Global North. While it would not be incorrect to think of that night in the airport as a new beginning, it also marked the end of four years of exile in Egypt as well as the continuation of events set in motion years earlier, perhaps with the US- and UK-led invasion of Iraq in 2003, perhaps with the brutal sanctions regime that lasted more than a decade and killed an estimated 500,000 children (Saleh 2020), perhaps with the Gulf War of 1990–91, perhaps even earlier. In order to make sense of the significance of Iraqi displacement and, for a few, resettlement, we have to follow these threads of recent and not so recent history. How did Um Muhammad and her family get to this threshold? What does it mean to attempt to rebuild lives shattered and dispersed by empire in the heart of the very empire that did the shattering? Does conceiving of Um Muhammad and her family's departure as a fresh start deny the multiple entanglements, the existing relationships, they already had with the US?

This book is an ethnography about war, displacement, and the possibilities or foreclosures of refuge, written not from the point of view of humanitarian organizations or from the vantage point of states that style themselves either, as the United States sometimes does, as "nations of refuge" or, as Egypt does, as "temporary hosts." Instead, in this book I foreground the experiences and stories of Iraqi refugees living in Egypt and take seriously their assertions of the kind of problem displacement represents and the kinds of solutions appropriate to it. Indeed, in the copious writing on the invasion and occupation of Iraq and in the smaller but still significant body of literature on the so-called Iraqi refugee crisis that the war precipitated, Iraqis' voices have been consistently underrepresented.[3] The absence of Iraqi voices is more than a question of representation. As in other circumstances where those most affected by an event or process

6   INTRODUCTION

are conspicuously missing from much of the discussion, their omission colors how one of the most controversial wars of the twenty-first century and the histories of violence that preceded and followed it are broadly understood and remembered, making it possible, at least in the West, for the Iraq War to be dismissed as a foreign policy blunder of the past and for Iraqi displacement to be represented ahistorically and apolitically as nothing more than a humanitarian crisis. The Iraqis I came to know in Egypt, such as Um Muhammad and her family, were living with two interconnected imperial interventions, war and humanitarianism, both of which explicitly or implicitly disavowed their understandings, aspirations, and experiences. Despite these elisions, Iraqis regularly drew my attention to forms of relatedness, including relations of obligation and indebtedness, that US imperial violence had generated but also sought to obscure. In what follows, I seek to understand how such erasures took place and their effects on Iraqis' lives.

Of the estimated thirty-seven million people displaced worldwide by the US-led War on Terror since 2001, more than nine million are from Iraq, the most of any single country (Vine et al. 2020). Between 2003 and 2018, at least three hundred thousand Iraqis were killed (Crawford 2019), a number that does not include the hundreds of thousands of people whose deaths could be attributed to the war-induced breakdown of infrastructure and associated illness, injuries, and malnutrition (Mazzarino et al. 2019; Savell 2023). It also does not include the lives lost—including nearly half a million children—during the devastating sanctions regime from 1990 to 2003, which Joy Gordon has referred to as an invisible war (Gordon 2010, 2020), though these sanctions were, of course, very much visible for Iraqis like Um Muhammad.[4] For those who remain in Iraq, the material infrastructure of the country and its very ecology bear the "toxic legacies of war" with attendant long-term health effects for current and future generations as well as for the larger environment (Rubaii 2020). Iraqis still grapple with the sectarian divisions imposed during the US-led occupation. The 2019 popular uprisings in Iraq, led by young Iraqis who would have been children during the 2003 invasion, were in part a rejection of those sectarian politics as well as the conditions of life (or lack thereof) in a state that has been systematically destroyed by decades of foreign intervention (Z. Ali 2020).

How do these examples of imperial violence as well as efforts to resist it relate to Um Muhammad and her family's travel? Refugee resettlement is often imagined as a benevolent form of rescue and an exceptional, if rare, humanitarian mechanism of protection. Resettlement is construed as a "solution" to displacement and, in the diplomatic and humanitarian language often applied to refugee situations, is understood as one important mechanism of what is known as "burden-sharing"—or the idea that countries unaffected by refugee crises should carry some of the responsibility either through hosting refugees directly or providing aid to refugees located in other countries (Betts 2015). Aside from the problematic and empirically untrue implication that refugees inherently constitute a burden on the states and societies that they join, this framing contains another troubling implication that I take on squarely in this book. Namely, the use of constructs such as "burden-sharing" helps to create metaphorical and literal distance between resettlement and the regimes of imperial war-making that cause displacement and motivate humanitarian responses. But, as Zainab Saleh (2020, 4–5) aptly argues, Iraqis have long been "imperial subjects," stretching back to the period of British colonial rule as well as more recent histories of US intervention. It is no coincidence that lines of resettlement often, but not always, follow lines of imperial war, occupation, and colonization.[5] It is also no coincidence that the irony and emotional weight of being resettled to the country responsible for their displacement was never acknowledged in the formal resettlement process. Part of the work of imperial violence is to untether and obscure these forms of relatedness. Drawing largely on displaced Iraqis' own understandings and demands, the work of this book is to surface and render visible the undeniable and fraught relationships that are forged by the violence of imperial intervention.

In the book's title, I reappropriate and reconfigure a common military euphemism to offer the concept of *collateral damages* as an analytic that foregrounds forms of relatedness that are integral to imperial war and its aftermaths, humanitarian and otherwise. In its singular military framing, *collateral damage* represents civilian casualties as a tragic yet inevitable consequence of war. In common parlance, it is often used to refer to accidental and unintended negative effects or harm. But this common understanding belies the way the military term is in fact quite calculating;

8   INTRODUCTION

militaries write collateral damage into their manuals, engage in legal training to avoid liability for civilian harm, and develop equipment and models to estimate and account for it. Instead of thinking of collateral damage as accidental harm to civilians during war, it can be better understood as "calculated indifference"—a planned and integral part of contemporary war that allows perpetrating states to simultaneously claim compliance with international law while also killing and injuring civilians (Whyte 2019).[6] In its military usage, collateral damage traces its history to the US war in Vietnam, where it was first used to describe incidents of friendly fire and the killing and injuring of civilians by US forces. However, it was not until the Gulf War of 1990–91 in Iraq that the US began using the language of collateral damage to justify the killing of civilians, blaming the Iraqi government for putting civilians in the way of their attacks (Whyte 2019). The concept of collateral damage has subsequently become a well-worn tool used to avoid responsibility for civilian harm in the armed conflicts associated with the Global War on Terror, including the 2003 invasion of Iraq.[7]

In a sense, the military euphemism of collateral damage is paradigmatic of the epistemological formations I excavate and challenge because it includes a twinned relationship between obfuscation and self-absolution, one that seeks to obscure and abnegate any sense of relatedness and responsibility. In its common usage, collateral damage seeks to render civilian deaths and injuries on the battlefield agentless and blameless if they are judged to be unintentional and/or a byproduct of military necessity. Importantly, collateral damage does not account for the damage to the infrastructure and land on which civilian life depends. Militaries can claim that they take measures to avoid collateral damage by moving populations or offering warnings while simultaneously destroying the conditions for civilian life and flourishing. Collateral damage, to the extent that it is part of the laws of war, seeks to "humanize" war. In the Global War on Terror, military planners promoted counterinsurgency doctrine as the "softer" side of war (Stone 2022). Yet despite these claims to softness and humanity, far more civilians than combatants have been harmed by the Global War on Terror. Counterinsurgency and terrorism rhetoric destabilizes and erodes the category of the civilian at the same time as it legitimates war and seeks to conceal war's violence (Khalili 2012; Stone 2022).

In the war on terror, collateral damage allows state perpetrators of violence to claim that they care about civilian harm while also abdicating their responsibility for the harms they commit (Whyte 2019).[8]

By contrast, *collateral damages* as I use it here returns to the root meaning of collateral, "together with," to trace Iraqis' multiple, changing, and enduring relationships with US empire, especially as they have been formed through military and humanitarian intervention.[9] In thinking with this togetherness, I ask difficult questions about the lived obligations, legacies, and relationships of imperial war and its aftermath and consider humanitarian responses, such as refugee resettlement, as inseparable from the conflict and displacement they claim to address.

Collateral damages as I conceive of it here is not only a reframing of relationships but an attempt at a radical shift of perspective. In his novel *The Book of Collateral Damage*, Sinan Antoon (2020) writes about an Iraqi bookseller, Wadood, who labors quixotically in occupied Baghdad to build an archive of war that captures the violence that is left out of more conventional accountings of collateral damage. In Wadood's archive, we read about how the war is experienced by beings, objects, and places as each narrates their own injuries and losses. We learn how the war looks and feels from the perspective of a bird, a horse, a tree, an artifact in a museum, a stamp album, and a rug, among others. The novel expands, specifies, and multiplies how we think of the damages of war—moving from an abstract and military-defined concept of collateral damage to one where those affected by war narrate their own relations to it. Inspired by Antoon's intervention and approach, I seek to compile a different kind of archive of war and displacement in which Iraqis' experiences and narratives, as they prioritize them, are foundational to an accounting of war's damages.

As a field, refugee studies has been criticized for being insufficiently historical, even "averse to history" (Marfleet 2007, 136). This tendency to theorize refugees outside of history contributes to the view of displacement as episodic crisis events, separate from histories of colonization, empire, and extraction (Mayblin 2017). In its military usage, collateral damage is also a static concept, focused on the immediacy of injury at the moment of violence. But the Iraqis I came to know in Egypt reminded me that the impact of war on their lives was not constrained by such limited temporal or spatial horizons nor, in their views, were the relations of debt,

10   INTRODUCTION

obligation, and responsibility that accrued as a result, regardless of whether or not the US acknowledged them.

Collateral damages, then, is not only about enumerating the many unacknowledged harms of war, but it also invokes damages in a reparative sense—that is, the compensation or restitution owed by the party that caused the harm. What is more, as Indigenous scholar Eve Tuck (2009) writes, research that aims to address the harms of colonization and imperialism all too often portrays affected communities as inherently damaged, which denies how people are so much more than their losses and also elides the forces of racism, colonization, and imperialism that are the cause of damage. At the same time, the lack of acknowledgment and accountability for the decades of serial war on Iraq and Iraqis cannot be disregarded.[10] Following the emerging field of critical refugee studies (Espiritu et al. 2022),[11] I have endeavored to attend to the unequal relationships that facilitate imperial war and displacement, to draw on refugee epistemologies especially when they are counter to or refuse militarized or humanitarian ways of knowing, and to attend to the ways that Iraqis struggled to rebuild livable lives on their own terms in the aftermath of war and displacement.

The call to collateral then, brings imperial war and humanitarianism together to both illustrate and counter how empire itself works to separate out regimes of war-making and humanitarian aid as discrete projects. To do so requires a double vision: to attend to experience on the specific terrain on which such politics are enacted—urban Cairo and Iraq, in this case—as well as to open a wider lens on the intertwinements of imperial war and humanitarianism in order to bring into a shared frame imperial war-making and the displacements it engenders. Situating Iraqis in both the urban space of Cairo and the geopolitical frame of empire within the context of the Global War on Terror challenges prevailing assumptions about refugees and provides evidence for new ways of thinking about displacement, humanitarianism, and empire. In addition, this book's focus on the intimate experiences of imperial relations over time moves away from a tendency to view refugees as humanitarianism's anonymous "third world" Other to instead trace the entanglements and complicities that tie us—those who are variously positioned in relation to the exercise of imperial violence—together in historically specific and uneven relationships.

INVASION AND OCCUPATION

On March 20, 2003, a US-led coalition invaded Iraq in what the US armed forces called, without any apparent trace of irony, "Operation Iraqi Freedom." The "coalition of the willing" was made up of some forty countries; after the United States, the most ardent supporter of the war was the United Kingdom, which had governed Iraq under the League of Nations mandate system during the early twentieth century. In the aftermath of the attacks of September 11, 2001, then US president George W. Bush justified the war on the pretext of Iraqi president Saddam Hussein's alleged possession of weapons of mass destruction, an assertion that has been shown to have been untrue. Other allegations, such as that Saddam Hussein's government supported al-Qaeda, also proved false. These representations of Iraq, and specifically Saddam Hussein, as a threat to international security were delivered alongside claims that the war was necessary to liberate and bring democracy to the Iraqi people. War was presented as a gift to Iraqi people, a framing that has been central to US empire building and to liberal war-making more generally and one that inevitably comes with the expectation of a debt to be repaid by those on the receiving end of these wars (M. T. Nguyen 2012).

The invasion was vigorously and vociferously opposed on a global scale. Even before the war began, it was clear to anyone paying attention that the claims of weapons of mass destruction as well as the likelihood that an invasion would be experienced by Iraqis as a gift of freedom or democracy were both unlikely to be true. On February 15, 2003, millions of people around the world demonstrated against the war.[12] It was, at that time, the largest mass protest in human history. Despite campaigns to mislead, intimidate, and otherwise coerce other states to participate, the invasion also failed to receive endorsement from the United Nations Security Council, clearly marking the war in contravention of international law. When politicians would later claim innocence at how long the war dragged out, how much it cost in resources and human lives, and how poorly it went, it is important to remember that there were plenty of voices warning against many of these consequences both before the invasion and during the occupation. These voices were disregarded, or in some cases silenced, by those intent on embarking on war.[13]

12   INTRODUCTION

The invasion, televised live and broadcast around the world, was rapid and forceful. In now-famous footage, explosions lit the still-dark sky over the Tigris River in shades of red and orange. I was a university student at the time. I watched the invasion unfold on live television from my parents' house in a suburb of Toronto, feeling helpless and realizing that neither the global antiwar movement, in which I had participated locally, nor admonition from the United Nations and other states had succeeded in stopping the invasion. As an Egyptian-Canadian from a Muslim family, the growing Islamophobia in the aftermath of 9/11 and the ever-present public debates around the war had a profoundly unsettling effect on me. Although the Canadian government had refused to formally join the coalition of the willing, Canada was not outside the ambit of empire.

The aerial bombardment was followed by troops flooding over the border from Kuwait, and by April 9, US forces had advanced on Baghdad. Despite more resistance than anticipated, the occupying forces seized the capital, taking over government facilities and ministries and ending Saddam Hussein's twenty-four-year rule. In a controversial and symbolic move, an iron statue of Saddam Hussein in Baghdad's Firdos Square was, after an unsuccessful attempt by a group of Iraqi men to fell the statue, toppled by US marines, its head covered with a US flag. The video was circulated widely as both visual metaphor of the toppling of the regime and alleged evidence of Iraqis' support for the invasion. For Iraqis abroad who had fled the persecution of the Saddam Hussein regime from the 1970s through the 1990s, the collective live viewing of the statue's fall represented a possibility for a new relationship with Iraq and the imagination that they might be able to return (Saleh 2018). For most Iraqis in Iraq, who were prohibited from owning satellite dishes by the sanctions and who had only sporadic access to electricity, the event was not experienced with the same immediacy. While it is true that many Iraqis both in the country and among the large diaspora were happy for the end of Hussein's authoritarian rule, this did not necessarily mean they welcomed the war. By May 1, 2003, George W. Bush stood on an aircraft carrier under a banner that read "mission accomplished" and proclaimed the war over.

President Bush was, of course, wrong. For millions of Iraqis and, indeed, for the US military and its allies, the war was far from over. While the date of the invasion can be pinpointed to the minute, the end (and, indeed, the beginning) of the war itself is much harder to locate and depends on the vantage point one takes. Many Iraqis I met traced a direct line from the Iran-Iraq War through the Gulf War of 1990–91 and the period of economic sanctions to the 2003 war and its aftermath. Some went even further back, speaking of the British Mandate period and its ongoing effects on their lives. While the 2003 invasion and occupation as well as the violence that followed may have been the proximate causes that compelled Iraqis to flee, to understand their experiences requires a longer view of this history. It is likewise difficult to pinpoint an end to war. Many analysts trace the rise of the Islamic State, the conflict in Syria, and subsequent unrest in the region as a whole to the 2003 war. The United States formally withdrew troops in 2011, but US military presence in Iraq continues. After an initial reduction that was in no way complete, US troops returned to Iraq in larger numbers in 2014 at the Iraqi government's request to lead an international coalition against the Islamic State. When the United States assassinated Iranian general Qasem Soleimani at the Baghdad airport in January of 2020, Iraq's Parliament (an institution itself founded under US occupation) passed a nonbinding but significant bill demanding that US troops leave the country (Baker 2020). While troop numbers have subsequently decreased, there is an "enduring presence" of the US military, State Department personnel, and private contractors (Baldor 2020). Liberal war is best understood not as a finite event but, as Mimi Thi Nguyen (2012, xi) writes, a "vital presence permeating our everyday." For the Iraqis whose stories I share here, their lives were forever changed by war and displacement. Many described the US invasion and occupation as among the most significant events of their lives, ones with enduring effects.

IMPERIAL UNKNOWING

Much has been written about the failures of the invasion and occupation of Iraq, including perhaps most notably the deceptions that were used to justify the invasion, the unwillingness of the media in the United States, Britain, and elsewhere to offer critical reporting during the lead up to the

14 INTRODUCTION

war, and the disastrous effects of the US-led administration's hubris in occupying the country, especially in the immediate aftermath of the invasion (Chandrasekaran 2006; Isikoff and Corn 2007). These critical perspectives have, over time, come to be the dominant narrative of a war that remains one of the central conflicts in the ongoing, geographically shifting US-led Global War on Terror. The controversial nature of the invasion as well as its seemingly interminable status as a "forever war" have spurred a plethora of accounting and accountability projects, seeking to document the costs, broadly defined, of the war.[14] Such efforts seek to counteract what is perhaps the prevailing sentiment, especially in the United States, that frames the war as a mistake, one that Americans would mostly like to forget.

To treat the Iraq War as a mistake or even as a failure is to participate in a form of imperial amnesia, which is especially troubling because of the ways that the war's ramifications continue to be felt and because of how the processes, institutions, and even people central to it remain influential in the political life of Iraq, the United States, Britain, and elsewhere, and, most crucially for the purposes of this book, in the everyday lives of Iraqis, both within Iraq and in the diaspora.[15] In this book, I argue that instead of conceptualizing the war as something that was known and might now be forgotten, the invasion and occupation of Iraq as well as its aftereffects can be better characterized by an assemblage of orientations and practices that I call *imperial unknowing*. I conceptualize imperial unknowing as a set of imperial practices, techniques, and dispositions rooted in ignorance, aporia, denial, hubris, and other forms of antiepistemology that seek to obscure forms of responsibility and relatedness and are thus integral to liberal imperial violence and the critical reevaluation of its collateral damages.

This book's focus on imperial unknowing is inspired by the Iraqis whom I came to know in Cairo, who repeatedly drew my attention to the weaponization of epistemological practices and assemblages in the context of the war, in displacement, and in the resettlement process. Abu Muhammad critiqued the US resettlement program's insistence that the airplane ticket was a loan because it forced Iraqis into relations of very literal debt even before they arrived in the United States—and though he didn't say so explicitly, surely he considered that the relationship of debt might run in the other direction. He made this critique aloud in the airport, even though he likely knew that the IOM workers would not acknowledge it or respond. Iraqis' theorizations connected these practices to their own experiences of displacement. They were therefore also the ones who encouraged me to see the imperial dimensions of unknowing, how unknowing is not simply an absence of knowledge but rather, as Eve Sedgwick (1988) writes, part of power's "magnetic field."

During my fieldwork in Cairo, where I conducted participant observation of the resettlement process and interviewed Iraqis about their experiences, I saw firsthand some of the ways that imperial unknowing, so present in the selling and prosecution of the war, persists in humanitarian spaces. I also saw the consequences of unknowing on Iraqis' lives. For example, Iraqis were subjected to humanitarian processes that allocated aid and resettlement on the basis of vulnerability, prioritizing some over others and pitting Iraqis against refugees of other nationalities in Egypt. Some Iraqis who either easily fit humanitarian categories of vulnerability (e.g., victims of torture, single mothers with multiple children, or unaccompanied minors) or who could effectively perform vulnerability benefitted from such categorizations, but many others were excluded. Vulnerability assessments were rarely accompanied by any form of discussion about how people became vulnerable in the first place, much less practices to try to repair the damages of imperial intervention and occupation. In this way, as I will show in more detail in the chapters to come, humanitarian processes in exile built on, reinforced, and extended forms of imperial unknowing that Iraqis encountered during war.

These same humanitarian processes sometimes figured Iraqis as unworthy or, worse, dangerous. In Cairo, there were only two official relationships Iraqis could have within the humanitarian order: they could be threatened, in need of rescue by humanitarian organizations or benevolent states, or they could be categorized as a threat. Iraqis were treated with suspicion by some humanitarian organizations and aid workers, imagined by some Egyptians as causing rents to rise, surveilled by the Egyptian state, which feared they might bring sectarian violence with them to Egypt, and subjected to extensive security screenings as part of the resettlement process by states, like the US, that represented them as possible national security threats. Sometimes, as I'll discuss in later

16   INTRODUCTION

chapters, Iraqis were simultaneously understood as both threat and threatened. But throughout my fieldwork, the Iraqis I came to know rejected these categories and insistently surfaced other forms of relatedness, ones that disrupted official attempts at unknowing and forgetting.

Iraqis have often been figured as objects of military or humanitarian intervention, and this tendency has been, perhaps unintentionally, reinforced in much scholarship that, as Omar Dewachi (2017, 10–11) has argued, in its paucity and its distance from the lives of Iraqis, inadvertently reifies imaginaries of Iraq as "dangerous," "unstable," or "ungovernable." Indeed, this characterization of Iraq and Iraqis is itself a form of imperial unknowing. In this book, I reject these tropes by reversing the direction of inquiry to read imperial intervention, both military and humanitarian, through the narratives and experiences of Iraqis who have been subject to it. To this end, I both catalog and elaborate *imperial unknowing*—and also amplify the forms of relatedness that Iraqis sought to make visible and knowable. Here then, is the second important dimension of imperial unknowing: how the forms of violence that it engenders are not only foundational to war and displacement but also persist and reappear in the humanitarian responses to that very displacement. Imperial unknowing seeks to obscure the relationships between war and displacement, imperial violence and humanitarianism. Tracing Iraqis' experiences from Iraq to exile and, in some cases, into resettlement renders visible what empire would prefer to keep hidden.

EXILE

To make sense of the imperial relations that Iraqis foreground and to consider how they help us to unsettle dominant ideas of imperial war, humanitarianism, and refugees, we need to consider how Iraqis like Um Muhammad and her family ended up living in exile in Cairo. The path they took to Egypt was not the one that humanitarian agencies or governments had imagined or planned. In 2002, when it became clear that the Bush and Blair administrations were going to launch an invasion, the UNHCR, NGOs, and analysts predicted a massive refugee exodus from Iraq. Accordingly, the UNHCR developed camp infrastructure, coordinated humanitarian responses, and stockpiled aid in neighboring countries. The US government, meanwhile, eager to present the invasion as a success and support its narrative that the war would bring liberation to Iraq, focused its efforts on facilitating the imagined return to Iraq of exiled Iraqis abroad by funding NGOs to assist with their repatriation (Chatty 2013). In the imagination of the US government, hundreds of thousands of exiled Iraqis would return and contribute to building a "free market" and "democratic" state in Iraq.[16] But the early displacement anticipated by relief and aid institutions did not materialize and, while some from the diaspora did return to Iraq, their numbers were much smaller than the US government had predicted.

Of those who were living in Iraq during the invasion and initial occupation, most stayed and tried to continue their lives, struggled to maintain their homes, jobs, and relationships, and in some cases, either fought against the occupation or found jobs with the occupation administration or among the media, aid organizations, and private contractors that suddenly had a huge presence in the country. But as the political and security situation worsened over time and sectarian violence increased dramatically, mass displacement did eventually take place, if not at the time or in the manner predicted by humanitarian agencies or governments. By 2006 and 2007, more than 4.5 million Iraqis, or about 15 percent of the total population of the country, fled their homes. Some 2.7 million Iraqis were displaced within Iraq while another two million became refugees in countries in the region. The majority of Iraqis who left the country traveled to Syria and Jordan, while smaller but significant numbers went instead to Egypt and Lebanon. At that time, only a tiny percentage of Iraqis made it to North America or Europe to ask for asylum.

Iraqi forced migration since the 2003 invasion has often been referred to as "the Iraqi refugee crisis." The numbers certainly supported the urgency in this claim; at the time, Iraqi forced migration represented the largest episode of forced migration in the Middle East since Palestinians were displaced from their homeland by the founding of Israel in 1948 (Fagan 2007). But Iraqis displaced after 2003 joined a large diaspora of Iraqis who had left Iraq prior to the invasion, many of them escaping Saddam Hussein's authoritarian regime. A small part of this diaspora lobbied the US and UK governments to overthrow Saddam Hussein, consulted on the invasion, and participated in the planning and politics of post-Saddam Iraq (Saleh 2020). Many of my Iraqi friends in Egypt had relatives all over the world who had traveled at different periods for a variety of reasons; some had left for work or education and stayed, others had been persecuted under Saddam Hussein's regime and had escaped the country. Most of the Iraqis featured in this book left Iraq in the years 2006–8. Although the humanitarian infrastructure and public discourse shifted as the Syrian war led to mass displacements beginning in 2011, Iraqi displacement has continued. The rise of the Islamic State in Iraq as well as the conflict in Syria that forced some Iraqis who had sought refuge there to move again has led to new or secondary displacement (El Dardiry 2020).

As I will discuss in chapter 3, displaced Iraqis confounded conventional categorizations of refugeeness, partly for structural, historical, and local reasons, but also because they themselves sometimes refused the label. In terms of policy, only Egypt even sought to categorize Iraqis as asylum-seekers. Syria, Jordan, and Lebanon all welcomed Iraqis as "temporary guests." Guest status partly emerged from cultural expectations of hospitality and political ideologies of Pan-Arabism and partly from the fact that of these countries, only Egypt has signed the 1951 Refugee Convention. Each of these states admitted large numbers of Iraqis, often with very little assistance of any kind from the international community, but the hospitality was not unconditional.

While the humanitarian imaginary had led the UNHCR to set up camps in anticipation of postinvasion displacement in 2003, once Iraqis began to leave, they settled in cities, especially Damascus, Amman, Beirut, and Cairo. During much of the time that I conducted fieldwork in Egypt, there were no refugee camps in the country at all. While some refugees lived in smaller towns or villages, the vast majority of refugees of all nationalities in Egypt lived in cities, most of them in Cairo.[17] Even though more than half of the refugees in the world live in cities and have for a long time, the refugee camp continues to dominate the public, policy, and, to a lesser extent, scholarly imaginaries of "refugeeness." Space has been a central way that scholarship has come to understand displacement, and the image and concept of the refugee camp has grown alongside some of the key theoretical concepts used to understand displacement and humanitarianism. Concepts such as "bare life" and "state of exception" (Agamben 1998, 2005) reinforce the primacy of the image of the camp, even as they fail to adequately capture the complexity of life in these spaces, let alone the reality of urban displacement. Yet if the camp has offered theorists a metaphor with which to think through the politics and power relations of displacement and humanitarianism, we might turn to how the spatial dynamics and lived experiences of urban exile can help us to consider differently both the existential and epistemological stakes of contemporary displacement.

IRAQIS IN EGYPT: LIVING IN A TRANSIT STATE

At the height of their displacement, some 150,000 Iraqis sought refuge in Cairo. These numbers were smaller than refugee populations in Syria and Jordan, reflecting the fact that to get to Cairo, people often, but not always, had to have access to air travel. This also meant that many Iraqis in Cairo came from urban Baghdad with its major airport, highlighting the important role that class and infrastructures of mobility play in determining where and how one is able to exercise mobility (Walters 2015). When many of my Iraqi interlocutors first came to Egypt, they imagined that their stay would be temporary. Weeks. Months, maybe. In this, their early hopes matched those of the Egyptian government, which also designated Iraqi presence as temporary. Iraqis expressed this temporariness in the way they described their time in Egypt as being a period or state of transit (*fatrat intiqālīa*). The Egyptian government expressed its version of temporariness through policy choices that made it impossible for Iraqis to imagine their time in Egypt any other way. In Egypt, most refugees are prohibited from working, attending public schools, accessing public services, or ever hoping for naturalization. Sara Sadek (2010) describes the Egyptian state's attitude toward refugees as "benign neglect" because Iraqis were able, at least initially, to enter the country, but beyond that the state offered them little aid or assistance. If Iraqis imagined their stay in Egypt as "a temporary place" or "a station" as some of my friends described it, they soon found, as Um Muhammad did, that their stay in Egypt was becoming much longer than they had hoped and that transit was taking on an indefinite, if not permanent, duration. Many Iraqis I knew ended up

20 INTRODUCTION

living in exile in Egypt for five, six, seven or more years before eventually being resettled, returning to Iraq, or traveling elsewhere. Very few Iraqis remain in Egypt today.

As displaced populations are increasingly immobilized and contained through racialized processes of "militarized global apartheid" (Besteman 2019), it becomes increasingly untenable to imagine displacement as a linear process with a discrete beginning, middle, and end. Instead, displacement has come to be as much about the control over or theft of time as it is about the loss of place. In this way, while refugees remain the paradigmatic figures of displacement as a sociotemporal phenomenon, there are existential and political conditions—waiting, uncertainty, abjection, precaritization—that extend far beyond people designated legally as refugees (Ramsay 2017b). As people are increasingly forced into conditions of longer displacement, the legal and social definition of a refugee continues to assume that this is a temporary status, one that is ideally resolved when the refugee once again becomes a citizen through repatriation, integration, or resettlement. This disjuncture between the actual experience of displacement and the spatiotemporal imaginary of displacement is one that is lived, and struggled over, by refugees.

When I began fieldwork in Egypt in 2007, I imagined that my work would focus on the existential and health effects of displacement for Iraqi refugees living in Cairo. As a student of anthropology and public health at that time, I was interested in understanding how Iraqis sought to cope and rebuild their lives as urban refugees in Egypt. I understood that, contrary to how it is sometimes presented, migration and displacement do not in themselves inherently cause ill health, but I expected to hear about significant suffering caused by the violence that had precipitated Iraqis' flight and by the conditions of their lives in Egypt. What I did not expect to find was that when I began asking Iraqis about their health and well-being, they almost without exception told me that the most significant source of their suffering was their "unknown future." This was how I first came to center temporality and futurity in my research and how I came to understand the subjective effects of bordering practices—which include both exclusionary state border regimes and also policies that separate refugees from other populations by limiting their ability to inhabit or dwell in space (Davidson 2009). One feature that these bordering practices share is the way they function not only to exclude people from particular spaces, rights, and possibilities but also to suspend them temporally within regimes of waiting (Haas 2017; Khosravi 2021; El-Shaarawi 2015). In this regard, the process of third-country resettlement was exemplary, if not exceptional.

THE AMBIVALENCES OF RESETTLEMENT

When I first met Shams, she was midway through the lengthy bureaucratic resettlement process. She was in her early thirties, single, and had come to Egypt alone—with the blessing of her family, she would note. Shams's work with a US-based women's rights organization was both the reason she had been forced to leave Iraq and the reason she was being considered for resettlement under a then new program to resettle "Iraqi allies" in the United States. Shams herself drew another direct line from her experiences under occupation in Iraq to urban exile in Egypt and then to her hoped-for resettlement in the United States. She described the common thread in terms of paralysis, a corporeal metaphor that for her referenced both enforced immobilization and a dulling of sensation.

> SHAMS: In Iraq I felt paralyzed. I had so many ideas and activities I wanted to do, but I was paralyzed. Maybe I would want to do something, like work for women's rights, but there would be an explosion or no electricity. So always I was paralyzed in this circle that I could not get out of. Here I am also paralyzed.

> NADIA: What do you mean by paralyzed?

> SHAMS: For me, time has stopped here [in Egypt]. For other people it is moving, but for me it is stopped.
>
> Sometimes when I am praying, I ask God to please give me more patience because I think it has run out long ago. Can you imagine your life paralyzed, all about waiting? Imagine someone takes your hands or legs and holds them still and says, don't do this and don't do that. Don't move.

22 INTRODUCTION

> So I have a lot of time and I am not using it. This is
> making me paralyzed. It makes the idea of getting out of
> here the main idea in my head, the dominating idea that is
> controlling me. You can't imagine life with this waiting.

The UNHCR—the intergovernmental organization tasked with global refugee protection—defines resettlement as "the selection and transfer of refugees from a state in which they have sought protection to a third state that has agreed to admit them ... with permanent residence status" (UNHCR 2011, 3). If refugees are designated legally and discursively as a "temporary problem," resettlement is intended to be a solution to displacement, ideally transforming them into citizens in the state that has accepted them. Indeed, in the language of the UNHCR, resettlement is considered one of the three "durable solutions" to displacement alongside repatriation and local integration. Resettlement is increasingly described by the UNHCR and states as the last of these three options—the durable solution of last resort. This reflects how, as a humanitarian gift and not an entitlement, resettlement is governed by a logic of scarcity.[18] Only about 1 percent of refugees are ever resettled.

Currently, thirty-seven states have resettlement programs, although the US, Canada and Australia take the majority of cases. In many of these "resettlement countries," recent shifts toward illiberal politics scapegoat refugees as threats to borders, public safety, or the economy, even though 85 percent of refugees live in the Global South. Unlike asylum, where a person enters territory on their own before requesting protection, resettlement allows states to select whom to protect and include from a distance. As such, resettlement sits at the nexus of humanitarianism and bordering.

Triage—a practice in which a commitment to saving life itself leads, in practice, to valuing some lives over others (V.-K. Nguyen 2010; Redfield 2008)—justifies why and how some refugees are selected while others are not. According to the UNHCR, the scarce good that is resettlement should be allocated to those refugees who, by virtue of extreme vulnerability, are most in need of the protection that resettlement affords. The resettlement process, then, produces some refugees as more vulnerable than others, more in need of humanitarian protection, and these few are then designated possible mobile subjects, potential citizens-in-waiting (Haas 2017) of resettlement states. By extension, it also produces those who are rejected as immobile and destined to dwell in "stuckedness" (Hage 2009) or wait in a state of transit. Because the distinction between these groups was not always clear, Iraqis found themselves living for extended periods within the resettlement process itself but often not even knowing for certain if they were under consideration.

Most of the scholarship on resettlement focuses on refugees after they have been resettled. In this way, scholarship and public discussion of resettlement tends to take the perspective of resettlement states, considering questions related to the ethics and politics of states' obligations to resettle refugees or investigating how refugees fare in their new homes. Such scholarship, while important, misses a crucial dimension of the social and political effects of resettlement, which occurs not in the so-called resettlement countries but in places like Cairo, where refugees spend years going through often arduous resettlement processes, and many more refugees seek resettlement than will ever be resettled. Shams's theorization of the resettlement process as enforcing a "continuity of paralysis" through the theft of time and indeterminate waiting is left out of scholarship that begins after resettlement is assured. The experiences of Um Muhammad and her family are similarly excluded as are the many more people who seek third-country resettlement and perhaps inhabit the process for months and years of their lives but are never actually resettled. An accounting of the social and political effects of resettlement must consider the effects that resettlement has on these larger populations and should, in my view, take refugees' experiences as its starting point.

METHODS AND APPROACH

I had been to Egypt many times before I returned for fieldwork. My father, born in a small agricultural village in the Nile Delta near Zagazig, had moved to Cairo to study at the Faculty of Economics, Statistics, and Political Science at Cairo University. When his father passed away, my dad was still completing his studies. As the oldest son, he moved the family, including his mother and nine siblings, to Cairo, where they all settled into an apartment in the Dokki neighborhood near the Cairo University

24 INTRODUCTION

campus. In the 1960s, my father traveled to Canada alone, with almost no money and even less English, in order to study for his PhD. There he met my mother, who had herself completed a rural-to-urban migration by leaving her family's farm in northern Saskatchewan to move by herself to Ontario for university and later her own graduate studies. They eventually married and stayed in Canada. We visited my large extended family many times when I was a child, staying in the same Dokki apartment, which was always full of aunts, uncles, and cousins. When I returned for fieldwork, I briefly entertained the idea of living alone or with an Iraqi family before it became very clear that there was only one living arrangement that would be appropriate and acceptable to my family and within the larger bounds of Egyptian propriety. I moved into that same Dokki apartment, where my beloved aunt, or *tant* as I call her, now lives alone.

The apartment was accessible by metro to the legal aid clinic where I did some of my fieldwork as well as to other organizations located in the urban core of Cairo. Most Iraqis lived spread out in suburbs surrounding the city, most notably 6th of October City, Nasr City, and Giza, so the apartment was as good a place as any from which to travel. I settled into life with my tant and the lengthy, unpredictable commutes by microbus, metro, and taxi that characterize urban mobility for many Cairenes. The ethnographic record is filled with the isolation and loneliness of extended fieldwork and, although there was of course some of that, I was fortunate to be supported, nourished, and cared for throughout much of my time in Egypt. This care came not only from my kin but from deep relations of friendship developed with Iraqis and humanitarians during my fieldwork.

However, my position as half-Egyptian, half-Canadian occasionally came with challenges. I was expected by my family, who like many Egyptians have become increasingly pious over the years, to maintain moral standards of feminine propriety. When I failed to meet these standards, I was gently corrected. At times, my identity created moments of conflict, such as when my tant insisted that I be accompanied, for my own safety, to my first day at the legal aid clinic by my sixteen-year-old cousin, Noha—hardly contributing to the competent professional image I hoped to project! I found it difficult to integrate into expat circles, which often included the humanitarians I hoped to know, because to stay out late in the evening drinking or attending parties contravened my family's expectations for pious and moral behavior. I also wanted to spend evenings visiting with Iraqi families and often found myself arriving home unacceptably late. On the other hand, there were many benefits to my status, not least of which was a greater understanding of and intimacy with my family and Egypt. Spending time with Egyptians and Iraqis gave me insight both into the social milieu in which my Iraqi interlocutors found themselves and also into the relationships between Iraqis and Egyptians in Egypt.

The analyses in this book are based on ethnographic fieldwork in Egypt from 2007 through 2017. The bulk of my fieldwork took place in 2007 and 2009–10, followed by several return visits in the years that followed. In addition to participant observation at the legal aid clinic, other humanitarian organizations, community events, and in peoples' homes, I conducted interviews with more than 120 Iraqis and humanitarians. Some of these interviews were single encounters, while in other circumstances I came to know people very well over time and across different settings.

I first came to work with and alongside Iraqis in Cairo under the supervision of the late anthropologist, educator, and refugee advocate Barbara Harrell-Bond. Barbara was a complicated, feared, and respected figure and one example of what it can mean to take anthropological training and scholarship into the public realm. I first learned the basics of refugee legal aid from her, and my ethnographic immersion in this very specific form of knowledge production shaped my understanding of the resettlement process as well as my ethnographic sensibilities and methods.

By the time I worked with her in Cairo in 2007, Barbara was in her seventies, formidable, in what she called her "second retirement," and running a team of lawyers and advocates from inside her Cairo apartment with the persistence, doggedness, and democratic spirit of a drill sergeant. Located in Garden City, a neighborhood of winding streets, grand, faded villas, and heavily fortified embassies bordered by the Nile, Tahrir Square, and Qasr el-Aini Street, Barbara's apartment was located on the ninth floor of a nondescript apartment building. The apartment was set up for its dual purpose; Barbara did live there, and guests frequently stayed with her for short and long periods, but the apartment was also a workspace and hub for everything related to refugees in Cairo. On any given day, the

26   INTRODUCTION

heavy, dinged wooden dining table would be populated by lawyers, law students, and refugees who had themselves been conscripted into refugee legal aid work, often in the role of interpreter or assistant.

THE RESETTLEMENT LEGAL AID PROJECT

When Barbara eventually left Cairo in 2009 and returned to England, moving from her second retirement to her third, young expat volunteers wanted to keep the project from ending. The Iraqi Information Office, later dubbed the Resettlement Legal Aid Project (RLAP), grew out of the more informal legal aid project in Barbara's apartment. Yet setting up an NGO in Egypt was, and is, a challenge. The Egyptian state is suspicious of NGOs, and although there is a formal process to create and register one, it was likely that an application would go into the state bureaucracy and never come out the other side with either approval or rejection (in this it paralleled many resettlement cases). No answer was the government's way of keeping people, citizens and foreigners alike, from working on sensitive topics like refugees. In order to move the project outside of Doktora Barbara's apartment, it needed another host, one with sufficient standing that it would be relatively safe from government interference. The project found its home in St. Andrew's Refugee Services, a church that had long been providing education services and humanitarian aid to refugees in Cairo.

In 2009, the Office decided to broaden its services from Iraqis exclusively to include refugees of other nationalities. The Office was then renamed the Resettlement Legal Aid Project. At the time that I returned to Cairo for more long-term fieldwork and joined RLAP in the summer of 2009, the Office had expanded its purview to include both legal and psychosocial services. It was an ideal field site because, although RLAP had begun to include refugees of other nationalities, the clientele remained about 80 percent Iraqi. Iraqi refugees had been extremely limited in their ability to form organizations by the Egyptian government, and previous attempts by Iraqis to form community-based organizations had led to the forcible closure of the organization as well as arrest and detention of its leaders. By virtue of its location in the apartment of a well-respected foreign professor and later inside the walls of a church, RLAP remained relatively unmolested, although the specter of security involvement was always present.

During my time at RLAP, I volunteered in both the legal and psychosocial departments. In the legal department, I worked individually with refugees from many nationalities, mostly Iraqi and Sudanese. I wrote testimonies and appeals, completed applications, followed up on cases, prepared clients for interviews, and helped out in a number of other areas. In the psychosocial department, I assisted in the formation and implementation of an Iraqi youth group and organized workshops and community events. From there, my ethnographic work radiated outwards to include other sites. I spent time in the homes, neighborhoods, and businesses of Iraqis in Egypt. I also visited other organizations that provide a range of services to refugees and interviewed aid providers.

ARC OF THE BOOK

Each chapter of the book foregrounds a set of relations forged through war, occupation, and humanitarian intervention. Chapter 1 theorizes the relationships that emerge from imperial unknowing and illustrates the effects that unknowing had on Iraqis' lives during wartime. Imperial unknowing draws our attention to how imperial intervention in Iraq relied on diverse and not always coherent forms of unknowing, inattention, hubris, and denial. I begin the chapter by tracing imperial unknowing in the lead-up to the war before moving to center Iraqis' stories of war and violence, placing those stories in the larger context of the US-led invasion and occupation of Iraq. Far from being limited in time and space, the epistemological violence that characterized the US-led war would shape Iraqis' displacement and subsequent experiences of humanitarian interventions in the aftermath of war.

Chapter 2 asks, How do we come to know what we know about war? How is unknowing produced by the stories we tell and don't tell about conflict and its aftermaths? In this chapter, I focus on the experience of Mazen, whose journalist brother was killed in the streets of Baghdad by American forces for seemingly no reason at all. Mazen's account of his

28   INTRODUCTION

brother's murder, which he narrated to me in the context of the resettlement process in Cairo, is an archive of war and its effects that illustrates what is often missing from scholarly and public discourse on displacement: how the wounds of empire are constituted by complex entanglements and histories that cannot be reduced to a single narrative of conflict. Mazen's telling is not the only account of his brother's death. Mindful of the work by Indigenous and postcolonial scholars that reminds us how the production of colonized peoples' voices and stories can serve to reify and reinscribe imperial projects, I do not offer Mazen's narrative as a recovery project; instead, I argue that by attending to his experiences and, in particular, the moments of unknowability within his narrative, we can think differently about how war is archived and known.

Chapter 3 lays the foundation for recognizing what is so important about the experience of *urban* displacement in Cairo in order to understand Iraqi refugees' experiences of living in prolonged transit and their desire for a solution to their plight. Cairo is host to one of the largest urban refugee populations in the world. Beginning with a close ethnographic reading of life in Cairo that maps the structural challenges and organizational complexity that urban refugees experience, the chapter telescopes out to situate Egypt within the region, the Global War on Terror, and the larger network of state and nonstate actors sometimes referred to as the global refugee regime.

In this chapter, I also attend to questions of class, gender, and national origin among urban refugees living in the "throwntogetherness" (Massey 2005) of urban Cairo. For example, I consider how Iraqi refugees were perceived, often disparagingly, as "five-star refugees"—a population who, in contrast to some other refugee populations, were able to move and settle temporarily with limited humanitarian assistance and who in some cases were better off financially than the local Egyptian population. I demonstrate how an attunement to the specificities of Iraqis as urban refugees challenges public and scholarly assumptions about refugeeness. First, through their own occasional, strategic refusal of the refugee category and their class status, Iraqis challenge the imaginary of refugees as passive victims in need of protection or rescue. Second, I consider the imperial relations that structure Iraqis' experiences of displacement in Egypt, focusing on the role of refugees and displacement in imperial politics.

Ethnographic attention to Iraqis' lives in exile illustrates the insufficiency of the methodological nationalism that remains so central to much research on refugees.

Chapter 4 introduces refugee resettlement in the context of humanitarian "solutions" to displacement and the larger global response to refugees. The UNHCR's durable solutions framework prescribes three ideal ways in which the problem of displacement can be resolved: voluntary repatriation, integration, and resettlement. But these frameworks represent solutions to displacement for states and the international system. How do Iraqis conceive of displacement as a problem and how do they evaluate resettlement as a possible solution, or not?

For some Iraqis, third-country resettlement offered a possible alternative or escape route from the prolonged experience of transit that characterized their lives in Cairo. But resettlement—in which refugees are "selected and transferred" by a third country that offers them residence and, usually, citizenship—is available to less than 1 percent of refugees. Much of the existing scholarship on refugee resettlement focuses on this tiny fraction of refugees who have been resettled, usually to countries in the Global North. As a result, significantly less attention has been paid to the resettlement process's larger social and political effects in places like Cairo, where seeking resettlement may take years, shaping life in exile and simultaneously rendering mobility and citizenship both possible and yet unlikely.

Iraqi refugees' engagement with durable solutions, especially resettlement, illustrates the bureaucratic complexity that refugees must navigate in order to access a "solution" and the ways in which they experience and negotiate the possibilities available to them, sometimes speaking back to the framework of durable solutions and other times creating alternative solutions. Centering Iraqis' experiences of seeking resettlement, regardless of whether or not they were ever resettled, troubles its designation as a "durable solution" and reveals ambivalence not only about bureaucratic processes but also about the very possibility of humanitarian solutions to displacement.

While chapter 4 investigates Iraqis' engagements with humanitarian resettlement programs that seek to rescue and protect vulnerable, "suffering bodies" without regard to their affiliation, chapter 5 offers a counterpoint by

30   INTRODUCTION

analyzing a particular resettlement program: the Direct Access Program to resettle "Iraqi allies" who assisted the US forces in Iraq and were persecuted as a result. This chapter develops the themes of collaboration, complicity, and obligation by beginning with the logic of "moral duty" to resettle refugees used by the US government before illustrating how these logics played out in Cairo. In thinking about imperial knowing in the context of war and humanitarianism, I follow the circuits (as first described in chapter 1) of knowledge that Iraqi "allies" provided for the US military in Iraq and the challenges Iraqis faced in proving these relations in the resettlement process in Cairo. I also explore how Iraqis were figured simultaneously as allies and enemies by the US program and the political and subjective effects of having to navigate these frames. To do so, I untangle the multiple valences of collaboration to reflect on the complex, conflicted, and unequal relationships Iraqis cultivated with US empire. What emerges are the diverse and diffuse ways that Iraqis were both injured by US intervention and how they themselves understood imperial obligations in the wake of these injuries.

In the conclusion, I show why Iraqis' experiences of displacement and humanitarianism matter in a context of protracted and polyvalent conflict and forced migration. Refugees' experiences and expressions of temporal displacement and their engagement with humanitarian "solutions," such as resettlement, provide insight into the politics of empire refracted through the lived experiences of the individuals who live with and navigate these politics.

1 "Bad History"

IMPERIAL UNKNOWING AND THE IRAQ WAR

History is the fruit of power, but power itself is never so transparent that its analysis becomes superfluous. The ultimate mark of power may be its invisibility; the ultimate challenge, the exposition of its roots.

MICHEL-ROLPH TROUILLOT (2015, xxiii)

This is the project of a lifetime, an archive of the losses from war and destruction. But not soldiers or equipment. The losses that are never mentioned or seen. Not just people. Animals and plants and inanimate things and anything that can be destroyed. Minute by minute. This is the file for the first minute.

SINAN ANTOON (2019, 46)

It was February 12, 2002. Donald Rumsfeld, two-time US secretary of defense, was answering questions from reporters in the Pentagon briefing room in Arlington, Virginia. Five months after the September 11, 2001, attacks, the "war against terrorism" was already well underway. The Bush administration had begun military intervention in Afghanistan mere weeks after the attacks and had subsequently turned their efforts to constructing a link between Iraqi president Saddam Hussein and al-Qaeda, and by extension to 9/11, despite the absence of any evidence. It was about precisely this lack of evidence that Jim Miklaszewski, the Pentagon correspondent for NBC News, was inquiring. Addressing the defense secretary, Miklaszewski noted that reports had uncovered no connections

32   CHAPTER 1

between Hussein's government and al-Qaeda and asked Rumsfeld if he knew of any information that would suggest that Iraq had supplied or would be willing to supply terrorist organizations with so-called weapons of mass destruction. Rumsfeld's infamous answer, in which he referenced "known knowns," "known unknowns," and "unknown unknowns," would come to be indelibly identified with the war and with the defense secretary himself:

> Reports that say that something hasn't happened are always interesting to me, because as we know, there are known knowns; there are things we know we know. We also know there are known unknowns; that is to say we know there are some things we do not know. But there are also unknown unknowns—the ones we don't know we don't know. And if one looks throughout the history of our country and other free countries, it is the latter category that tend to be the difficult ones.

Rumsfeld's response could be understood as a nonanswer, which it certainly was, and as an attempt to sow doubt about reports and investigations that had failed to find the weapons of mass destruction that the Bush administration hoped they could use to justify invading Iraq. But might the quote hint at something deeper about how the Bush administration approached the war in Iraq as well as the role of unknowing in imperial power more generally? Studies of imperialism have focused on the myriad ways that empire seeks to know, enumerate, master, and domesticate as part of strategies of military, cultural, and economic extraction. But a critical reading of Rumsfeld's unknown unknowns suggests that we might also consider how unknowing buttresses, facilitates, and enables—but also sometimes undermines—imperial power.

In this chapter, I depart from a conception of power that emphasizes the construction, accumulation, and deployment of knowledge to trace instead the possible relations of force and subjective experiences that emerge in a context where imperial power emerges as much from unknowing as it does from knowing. To do so, I follow a linked set of imperial practices of unknowing, each of which centers the production of unknowing as an integral epistemological strategy of imperial war and occupation. I call this assemblage *imperial unknowing* and I argue that it has been central to the war in Iraq and, more broadly, to the diffuse, global,

"BAD HISTORY"   33

and ongoing War on Terror. In the context of the Iraq War, the production of imperial unknowing includes the willful destruction or disregarding of knowledge, the refusal to collect data, the managing, coopting, and even murder of journalists, the production and dissemination of falsehoods, and other efforts to create a sense of uncertainty and unreality among diverse publics. Each of these practices has been considered separately, but I argue that thinking with them together as an armament of imperial power helps us to understand the character of that power. Because one of the key effects of imperial unknowing is the denial, denigration, and devaluing of Iraqi lives as well as their experiences of war and displacement, I am particularly interested in considering how taking Iraqis' experiences seriously can challenge imperial unknowing. The ways that imperial unknowing is felt, experienced, navigated, and refused by Iraqis, both during the war in Iraq and in exile in Egypt, are at the heart of this book. The relationship between imperial practices of unknowing and their subjective effects might be understood as what my friend Suad has called "bad history."

Suad and I met in Cairo in 2009. But it was not until 2016, on an autumn walk in the midsize American city where she had recently been resettled, that she narrated the longue durée of living with, and through, this bad history to me. By then, our friendship had been cemented by long years of mutual aid and support while living both in and out of physical proximity, but I realized that there was much I still did not know about Suad's life. It had been nearly fourteen years since Rumsfeld had given the "unknown unknowns" monologue, thirteen since the invasion, ten years since Suad had left Iraq, and almost three years since she had come to the United States as a refugee. Since leaving Iraq in 2006, Suad had not been able to return, even to visit. Anniversaries have a way of opening space for contemplation, and perhaps it was the decade of exile that prompted reflection. But Suad's phrase also stuck with me because it seemed somehow disruptive of the frames through which the Iraq War is often viewed, even if the dominant historiography and, indeed, much public discourse about the war now also overwhelmingly portray it in critical terms. What does it mean to have lived through and to live with bad history? How do we unsettle imperial techniques of unknowing—from the obfuscation of Rumsfeld's unknown unknowns to the ways that the war is remembered

34   CHAPTER 1

or not remembered today—and how might we come to understand US militarized intervention in Iraq differently? In what follows, I further theorize imperial unknowing, tracing its different faces as they emerged in the distinct phases of the US-led war in Iraq—from selling the war through invasion and occupation to counterinsurgency and ethnicized civil war—turning throughout to Iraqi experiences that challenge the erasures of unknowing.

IMPERIAL UNKNOWING II

The blatant, explicit, and even celebratory disregard of knowledge that characterized the Bush and Blair administrations' approach to the Iraq War, which lead to the deaths of hundreds of thousands of people and the displacement of millions more, serves as an invitation to critically investigate not only knowledge production in war but the social production of unknowing and its effects on the Iraqis who lived through it. In thinking with unknowing, I do not mean to suggest that intervention in Iraq does not have its own forms of knowledge production. However, I argue that while the production of forms of imperial knowledge has been well documented and analyzed, the role of unknowing in imperial intervention has not yet received the attention that it deserves. Unknowing, I contend, exists alongside and in tension with forms of knowing—and deserves to be attended to in its own right as an epistemological formation because of its centrality to US-led intervention in Iraq specifically and to US empire more generally. Unknowing also produces subjective and political effects that cannot be understood with a focus on knowledge alone. Such effects, in the context of intervention in Iraq, have been disastrous for millions of Iraqis as well as for many Americans. What do I mean by imperial unknowing? In thinking with unknowing, I am inspired by Eve Sedgwick (1988), for whom unknowing affords its own kind of power, which she calls the "epistemological privilege of unknowing." Sedgwick distinguishes the privilege associated with unknowing from the power more conventionally associated with knowledge as something produced, possessed, and circulated. Unknowing lurks in the shadows of knowledge production—unlike knowledge, it provides the possibility of a moral alibi, however shaky: "I didn't know."

The connections between US imperial formations and epistemology are manifold and not uniform. US empire has long conscripted scholars, including anthropologists, into relation with its projects (McGranahan and Collins 2018). In the aftermath of World War II, the United States turned its geopolitical focus to the Middle East and North Africa, leading to a proliferation of scholarship on the region as well as forms of imperial silencing and surveillance of scholarship (Deeb and Winegar 2016).[1] Perhaps one of the most enduring silences is the reluctance to name the United States as an empire—and an increasingly militarized one at that. But what else should one call a power that has appointed itself the world's police, anointing itself with the authority to decide which governments around the world are legitimate and which are not and to implement those decisions through coups and wars, even while claiming to promote democracy (Harvey 2003)? Or that has the largest economy and a massive military that divides the world into segments and rules through a decentralized network of bases and outposts in other countries that it patrols and monitors (Lutz 2006; Vine 2015)? Or that claims the prerogative to identify and impose consequences for violations of human rights and international law while simultaneously exempting itself from the same rules?[2] That claims it is dedicated to peace even as it makes war (Hardt and Negri 2001)? That alternately claims to know and also not to need to know?

As a collection of epistemological forms, imperial unknowing is produced through myriad practices, strategies, and processes. Perhaps the most obvious and well-studied example of unknowing is ignorance.[3] While Sedgwick is clear that unknowing cannot be reduced to ignorance, I would argue that ignorance is a crucial point in unknowing's larger constellation. Ignorance too is associated with power and privilege; to be ignorant and survive, even thrive, is a possibility only available to some. Charles Mills, in his essay "White Ignorance," takes on these differential politics of ignorance when he writes that "what people of color quickly come to see—in a sense, the primary epistemic principle of the racialized social epistemology of which they are the object—is that they are not seen at all" (Mills 2007, 18). Mills's intervention is so powerful for precisely the way that it subverts the taken-for-granted enlightenment precept that knowledge is the purview and weapon of the powerful. Alongside the

36   CHAPTER 1

ability to claim and deploy knowledge as a form of authority, power also enables ignorance. For Mills, ignorance forms a crucial part of a racialized social epistemology in which white people are afforded the privilege of ignorance while people of color must become "lay anthropologists" of white society and culture in order to survive. Mills notes, however, that the relation between ignorance and knowing is not only one of bare survival; at times, ignorance and invisibility can be subverted, taken advantage of, relished, and encouraged by people of color for survival, yes, but also for creative expression, freedom, and joy. This other side of white ignorance, these spaces of subversion, flight, and refuge that it opens up, makes sense when we consider the possible freedoms associated with becoming illegible to power especially in contexts of hypervisibility and surveillance.[4]

In addition to ignorance, unknowing may also indicate a process of coming not to know, that is to say, forgetting, obscuring, or looking away (Stoler 2011; Edwards 2016). In this vein, unknowing may be productive or conciliatory, as when it allows relationships to continue despite potentially unsettling or rupturing differences that must remain unarticulated (Geissler 2013). It may likewise encompass what Michael Taussig (1999) terms "public secrets"—those things that are widely known but that must be treated as though they are not known by not speaking about them or addressing them.[5] Thinking with secrecy, especially public secrecy, reminds us of the importance of position and location in relation to unknowing. When we consider the production of unknowing, we might ask: In whom and for whom is unknowing produced? By whom and with what effects? In her book on Hmong refugee epistemologies in the aftermath of the US "Secret War" in Laos, Ma Vang (2021, 33) explores these questions in relation to secrecy, displacement, and empire. She writes: "State secrets are not secret to refugees or those who survive the material violence enacted by policies of secrecy." What is secret to some may be deeply felt and shared knowledge for others.[6] Secrets are not only about what is hidden but rather about the pull between what is obscured and what is revealed; secrecy and revelation produce one another and in doing so constitute differentially positioned publics.

Unknowing may also involve indifference, neglect, or abandonment. Jason De León (2015) writes about how the necropolitical power of US border policies derives not only from how they put migrants' lives at risk but also how migrants are doubly disappeared. The first disappearance takes place with the euphemistic language of "prevention through deterrence" that intentionally obscures, for the US public, how border-enforcement policy pushes migrants from safer routes into more dangerous terrain. Second, migrants are literally disappeared when they die while trying to cross this inhospitable desert terrain. The combination of US border policies and the harsh desert landscape not only kills, but it also creates a context in which migrants' remains are often not found, leaving their loved ones without answers and creating an incomplete archive of the cost of border violence. Indifference does not remain in the realm of the epistemological but also has very material, in this case necropolitical, effects.

Unknowing therefore works to prevent an awareness and enactment of forms of relationality and mutuality. This is especially true in contexts of settler colonization and imperial intervention. "Colonial unknowing endeavors to render unintelligible the entanglements of racialization and colonization, occluding the mutual historicity of colonial structures and attributing finality to events of conquest and dispossession" (Vimalassery et al. 2016). Processes of colonial unknowing accomplish two simultaneous, imbricated effects: (1) They obscure ongoing relationships of colonization, including the connections between imperial processes of subjugation across time and space, and in doing so, (2) they seek to represent colonization as complete, in the past, and unable to be redressed. In the context of US empire, we see a similar politics in what Ann Stoler and Carole McGranahan (Stoler 2018; Stoler and McGranahan 2018) call *disassemblage*, or the cultivation of unrelatedness between US imperial formations. In contexts of imperial intervention, especially in Iraq, I would add that alongside denying relationality, unknowing can involve a flattening and a fixing that denies people and places historicity and multiplicity. For example, to prepare for war, the US military held screenings of *The Battle of Algiers* (Kaufman 2003), circulated texts about Iraq written during World War II, and took inspiration from T. E. Lawrence (Stone 2022, 223), as though Iraq and Iraqis could be reduced, through Orientalizing representations and discourse, to people out of time and place; as Zainab Saleh has noted, the invading forces sought

38 CHAPTER 1

to govern partly through an ahistoricizing "politics of erasure" (Saleh 2020, 14–19).

Just these few examples make clear that thinking with unknowing presents itself as an epistemological challenge: Can one group together a range of practices, technologies, and modes of imperial power under a rubric of unknowing? And what does such an exercise accomplish? What would an ethnography of unknowing look like? Although different, the strategies described above each clearly link the social production of unknowing to forms of power that derive from the ability to induce epistemological instability in another, whether through denial, indifference, deception, secrecy, or willful ignorance. As Vang illustrates in her work on US imperial intervention in Laos and as I will show in relation to the US-led invasion and occupation of Iraq, the production of unknowing is an important form of imperial power, one that has lasting effects for imperial subjects both within the territorial borders of empire and beyond. These practices are also all active processes of subjective becoming; unknowing is made in particular contexts, reproduced, distributed, and comes to be how things are felt, understood, and experienced on both sides of imperial divides. These are not passive omissions or forgettings but rather disavowals or occlusions that work to make the world as it is seem fixed and inevitable, preempting other forms of relationality and obscuring how things might have been, and perhaps could still be, otherwise.

The role of ethnography in this project is not to provide a classification or taxonomy of unknowing but rather to elucidate specific practices and relations of imperial unknowing as well as consider how they are lived and negotiated in the everyday—and how they have been or could be disrupted. The relationship between anthropology and imperial unknowing is not necessarily a straightforward one. As I discuss in the introduction, ethnography and anthropology, as forms and practices of knowing, have long been complicit in and integral to colonial and imperial objectification as well as in the turn toward the neoliberal security state. Yet paradoxically, as a methodology ethnography may be particularly well suited to documenting the particularities, inconsistencies, and details that characterize specific imperial practices and institutions at particular times—it is perhaps through this detail work that empire might be challenged (Lutz

2006). This chapter is neither a comprehensive history of the war nor an exhaustive catalog of imperial unknowing. However, it is helpful to recognize that imperial unknowing may take many different shapes and to follow some of these forms, practices, and moments before, during, and after the war in order to consider how Iraqis lived with the effects of these practices—as well as how they challenged them and insisted on other ongoing relationships and other possible reciprocities.

To do so, I consider several key examples of imperial unknowing in the conduct of the war and occupation alongside the lived consequences as narrated by my interlocutors Suad, Hassan, Entisar, and Hatem. My goal is threefold. First, I describe the role of unknowing in the Iraq War as a way of considering its role in liberal militarized imperialism. Second, I illustrate how the politics of imperial unknowing were central to the specific forms of violence that ultimately forced Iraqis to flee to Egypt. Inspired by scholarship that seeks to understand how people unmake and remake social, moral, and individual worlds in the aftermath of political violence and terror (Das et al. 2001, 2000), I am interested in how Iraqis have experienced, reckoned with, and struggled against the war and subsequent violence. Third, by sharing these narratives, I offer a glimpse into a possible alternative history of the Iraq War, one that foregrounds the lived experiences of Iraqis themselves and highlights experiences and relationships that are often ignored or discounted. With this objective, I seek not only to describe unknowing but to intervene directly against it.

Ultimately, the fact that so many accounts of the Iraq War center the perspective of the occupation and not of Iraqis is, in my view, both a symptom and consequence of processes of imperial unknowing. I hope to both reveal these dynamics and begin to offer an alternative, one that affirms Iraqis' experiences as foundational, not peripheral, to the history of war and displacement in Iraq. Such an alternate history is not only a matter of setting the record straight. It is the necessary foundation from which we might begin to recognize the relationships that the war created between Iraqis and Americans—relationships that so many of my interlocutors insisted upon in their descriptions of the war and in their struggles in exile. Before turning to Iraqis' accounts of their own experiences during the invasion and occupation, I want to briefly consider the role of imperial unknowing in the period just before the 2003 invasion.

40   CHAPTER 1

"WHEN WE ACT WE CREATE OUR OWN REALITY"

On March 20, 2003, a US-led coalition invaded Iraq. The so-called coalition of the willing—made up of some forty countries—went ahead despite failing to secure United Nations authorization for the invasion. The United States' most committed partner in the war was the United Kingdom, which, after the dissolution of the Ottoman Empire, had colonized Iraq under the League of Nations mandate system beginning in 1920. The attacks of September 11, 2001, in which nearly three thousand people were killed, became the justification for the decades-long Global War on Terror, including the wars on Afghanistan and Iraq. In the case of Iraq, the Bush administration relied on baseless accusations that the Iraqi government was linked to al-Qaeda and possessed weapons of mass destruction to make an argument for war. They also claimed that the war had a humanitarian aim: to bring democracy to the Iraqi people.

Although none of the 9/11 hijackers were Iraqi, and there were no clear links tying the Iraqi government to the attack, George Bush and the neoconservatives around him saw September 11 as an opportunity to justify the invasion of Iraq.[7] As has been well documented, the desire for war with Iraq had been in place long before 2001; the 9/11 attacks offered the pretext for the invasion, and a fearful American public was mostly willing to support it. For a year before the war, the Bush administration made repeated public statements accusing Saddam Hussein of having or seeking to develop "weapons of mass destruction" despite growing concerns that the evidence for the claims was mistaken at best and fraudulent at worst. However, when efforts to find evidence to support the administration's claim that Saddam Hussein had "weapons of mass destruction" or supported terrorism failed, the administration manufactured evidence, which was repeated by politicians and a media willing to put their faith in official calls for war. The UK government, led by Tony Blair, was actively complicit in the development of the case for war based on false information and rumor (Robinson 2017).

The examples are many and well known. While Rumsfeld essentially deflected and refused to answer the question he was asked, unknowing was also promulgated in the buildup to war through other falsehoods. Famous examples included Colin Powell's appeal to the UN Security Council to preempt the threat of weapons of mass destruction that did not exist. Lies and misinformation also involve an imbalanced relation of knowing and unknowing; falsehoods were used to build a case for war by either planting inaccurate information or sowing doubt and uncertainty in a variety of publics. Such lies supported other falsehoods such as that the war was being fought to secure freedom and democracy for Iraqis or about the larger role of the US as an empire. The US government played on the fear generated by 9/11, suggesting that it was better to attack Iraq than to risk the possibility that Saddam Hussein might attack the US or Britain, even though there was nothing to suggest that any such attack was planned or even possible. For example, in January 2003, Condoleezza Rice, then national security advisor, famously said, "The problem here is that there will always be some uncertainty about how quickly he [Saddam Hussein] can acquire nuclear weapons. But we don't want the smoking gun to be a mushroom cloud."

The mainstream media in both the US and the UK mostly repeated the administrations' allegations unquestioningly, by and large supporting the war and failing to investigate or substantiate claims made by administration sources. There were real consequences to dissent, as I will discuss in chapter 2. Presenters who opposed the war found themselves fired or their shows cancelled (Kumar 2006). Although some news outlets, such as *The New York Times*, would later admit to having published false or misleading information, the corrections and apologies received much less attention than the initial inaccurate stories. Given the propaganda campaigns coming from the government and the press, it is not surprising that polling suggested that some 60 percent of the US public supported the invasion.

Related but less discussed was the administration's wholesale devaluing of knowledge as an instrument of government. This attitude of imperial hubris, central to the neoconservative approach to the war, was characterized by the deliberate disavowal not of particular ideas or facts but of knowledge itself. Perhaps the most telling example of this disavowal also occurred before the war, when journalist Ron Suskind interviewed an unnamed senior Bush administration advisor. Suskind later described the encounter in a 2004 *New York Times* article:

> The aide said that guys like me were "in what we call the reality-based community," which he defined as people who "believe that solutions emerge

42   CHAPTER 1

from your judicious study of discernible reality." I nodded and murmured something about enlightenment principles and empiricism. He cut me off. "That's not the way the world really works anymore," he continued. "We're an empire now, and when we act, we create our own reality. And while you're studying that reality—judiciously, as you will—we'll act again, creating other new realities, which you can study too, and that's how things will sort out. We're history's actors . . . and you, all of you, will be left to just study what we do." (Suskind 2004)

The quote, widely attributed to Senior Advisor to the President Karl Rove, though he denies it, is both a stunningly bald-faced description of imperial power—"when we act we create our own reality"—and an explicit disavowal of knowledge in the context of the approach to the Iraq War. Instead of faulting critics of the regime for having inaccurate knowledge, "the aide" questioned the relevance of knowledge entirely. The conventional empiricist account of knowledge, which is evident in, for example, the fetishization of evidence-based approaches or the appeal of "big data," is that knowledge of the world precedes and enables action. But for "the aide," action is the primary domain of empires, with those who cling to the "reality-based community" following meekly behind, gathering information even as empire acts again and again, changing the world faster than the knowledge-seekers can keep up.[8]

To dismiss the unnamed aide's words as simply imperial hubris is too easy, I contend, and too comforting in a world where unknowing has epistemological and ontological effects. I argue that they indicate something characteristic about imperial power generally and the specific nature of US imperial power in the War on Terror. Hubris, in the ancient Greek origin of the term, implies wildly overconfident action that leads inevitably to downfall. Certainly, the administration's assertions about the war proved to be both overconfident and spurious. But the downfall implied in the term hubris has never been experienced by those who perpetrated the war. Despite a general consensus that the war was illegal, a failure, and that it has left the world more dangerous, its consequences have been borne almost exclusively by ordinary people, especially Iraqis; those responsible have evaded any meaningful forms of accountability.

EMPIRE'S OPTICS AND BLIND SPOTS

If the case for war could be built on falsehoods, deflections, hubris, and unsubstantiated claims of knowing, once the invasion began in earnest the relationship between militarized liberal imperialism and unknowing changed, reflecting both continuities but also differential relations to knowing and unknowing held by the multiple institutions and actors involved in administering the invasion and occupation. These actors, including the US military, the Coalition Provisional Authority (CPA), private contractors, and journalists, among many others, each had different ways of relating to unknowing and knowing at different moments. The relative power—and the respective practices of unknowing—shifted over time, especially in the shift from the initial military campaign against Saddam Hussein's regime to the occupation to a grinding counterinsurgency and finally to an interethnic civil war.

War is often imagined as one of the most paradigmatically uncertain of human activities (Lutz 2019). Perhaps the most obvious metaphor of the ascribed uncertainty associated with militarized conflict is the concept of the *fog of war*. The fog of war refers to experiences of ontological uncertainty associated with the relations between participants in military conflict and, variously, time, space, co-combatants, and adversaries. In the fog of war "personal agency, personal responsibility, and personal epistemology—that is, doing things, being morally responsible for things, and knowing about things—are all blurred together" (Rubaii 2018, 85). In Iraq, as in other conflicts, this uncertainty was often represented through the use of visual metaphors. Yet the optics of war are not only metaphorical but are tied to specific practices and technologies. Militaries often seek to reduce or manage war's uncertainty through the use of visual technologies (Gregory 2010). The proliferation of technologies in warfare, such as drones, unmanned ground vehicles, and satellite imagery, seeks to cut through the fog and create clarity for military planners and commanders.

Drawing on the experience and narrative of the Gulf War of 1990–91, the US military touted its technological supremacy and visual acuity, especially in its systematic destruction of Iraqi defenses in the course of the

44　　CHAPTER 1

invasion, claiming that new technology would allow the war to be fought quickly, primarily from a distance, and with few costs to the invading forces. The invasion itself, beginning on March 20, 2003, was largely slotted into this narrative. The "shock and awe" aerial bombardment campaign was timed to be both shocking for Iraqis, beginning at 5:34 a.m. Baghdad time without a customary declaration of war, and awe inducing in a different way for Americans, who could watch the air strikes and then the subsequent ground invasion happening live on prime-time television.[9]

Shortly after the invasion, however, the reality of war became much murkier and the importance of "local" knowledge much more important to the occupying forces, at least those who had to leave the Green Zone. Derek Gregory (2010) notes the tensions that emerge between forms of vertical warfare, such as traditional command-and-control structures or technologies of distanced surveillance, and forms of counterinsurgency, in which the emphasis is instead on contingent, unfolding on-the-ground relations with local populations who are understood simultaneously as a potential threat and as essential to the conduct of war. In Baghdad especially, as the occupying forces were forced to accept that their technology was not sufficient for fighting a growing insurgency in which they struggled to identify the enemy, the military adopted other technologies of information-gathering, such as the use of patrols, surveillance, intelligence-gathering, and simulations. These technologies sought to gather information with the goal of reducing uncertainty and gaining tactical advantage.

But military practices of combating and managing uncertainty for soldiers in Iraq—especially in the transition from destroying the Iraqi military to combatting a growing insurgency—had the effect of passing uncertainty on to civilian populations. It is the experiences of civilians that illustrate that the distinction between optical technologies and human technologies does not always hold on the ground. Hassan found this out the hard way when his family and their home were unwillingly conscripted into the occupying forces' project of surveillance.

Before coming to Cairo in 2007, Hassan and his family had lived in the al-Hurriya neighborhood of Baghdad for many years. Hassan had worked as a school principal for nearly his entire adult life. He loved the job and he was good at it, but as he aged his eyesight progressively faded. Soon it began to interfere with his work and he was forced to retire, which he accepted with great reluctance. By the time I met him in Cairo, Hassan was almost entirely blind but got around with the assistance of his wife, Fatima. Neither retirement nor exile had undone his schoolmasterly air, and in our conversations I often oscillated between feeling like I might either receive a kindly didactic lecture or be chastised as a misbehaving student.

In Baghdad, the family house, taller than others in the neighborhood and on a corner lot, was a source of pride and comfort that housed Hassan, Fatima, and their children and, over time, their children's own growing families. But pride became misfortune as the house's height and location, once prized features, became liabilities under occupation. "It could be a very good checkpoint," Hassan said ruefully, as he explained the layout of their lost home to me with his exacting precision in one of our first conversations in Cairo. Hassan's house overlooked the only road that connected Baghdad International Airport to the city as well as to the Green Zone, the highly fortified center of the occupation administration. Iraqis call this road the Airport Road (*Tariiq al-maTaar* or *Shār ʿ al-maTaar*), but the US military, which renamed many of Baghdad's main roads in English in lieu of learning and employing the Arabic names, dubbed the road Route Irish.[10] Tariiq al-maTaar was an essential artery of movement through the city, traveled especially by taxis, Iraqis who worked at the airport, and those who either were traveling themselves or were picking up or dropping off passengers. During the occupation, the road also became an essential supply route; personnel and equipment all had to travel the ten-mile Tariiq al-maTaar to enter or leave Baghdad. Insurgents were well aware of the importance of the route to the occupation as well as its vulnerability and began targeting convoys along the road, which soon earned it another nickname among US soldiers: "IED Alley." The road was dangerous for everyone who traveled it, but Iraqis, who had to navigate the road while avoiding attacks from insurgents, IEDs planted in medians, and American convoys that might open fire if a driver got too close, suffered the greatest casualties. Occupation forces, contractors, journalists, and humanitarians also suffered injuries and lost their lives along the road. Casualties were so great that the US military sought to obscure the number of attacks, redacting them from reports.

46   CHAPTER 1

To protect themselves from attacks and secure their uninterrupted passage along Tariiq al-maTaar, occupation forces sought to control the neighborhoods that bordered the route and surveil the road from within these neighborhoods. At some point, someone must have noticed that Hassan's house, as he himself retrospectively noted with bitterness, "could be a good checkpoint." Because one day, a phalanx of soldiers arrived in the square in front of Hassan's house, parking their armored vehicles in full view of the neighborhood, and entered the house, fully armed. Spreading out around the interior of Hassan's home and onto the roof to observe the traffic on the road, the soldiers transformed the home into a temporary watchtower from which to observe the airport road.

Hassan described the experience of having their home occupied and transformed into military infrastructure as one of terror. The soldiers would order the family to wait in one room with the door closed while they took over the house. It was an experience that left the entire family cowering together for four or five hours at a time, unable to know what was happening in the rest of their home:

> The whole family was inside one room, terrified, until the job was finished. We could not go out of the room for all these hours to eat breakfast, drink water, or to go to the bathroom. Because they were coming in armored cars, and especially because they were armed, the whole family was terrified. My grandson, the son of my son, was a year and a half old, and from the scene of the soldiers roaming around the house, his psychological situation is [still] not good to this day. He was terrified. My wife and my daughters were so terrified too, and they were always saying that we may be killed at any moment.

Hassan's account illustrates the intimate terror of daily life in occupied Baghdad—how domestic spaces might become active sites of occupation and warfare nested within the larger context of the occupied city and state. The soldiers asked if they could use the house, and Hassan acquiesced, but only because he was afraid that they might kill him if he refused. Confined to one room, the family couldn't see what was happening in their own home. Meanwhile, throughout the house, including from the roof, US soldiers surveilled the neighborhood while the family listened and waited in terror for "the job" to be done. The military's fear of the hidden dangers of insurgent attacks on and around "Route Irish" and their efforts to manage these dangers transmuted into terror and uncertainty for Hassan and his family.

Alongside the soldiers' efforts to surveil the neighborhood and identify and contain insurgents, there is a concomitant blindness or indifference to how their actions affect Hassan and his family. Such indifference to the basic needs, dignity, and well-being of Iraqis is occasionally present in reports about counterinsurgency strategy in Baghdad, but when it does appear the focus is often less on the indignities themselves than on how they might create resistance among Iraqis to the occupying forces, hindering the war effort. More commonly, such experiences are invisible. The invisibility of Hassan and his family in the encounters recalls Mills's description of white ignorance: The combination of military power and anxiety about the uncertain danger of the road creates the conditions for a racialized social epistemology in which Hassan and his family simply do not exist for the soldiers. The confinement and sequestration of the entire extended family—Hassan, his children, and grandchildren—to a single room while the house is taken over as a watchtower renders this invisibility quite literal. Such experiences are also invisible to the archive of the war; as I will discuss in chapter 2, casualties are debated, denied, and counted as a diagnostic of the war. But who counts the loss of a home as it is forcibly transformed into military architecture and then eventually lost entirely? Who counts the lost sense of home when one's house is overtaken by armed soldiers multiple times—three times before the family was eventually forced to abandon the house entirely? Who counts the feeling, which Hassan describes in terms of terror, of not knowing if or when the soldiers might return to retake the home? The bitter irony of the situation in which the American forces sought to render threats visible by terrorizing and invisiblizing Hassan and his family was not at all lost on Hassan, who described the experience as a series of "traps" that ultimately sealed his fate and forced his family into exile.

For Hassan, the first trap was the occupation of the house itself and the coercion of having to "allow" the armed soldiers entry despite how terrifying it was for him and his family. But, as Hassan noted, "This is just the first trap. The second trap is that after each time the Americans used our house, people started to ask, 'Why did you let the Americans use your house?'" Hassan had tried to explain that he hadn't exactly "let" the

48   CHAPTER 1

Americans use his house—at least not voluntarily. But, as he described it, the situation was another trap. He wasn't free to say no to the heavily armed American soldiers, he explained. But being perceived as aiding the occupation, even under duress, put him and his family at risk of violence as well. Each time, shortly after the Americans came, Hassan's house was fired on by insurgents. "At first, we did not know that they were targeting us. We thought it might be random," Hassan said. "But once we started to receive threats, we began to realize we were targeted."

"YOU ARE BEHAVING LIKE TRANSLATORS!"

Roads could be renamed, at least for the occupation forces, simply by writing new English street names on satellite maps of Baghdad, but many other military operations required more proximity and contact with local populations. For this work, on which they were vitally dependent, the military hired and recruited local Iraqis who could speak English.[11] Nomi Stone (2017, 150) describes how these people are construed by the US military as *human technologies*—embodied reservoirs of cultural, regional, and linguistic knowledge. Iraqis were hired to work as interpreters, translators, mediators, proxies, advisors, and contractors by the military, the CPA, and contractors, as well as by other organizations such as human rights groups and foreign media outfits. For the military, such work represented an important part of the so-called *cultural turn* in warfare, which was heightened by the military's shift in Iraq from invasion, which the administration had argued would be met with popular acquiescence, if not gratitude, to a campaign of counterinsurgency in the face of the actual resistance to US-led occupation. The cultural turn involved a heightened reliance on the use of culture in an attempt to make an adversary and battle space increasingly perceived as illegible more understandable (Stone 2022). It represented the military's move away from the so-called revolution in military affairs, which was dominant early in the invasion and emphasized an increased reliance on technology and distance through the use of unmanned technologies and surveillance, toward counterinsurgency, a military philosophy in which the enemy was hiding within local populations and opaque and foreign landscapes.

In 2006, under the leadership of General David Petraeus, the US Army and Marines produced *Field Manual No. 3-24*, which sought to recharacterize the Iraq War as a counterinsurgency, a shift that brought culture more squarely into the center of the war as the military tried to make sense of, contain, and control what they termed the *human terrain*. It was within this framework that the military began recruiting anthropologists and other scholars to participate in the Human Terrain System—a program that sought to embed anthropologists within the military to conduct ethnography designed to generate the cultural knowledge that the military craved. The Human Terrain System provoked tremendous debate within the discipline of anthropology, and the American Anthropological Association condemned the program in 2007 (Deeb and Winegar 2016). The military's use of culture and anthropological expertise is one that should provoke ongoing, searching discussion of the role of anthropological knowledge production in liberal militarized empire and the role of anthropology and other scholarship in imperial unknowing.[12] However, it was Iraqis who ended up taking on most of the work and danger of the turn to culture and counterinsurgency. In a context of unknowing, "local wartime intermediaries emerged as militarized bodies to see the intimate unseen, to translate and furnish otherwise inaccessible, operationally useful cultural knowledges, and ultimately to produce the U.S. soldier as an insider within the war zone" (Stone 2017, 152). Unlike the technologically produced efforts at omniscience described earlier, counterinsurgency operations sought to see the unseen through, as Stone notes, intimate encounters, knowledge, and experiences. But there was much that the military refused to see and refused to know.

Such encounters became much-needed regular employment for some Iraqis during a time of tremendous unemployment induced by the war and occupation administration, but this work came with significant risk to them and their families as insurgents sought out and targeted those who were seen to be assisting the occupation. Most famously, Iraqis who worked as translators and interpreters for the occupying forces were at particular risk because of the ways they were often at the forefront of military occupations, acting as mediators between occupying forces and Iraqis in ways that left them exposed and vulnerable.[13] But there were also more ad hoc moments of relying on Iraqi linguistic skills, expertise, and

50   CHAPTER 1

assistance, moments that might likewise put Iraqis at grave risk despite their brevity. The risks and fallout of such brief encounters were often ignored by occupying forces who seemed oblivious and indifferent to the effects of their interactions on Iraqis' lives.

For Entisar, it only took one such brief encounter to radically change her life. Like Hassan, Entisar is from Baghdad. She was among the middle class, and like hundreds of thousands of Iraqis, she had worked for the sprawling government bureaucracy under Saddam Hussein's regime, in her case for the Ministry of Finance. "When the war began, violence came to our neighborhood almost immediately," she told me, describing how coalition forces bombed her neighborhood in an effort to target the Baathist resistance forces who were present. After two bombs fell close to their home, damaging it and terrifying the family, they moved into a nearby shelter that had been built during the Iran-Iraq War in the 1980s. The family who had built the shelter for an earlier war had left Iraq for Canada during the sanctions period, leaving their home empty and the shelter available for when it became necessary again in a new war, for a new family. Entisar and her family lived in the shelter for nearly a month.

Shortly after the toppling of Saddam Hussein's statue in Baghdad's Firdos Square, the family moved out of the shelter and returned to their bomb-damaged home. Once there, they had to, as Entisar put it, "live simply." They discovered that they no longer had electricity or running water. All the shops were closed. When they discovered that bread wasn't available, Entisar's mother dusted off an old recipe and started making the bread for their meals herself. They could not find anyone to hire to repair the house, so they had to live with whatever damage they could not fix. The family slowly worked together to mend what they could. With the Ministry shuttered, Entisar was unable to return to work and stayed home helping her family during this time, focused on rebuilding and survival. After several months, the Ministry reopened, and Entisar was able to return to work. As a near-fluent English speaker, she retained her job during the occupation; her linguistic skills made her an asset. Work was not as before though; the composition of the office staff was changing on sectarian lines, and after Entisar was selected to travel abroad as part of a delegation, she received death threats. She was shaken but thought maybe it was a cruel joke and continued working.

One day in December 2006, the Americans, as she called them, were walking around Entisar's neighborhood, entering each house and talking to everyone they encountered. "That was the day that Saddam was sentenced to death," she remembered. "They wanted to ask us what we thought about Saddam." Someone in the neighborhood must have told them that Entisar spoke English because they came to her house looking for her: "They were without a translator so they asked me to come with them and help them talk to people. But I refused to help them because I was scared of being seen with them. I am also terrified of the Americans. The man who came to speak to me was very nice but I felt that I couldn't trust them because they have weapons. I don't feel comfortable around weapons." Although Entisar refused to translate, people in the neighborhood had noticed that she had been asked. Neighbors asked her father what the Americans had wanted and if Entisar had acquiesced. Frightened, she asked him to tell them she'd been sick and that she hadn't talked to the Americans at all.

Entisar explained how under occupation, the loanword *translator* took on new, disparaging connotations.[14]

> The people in my area knew that I was a teacher and that now I am a translator of financial documents in the Ministry, but the word *translator* has become a bad word in Iraq, and anyone associated with it is at risk. Uneducated people had never heard this word before: *translator*. When the Americans invaded this word entered their vocabulary, and they began to associate it with bad things, and so it became a bad word. It was incorporated into Iraqi slang, and if you did something bad people would say, "You are behaving like translators!" when they meant, "You are not honest!"

Two days after she refused to translate, Entisar received a phone call from an unknown number. "The caller said, 'We told you to stop working, but you did not, so now we are going to kill you,'" Entisar recalled. "He told me to stop working with the Americans, and I told him that I do not work with them, and he said that I should not lie because they know my job very well and they know that I speak to foreign people." Entisar was angry but most of all scared. Not wanting to worry them, she did not tell her family about the phone call. But she quit her job and started preparing to leave for Egypt, where one of her relatives who had also been threatened had already fled.

Both Entisar's and Hassan's experiences in Baghdad suggest a paradox; while Iraqis were absolutely essential to the occupation, their experiences

52   CHAPTER 1

and the dangers the occupation imposed on them were also largely invisible. In each case, the dangers of military insecurity and unknowing were passed on, through technologies of knowledge production and generation, to the Iraqis on whose lives, bodies, homes, and neighborhoods these military ways of knowing relied. In both cases, war, and more specifically counterterrorism and counterinsurgency, transforms and reshapes the environments and relations in which people live (Rubaii 2018, 3). Both Entisar's and Hassan's experiences also complicate how we understand Iraqis' participation in the occupation. Both were seen to have collaborated with the Americans despite either refusing or acquiescing under the threat of violence; both were targeted as a direct result of their encounter with the occupation. But their relations to the occupation were not legible either to the soldiers who approached them without considering the consequences of the contact or to larger narratives about the war and Iraqis' place and role in it.

Counterinsurgency is largely about knowledge and visibility in a context where war is understood as uncertain and unpredictable, and adversaries are construed as foreign and illegible. It assumes a terrain in which threat is opaque; the role of counterinsurgency strategies is to identify who among a local population is an insurgent and who is a civilian. It implies a space where threat is omnipresent and unknown. While Iraqis were at once the object of the counterinsurgency gaze—at all times potentially suspect—they were also drawn into the everyday practice of it with sometimes disastrous effects. And it is clear that even if counterinsurgency doctrine states that it seeks to distinguish between Iraqi civilians and combatants—good Iraqis and bad Iraqis, according to the occupying forces—in practice, these distinctions were not made. Iraqis were either not seen or seen as instruments or seen as possible threats, regardless of whether or not they were civilians, whether or not they acquiesced or refused interpolation into the imperial project.

COLONIAL DENIAL AND HUBRIS

"I never could have imagined that the United States would colonize Iraq, especially not based on wrong information," Hatem declared. He was feeling combative. He was a passionate reader, a consumer of satellite news, and an opinionated debater of world politics in general, but understandably he reserved his choicest words for describing the US-led invasion and occupation of Iraq. I paused on the word *colonize* because I realized I had never heard this terminology used in official historiography of the war. Hatem set his cup of coffee down with a clatter on the table, jolting me back into the conversation. "I consider the United States a developed country that is supposed to care about human rights. How could they commit all these massacres in Iraq? I had hoped they would withdraw from Iraq after the invasion and then again after the killing of Saddam Hussein, but they stayed."

The United States is often described as an empire in denial (Collins and McGranahan 2018). Unlike the civilizing mission that was so central to the rationalization of European colonization, especially in the nineteenth century, US empire building has involved the acquisition and control of territory alongside the simultaneous disavowal of colonization and the obscuring of colonized territory and peoples from official narratives of the United States (Immerwahr 2019). Part of this denial is rhetorical and representational, so it should not be surprising that the occupation of Iraq is rarely described in the language of colonization. However, the United States also materially enacts the possibility of imperial denial through the use of strategies such as the development of a vast global archipelago of military bases or the reliance on other states to do the work of domination and control (Vine 2018). These approaches enable a plausible deniability within US public life in a way that the institution of direct rule would not and promote the fiction of empire without imperialism (Morefield 2014). But Hatem's argument illustrates that such deniability is less plausible for Iraqis who have lived with decades of imperial intervention in Iraq and felt that US actions, however ill informed, directly decided their fates. What are the implications of taking Hatem's argument seriously and thinking of the US invasion and occupation within the frame of colonization, even if such realities are denied in official histories?

Imperial unknowing has been buttressed by colonial, postcolonial, and neocolonial histories and epistemologies. Following the First World War, the Ottoman provinces of what is now present-day Iraq were combined into the British Mandate state of Iraq. Under the mandate system, Iraq became a "protectorate." Implemented by the League of Nations, the

54   CHAPTER 1

mandate system involved two different, at times competing, doctrines of development: economic development, in which resources were extracted and exploited, and development of the people, in which governed peoples were imagined to need protection from and tutelage in the ways of the modern world (Pursley 2019).[15] Under the mandate system, the state of Iraq was to be ruled by the United Kingdom until such time as it was deemed that the Iraqis could govern themselves and become a sovereign state.

There are of course material links and continuities between the Mandate period and more recent imperial intervention in Iraq. If the League of Nations described the Mandate period as one of tutelage, Sara Pursley (2019) notes that it was accompanied by significant violence—including aerial bombardment and among the earliest use of chemical weapons—which she describes as necropolitical. Certainly the Mandate period was characterized by colonial resource extraction; subsequent imperial wars in Iraq can also be at least partly understood as struggles to expropriate and retain access to resources, especially oil (T. C. Jones 2012). However, just as there are rhetorical and material dimensions that expose the United States as an empire in denial, there are also elements of the invasion and occupation of Iraq that evoke colonization and may help in thinking through the occupation and its effects. One clear parallel is the rhetoric of primitivity and associated paternalistic ideas, resonant of the Mandate period, that the US was better equipped to manage Iraqis' affairs than Iraqis themselves. In the case of Iraq, such discourses often center on themes of ungovernability, as Omar Dewachi (2017) has carefully documented, and serve to erase the reality of Iraq as a country with, at the time of US-led intervention, well-developed education, health, and other infrastructures.

It is not necessary to remain only in the realm of metaphor, however. For just over a year after the invasion, the United States ruled Iraq directly through an occupation administration called the Coalition Provisional Authority (CPA). Headquartered in the Green Zone in Baghdad, the CPA was led by Paul Bremer, who had previously headed the National Commission on Terrorism. The self-styled viceroy of Iraq famously wore combat boots with his suits and ruled by decree, issuing numbered orders. Moving into the Green Zone with an army of private American companies and Republican-affiliated aides, consultants, and contractors with no knowledge or experience of Iraq, the CPA sought to build "the Middle East's first democracy" along neoliberal lines, as if from a terra nullius.

The CPA's short rule was marked by a particularly pugnacious version of imperial unknowing that would have lasting legacies in a number of ways: First, struggles for control between the Pentagon and the State Department led to the marginalization of the State Department in the administration of postwar Iraq, and with it, the sidelining of Iraqis as well as US government employees who had traveled to Iraq or other parts of the Middle East, who spoke Arabic, and who had studied Iraqi society and history. Reports written by the State Department went unread and personnel were systematically excluded from CPA meetings and planning (Packer 2006). It has been estimated that most CPA employees got their first ever passport to travel to Iraq (Chandrasekaran 2006). Once in Iraq, most CPA employees stayed within the walls of the heavily fortified Green Zone. They ate American food, watched US cable TV, and listened to 107.7 Freedom FM. Second, Bremer's de-Baathification policy—Coalition Provisional Authority Order 1—which ultimately forced out a significant portion of the preinvasion government bureaucracy, meant that tens of thousands of Iraqis who had been involved in the functioning of the state were suddenly jobless, and their knowledge of the country and its institutions was also dispersed. Coalition Provisional Authority Order 2 disbanded the Iraqi military as well as the intelligence and security services, rendering an additional five hundred thousand Iraqis immediately unemployed. Third, the CPA relied heavily on a small group of mostly exile Iraqis who were returning to the country after decades away and whose participation they organized along ethnic lines: Sunni, Shia, Kurd, Turkmen, and Assyrian (Rubaii 2019). Knowing and understanding Iraq were not central goals of the CPA, nor was meaningfully involving Iraqis in the governing of the country.

OCCUPATION ADMINISTRATION, SECTARIAN DIFFERENCE, AND THE "LOSS OF TRUST"

Sectarian difference—which came to the fore during the 2006–8 period that is often characterized as an ethnic civil war—is portrayed as being

56   CHAPTER 1

"ancient," "irreconcilable," and "inherently violent" in many accounts of the war. Its history is much shorter, however, and in its current form, it can be traced to the actions of the Coalition Provisional Authority itself. The CPA calcified *sect* as a tangible category of social and political division in a way that was new to Iraq: The CPA-drafted constitution of 2005 explicitly codified "sectarian categories of citizenship" (Rubaii 2019, 126) for the first time, and ID cards were issued that listed sectarian identity. In an effort to stop violence by insurgents, walls were erected to block off neighborhoods. These walls only served to cement and accelerate the reconfiguring of the city along sectarian lines (Gregory 2008a). The CPA's decision to suddenly dismantle the Iraqi state bureaucracy, military, and security forces without having alternatives in place was a disastrous experiment in social engineering. Some disaffected and unemployed former military joined insurgent groups and militias, and Iraqis, finding themselves without a social safety net in place, relied more on tribal affiliations for support (Al-Mohammad 2010). So when Iraqis said to me, as many did, that "we didn't know *sect* before the war," it was less a literal statement than a rejection of the ways that their lives had been violently redefined on sectarian terms.

Hassan described this period in terms of a "loss of trust." During these months, their neighborhood and Baghdad as a whole were increasingly being redefined in sectarian terms. It had always been a primarily Shia neighborhood, and Hassan and his family were Sunni, but it had never been an issue for them before the war. Speaking about his neighborhood, Hassan explained:

> Before this, the Sunni and Shia were like brothers in the same area, but after the situation became worse, they started to establish some kind of struggle for life where the stronger would win. The problems started whenever a Sunni was killed, a Shia would be accused, and when a Shia was killed, Shia would accuse Sunni. That was when the problems started. So it became like a loss of trust between the two parties, and each was trying to kill the other to feel safe. So, it was normal that the Shia dominated because the government was Shia, and [they could more] easily get armed.

Hassan's description of loss of trust departs from conventional accounts of sectarian violence in Iraq and indeed in the larger Middle East (or

Muslim world), which tend to posit sectarian differences as irreconcilable, primordial, and inherently violent. By contrast, Hassan recounted a recent, incremental, and localized process in which sectarian difference was transmuted into sectarian violence in the context of US occupation. Thus, when we spoke in 2007, Hassan was doing the work of discursively denying the primordial hypothesis and reversing this process of turning difference into violence by calling my attention not to naturalized enmity but to a "loss of trust" and referring back to a time when "Sunni and Shia were like brothers."[16]

Entisar had not only refused the American soldiers' request that she translate for them, but she also refused the terms of the request, especially when the soldiers sought to categorize her in sectarian terms: "The Americans asked me if I am Sunni or Shia. I told them, 'I am Iraqi! It makes no difference if I am Sunni or Shia!' The man pointed his gun in my face and yelled at me, 'Tell me which one!' I told them that I wanted to see flowers and peace, not guns, and they calmed down and said they were sorry."

As its multiethnic, multiconfessional neighborhoods were redrawn by force along sectarian lines, Baghdad suffered some of the worst of the postoccupation violence, and many of the Iraqis I met in Cairo had first been forced out of their neighborhoods or the entire city before having to flee the country entirely. For Hassan, the feeling of being threatened mounted over time, the unraveling of his mixed-sect neighborhood, the terror of the Americans occupying his house, and the perceived association with the Americans all intertwining. Once, while sitting outside in their garden, the family heard people passing by the house, talking amongst themselves, but loudly. They were saying, "We are going to explode every Sunni house in this area," Hassan said, and "we know that they meant for us to hear it." Soon afterwards, someone fired on the house again, but this time it was worse than before. Bullets shattered the windows as the family cowered inside. When I asked him, Hassan told me that he didn't know who was shooting but recognized that they were using machine guns. After that, Hassan and his family escaped "very early in the morning so that no one could see us moving. And we left the house with its contents . . . We left in three separate groups so that if they found us, they would not kill us all at once."

58   CHAPTER 1

Just as Hassan would never know exactly who had fired on his house or why, Entisar likewise explained how the terror of that time was partly rooted in the uncertainty of not knowing where the threat came from. Shortly before she received the death threat, one of her close friends had been kidnapped. Her body was never found. Entisar imagined that she had been abducted because she was Sunni, but she wasn't sure. She similarly didn't know who had threatened her life. She felt surveilled by neighbors with whom she had previously lived closely. "I do not know if the people who threatened me were Sunni or Shia, but I know that both sides hate me because I hated their methods. It is not a question of religion, it is a question of violence," Entisar explained. "It is so difficult to know who the real enemy is. That is why we had to leave Iraq: because we had no way of knowing who would hurt us, who the enemies were. We could never be safe."

. . . . .

We can discern numerous forms of imperial unknowing across the stages of the US-led invasion of Iraq: from the disorienting deception central to the selling of the war to the coalition of the willing, through the insistent staffing of the occupation with administrators utterly unfamiliar with the historical, political, and cultural context of Iraq, followed by the Orientalizing decontextualization and indifference of US military counterinsurgency, to the willful ignorance of the complexities of interethnic relations in prewar Iraqi life that accelerated the descent into intercommunal violence. By foregrounding the lived suffering and experiential uncertainty that these interventions generated for Iraqis who were ultimately displaced by the war, I begin the work of this book; I listen to the ways that Iraqi experiences challenge imperial unknowing, not least by showing the human costs of these interventions, costs that have been consistently ignored, silenced, devalued, distorted, and denied. But just as importantly, listening to the words of Iraqis opens up what has been foreclosed: a recognition of the relationships—including the debts, obligations, and reciprocities—that have been created through imperial interventions.

One crucial relationship is the connection between imperial warmaking and humanitarian aid. We will see in the chapters that follow that

Iraqis found ways to insist upon a recognition of the debts, obligations, and other relationships that have been created between them and those who have intervened, invaded, and occupied, especially US empire. In the chapters to come, Iraqis will continue to try to assert other reciprocal obligations in the refugee resettlement process, which will insist on its neutrality and humanitarianism. However, politics of imperial unknowing extend from war into humanitarian processes as well. Accounts such as Entisar's were confounding in the context of refugee legal aid, where international protection required clear, specific threats with motives that could be attributed to one of the specific categories of persecution that are protected in the Refugee Convention. However, in Entisar's case, the threats were multiple and reflected more than anything the "epistemic murk" that Michael Taussig uses to describe political violence and terror. The failure of the resettlement process to accommodate Entisar's uncertainty about who threatened her and why illustrates how the politics of imperial unknowing travel from military to humanitarian intervention, while the lived consequences of imperial unknowing likewise retain relevance in Iraqis' lives as they themselves move from Iraq to Egypt to possible resettlement elsewhere.

For us, though, perhaps we can try to imagine something different, to sit with Entisar's uncertainty and see the narratives presented here not as a recovery project but as accounts and theorizations of an armament of imperial power that would not be discernable without seeing the war and occupation from the point of view of Iraqis. In this, I am inspired by Lisa Stevenson's (2014) provocation to consider uncertainty as an ethnographic mode, a way of listening that abides with our interlocutors and does not try to demand fixity in a world where some things are simply unknowable, ephemeral, uncertain. In building on my interlocutors' accounts and their own analyses of the occupation, I hope to foreground Iraqis' accounts and experiences of war as central. I intend this narrative as a counterhistory to that of an invasion and occupation that actively sought to discount and obscure the suffering of Iraqis. These elisions are part of the larger politics of unknowing that was integral to imperial intervention in Iraq; to attend to them renders imperial unknowing and its subjective effects visible. Accounts of war are of course situated, partial, and contested. Yet even if we accept that there may be no

60 CHAPTER 1

way to tell a "true war story" (Nordstrom 1997), I argue that there is something to be gained by attending to the stories people tell about war, especially when those stories diverge from dominant accounts of conflict, forcing us to question both what we know about war and how we come to know it.

2 War Archive

TELLING AND LISTENING TO WAR STORIES

"My troubles began when my brother Ali was killed by the American troops," Mazen begins. We sit opposite one another at the long wooden dining room table where, just days after arriving in Cairo, I have been transformed into a legal advocate in training. It is a chilly—by Cairo standards—January day in 2007. A slender pharmacist in his early thirties, Mazen has come for our interview dressed in pressed slacks and a button-down shirt. I find myself easily imagining him in his prior life behind the counter of his eponymous pharmacy, dispensing medicine and advice to patients as he used to do before he had to leave his native Baghdad. As Mazen talks, I listen and absorb, furiously typing every word I can catch into my laptop while trying to maintain eye contact. Mazen has so much to say that I abandon my prepared list of questions and just try to transcribe as much as possible. He is my first client at the legal aid clinic and I am both nervous and eager to do a good job taking his testimony.

Mazen was unusual in that some aspects of his testimony were, as he put it, "a famous story in the media." Mazen's brother Ali was one of two journalists killed by US forces in Baghdad in the spring of 2004. Unlike the experiences described in chapter 1, the killing of Mazen's brother was not entirely absent from the public record of the war. It was partially

62   CHAPTER 2

known, having been briefly covered by the international media. This media coverage created enough pressure that the US military conducted a short investigation into the killings. Unlike in the case of the vast majority of complaints brought by Iraqi civilians during the war and occupation, the military eventually admitted responsibility for the deaths, although they deemed them an "accident." They did not release any details of their investigation. It would be years before the military responded to a Freedom of Information Act request filed by the Committee to Protect Journalists, and even then they would make only some of the investigation records available, redacting and rejecting other parts.

In chapter 1, I described how relations of imperial unknowing colored Iraqis' experiences of trying to live through and with military invasion and occupation, eventually forcing them to leave Iraq and seek refuge in Egypt. Here, I focus on a different set of relational practices, namely telling and listening, to consider how war stories find or do not find audiences willing to receive them and what that means for how war is archived, remembered, or forgotten. I recount Mazen's narrative of his experiences during the war as shared with me during multiple conversations, both within and outside of the testimony process, beginning with our first meeting in 2007. I have chosen to anchor this chapter in Mazen's account for several reasons. The first is that it illustrates how the struggle over knowledge production and dissemination in war has life-or-death consequences for those engaged in the labor of producing and sharing knowledge as well for as their kin and communities. This is especially true for knowledge that challenges or at least does not conform to imperially sanctioned forms, practices, and figures. It also shows us that, much as the US military might wish to minimize or obscure certain kinds of war violence, counternarratives circulate, persist, and demand reckoning, even if they might struggle to find a willing audience. This is true even in humanitarian processes like resettlement or asylum adjudication, where one might imagine that the possibilities for such forms of resistance and refusal are significantly constrained. These counternarratives—all the more remarkable for how Iraqis insisted on them even in contexts that were unwelcoming or hostile to their accounts—offer historiographical and archival potential for seeing war differently. There can be no single archive of war; rather, there are ongoing and unequally positioned struggles over how war is historicized:

a war of archives, if you will. This struggle over war archives is not solely epistemological. On the contrary, the archival desires of people such as Mazen illustrate how significant the personal and political stakes are of the stories that dominant narratives of war seek to elide or obscure.

MAKING MYSELF USEFUL

Before sharing what Mazen told me, I want to recount the circumstances and setting in which we came to know one another because they raise important methodological, ethical, and epistemological questions about the possibilities for ethnography at the margins of legal adjudication processes and illuminate the material dimensions of the archive that I develop in this chapter. I also linger on my positionality and methods because one way to understand this chapter is as a layered and connected set of efforts to create and tell narratives about the Iraq War that empire would prefer to hide, an effort in which I am an active participant. Before turning to Mazen and his brother, then, I consider how I am implicated and constrained within the institutions and processes that render counternarratives of empire both possible and impossible and how these processes limit not only audiences for Mazen's accounts but also what I can know and share. Many of the other accounts and experiences I describe throughout this book relate to asylum and resettlement but emerge either at the margins of these processes or in informal spaces, such as people's homes or community events. However, in this chapter, significant parts of what I share emerged directly within the context of refugee legal aid and especially within the testimony process.

Mazen and I first met when I was volunteering in the informal legal aid clinic that Barbara Harrell-Bond established in her apartment, which would later come to be formalized as the Resettlement Legal Aid Project (RLAP). When I first proposed conducting ethnographic research with Iraqis in Cairo, I was generously welcomed but cautioned, first by Barbara and later by Iraqi friends in Cairo, that if I wanted to do research I would also need to "make myself useful." As a graduate student keenly aware of the ethical challenges and extractive possibilities of research, I was easy to convince. Over the years, this effort to be useful has led me to engage in a

64   CHAPTER 2

wide range of practices of mutual care and reciprocity, including helping with résumés, accompanying friends to doctor's visits or embassies, connecting people to services or resources, carrying gifts, writing reference letters, deciphering forms and rules, and organizing social events. The more formal way that I tried to make myself useful in the field was through volunteering, first as a legal intern under Barbara's supervision and then later in both legal aid and psychosocial support programming at RLAP.

"Write to Doctor Barbara," more than one person told me when I first expressed interest in traveling to Egypt to work with refugees. So began an email exchange that would, as I would later learn it had done for countless others, conscript me into the late Barbara Harrell-Bond's lifelong, worldwide network of activists, advocates, and scholars. "Dear Nadia, time is flying. Are you coming?" read one urgent early correspondence, sent at 2:49 a.m. Cairo time, with no subject line and no sign-off. I should have had an inkling then of what I was in for. But the emails, low on prose, full of instructions, and frequently in all caps, did not prepare me for working with the woman known by refugees and seemingly everyone in Cairo and beyond as Doktora Barbara.

Barbara Harrell-Bond was the author of *Imposing Aid: Emergency Assistance to Refugees* (1986), a landmark study and unsparing critique of humanitarian aid. She had gone on to found refugee studies programs and legal aid networks in the UK, Uganda, Egypt, Kenya, and South Africa alongside writing numerous books and articles on refugees and humanitarianism, combined with teaching, network building, and formal and ad hoc advocacy for refugees.[1] In Cairo, everyone seemed to find their way to Barbara's door. All day long the doorbell of her Garden City apartment would ring. Life for refugees in Egypt was and is hard. There is little humanitarian assistance available and the structures set in place sometimes seem designed to hurt more than they help, if they can be deciphered at all. But more on that soon. Doktora Barbara was who you sought out when your case was rejected, your husband was detained by state security, you had been subject to a racist attack in the streets of Cairo, you couldn't afford food or medicine, or you had been turned away by other organizations. Although famous in anthropology for her early critique of humanitarianism, Barbara's help was often solicited on exactly these grounds.

In the far left corner of the apartment, behind a perforated screen, was Barbara's workspace consisting of a computer and endless files, folders, and books. This was where Barbara worked, sending emails and orders out into the world, her electronic cigarette always in hand. On my first day in her apartment, I and the other new recruits, a Canadian master's student and American law student, huddled around Barbara on mismatched chairs as she gave us assignments. Barbara explained that she believed new policies, especially the Refugee Crisis in Iraq Act being passed in the United States, meant that many of the Iraqi refugees then living in Cairo were likely eligible for third-country resettlement but that no organization in Egypt was helping them with the process. She needed us to take their testimonies to advocate for their resettlement.

It was through learning and practicing testimony that I came to some of the questions that animate this book as well as some of the methodological lessons that I used when I returned to Cairo in 2009 for a longer stint of fieldwork. Volunteering while also conducting ethnographic research created an uneasy ethnographic positionality. To respect client privacy, I cannot write about the vast majority of my legal aid work, although my experiences of working in refugee legal aid are central to my understanding of the resettlement process. My consideration of epistemology is therefore partly based on the experiential, embodied act of coming to understand resettlement by learning to conduct legal aid and taking testimonies myself. I was both inside and outside of the resettlement process—on the one hand, working to help my clients seek recognition but on the other hand, noticing the limitations of the process in which I was involved, especially the ways it reproduced imperial violence and humanitarian hierarchies. There was so much that emerged during the testimony process that exceeded the humanitarian and security grounds of the process, geared as it was to convincing the United Nations High Commissioner for Refugees (UNHCR) and states to accept individual Iraqis as both in need of protection and not a threat. As a legal advocate, I found myself culling and editing out some of the details that my clients said were most important to them in order to conform to the requirements of the resettlement regime. Over time, I started to think of these excesses as an important archive of the violence of imperial intervention, an archive without an audience.

66   CHAPTER 2

In many ways I tried to separate my research from my legal work because I wanted to build relations with Iraqis in Cairo beyond and outside of the humanitarian sphere, and I was afraid that people might feel compelled to speak with me or that they might view me as a representative of the humanitarian system and, understandably, carefully guard what they told me. The former concern turned out to be almost completely unfounded as many people had no trouble whatsoever not talking to me. The second turned out to be partly well-founded, at least initially. However, as time went on and I developed deeper relationships, it became easier for me both to see when this was happening as well as to notice when—even in humanitarian spaces—practices, events, and narratives emerged that exceeded, undermined, and sometimes outright challenged humanitarian forms of government. Of course there were moments when I was unsure whether I was being viewed as part of the broader resettlement process and also moments when I was absolutely sure that I was. While I began my work in refugee legal aid as an accompaniment to research and out of an ethical commitment to practicing some form of reciprocity, however imperfect, it soon became clear that conducting ethnographic research from within the legal aid clinic, which operated on the margins of UNHCR and state resettlement processes but was deeply entangled with them, was one of the only ways that I would come to understand the opaque and bureaucratic resettlement system. It was also through participant observation of refugee legal aid that I came to understand how the resettlement system, despite its stated aim of protection and its reliance on refugees' testimonies, was unable to hear the stories that were of most importance to the people it was ostensibly aiming to protect. But, as I learned, this would not stop people like Mazen from insisting on telling them.

Throughout this book, I move awkwardly but intentionally between the roles of legal advocate and ethnographer. Although some of the practices of each look the same on the surface—interviewing, documenting, listening, and analyzing—they are ultimately shaped as divergent practices by their aims, contexts, forms, and audiences. The vast majority of my legal aid work is protected by agreements of client confidentiality, and I do not include it here. Of the many clients with whom I worked, I asked a small number if they would be willing to have their legal aid processes and their testimonies become part of my ethnographic research. I then conducted at least one separate interview with each of these people. Mazen was among them. Much of the ethnographic material I share in other chapters occurs outside of the refugee legal aid process and outside or on the margins of formal humanitarian spaces, but in this chapter I turn to some of what I learned within the practices and settings of the legal aid process itself.

To be clear, I do not subscribe to the view that ethnographic "data" is inescapably sullied by relations of obligation, care, and indebtedness that inevitably emerge throughout years of building relations with individuals and communities or even through institutional relations, asymmetric as they certainly are, such as that between legal advocate and client. Such a view presupposes some knowledge production that exists outside of relationships and structures of power and, equally concerningly, imagines interlocutors predominantly as exploitable victims and not as thoughtful, critical interlocutors and theorizers in their own right who may choose if and how they engage with an ethnographer. Humanitarian and scholarly structures and relationships often infantilize refugees instead of considering them as knowledge producers who are pursuing their own meaningful life projects (Espiritu et al 2022).

It is from these imbricated relationships, unevenly positioned in structures of power but not in pro forma ways, that I write this chapter out of a sense of obligation to Mazen. This obligation is not only grounded in our interpersonal relationship but references larger relations of indebtedness that emerge from research, from war, and from empire itself. One of the things that has most stayed with me, even years after first hearing this story, is how Mazen's account of the events has been dismissed, negated, or denied an audience. On top of the violence committed against Mazen and his family, I see this silencing as a second, related form of imperial war violence that persists long after war has allegedly ended. I came to understand the contours of this process of silencing as well as the content of what is obscured through Mazen's narrative and his commitment to entering what he knows into the record. In this sense, Mazen understood our relationship—both in the testimony process and then in the context of my research—as one of archive making.

68   CHAPTER 2

TAKING TESTIMONY

In refugee legal aid, a testimony is a chronological written account of a refugee's life, focusing on their experiences of persecution, flight, and their circumstances in displacement, that lays out a case for their refugee status or resettlement. It is intended as an attestation to the events that have forced a person into exile and led them to ask for protection and often includes various forms of supporting evidence including photos, letters, reports from experts, and other documents. Unlike some other more public forms of testimony such as those used in truth and reconciliation processes, it is an archive with a very small audience: it may be forwarded to the UNHCR, the International Organization for Migration (IOM), or resettlement country embassies in the hopes that it will convince one of these institutions to consider a refugee for resettlement. The testimony's importance lies partly in the fact that much of what a refugee will be judged on in adjudication processes cannot be verified independently from the account that refugees themselves provide. In the absence of further evidence, asylum officers and other adjudicators judge the content and form of a refugee's narrative, hoping to glean who is "deserving" of protection and who can, or should, be excluded (Bohmer and Shuman 2007).

The goal of testimony-based refugee legal aid, at least as I learned to practice it in Cairo, is to work with refugees or asylum-seekers to construct a narrative document that can then be sent to adjudicators—the UNHCR, the IOM, or more rarely directly to the authorities of a state with a resettlement program—so that the case for an individual's or family's resettlement is already made in a way that is palatable and legible to these gatekeepers. Although the testimony is a document that seeks to render people legible to the state or its representatives, documents are never one single thing. As Heath Cabot (2012) writes, documents have complex and contradictory lives that can also render people illegible or create opportunities to undermine the governmental purposes for which they are intended. In Egypt, neither the state nor the UNHCR offer asylum-seekers or refugees any form of legal assistance, and so a small number of nongovernmental organizations have sprung up to assist people in navigating the complex and often inscrutable bureaucracies that govern asylum and resettlement in Cairo. The role of these organizations is both collaborative and conflictual with existing asylum and migration-control regimes: On the one hand, in order to have their work taken seriously by the UNHCR or the IOM, organizations such as RLAP must carefully choose only "good cases" or risk losing credibility. Indeed, over the course of my fieldwork, as RLAP expanded from an office that worked only with Iraqis to include people regardless of nationality, their intake process became more and more formalized and selective.[2] On the other hand, legal aid organizations had a partially adversarial role with the UNHCR and the Egyptian state, which I will discuss more in subsequent chapters. Historically the UNHCR resisted allowing asylum-seekers to have legal representation and only permitted it after significant lobbying from NGOs, but even then only for refugee status determination (formalized as a right under international law) and never resettlement. NGOs also documented and sought to intervene in rights abuses by the UNHCR and the Egyptian state as well as critiqued discrimination against refugees and migrants in Egypt.

Taking testimony is a time- and labor-intensive process. After a brief initial screening to ensure the applicant fit within resettlement criteria, I would conduct multiple interviews with them, aided by an interpreter when necessary. To build the life story that would become the testimony and to prepare the applicant for the questions adjudicators would ask, I would ask detailed questions about all periods of a person's life: names, dates, addresses, places, and people. As I did this work, I was often struck by how difficult it was to present one's life in this way to a stranger. To this day, whenever I struggle to remember the date of an event or the precise address of a place I used to live, I am reminded of the impossibility of the task asylum-seekers and refugees face within hostile bureaucratic systems.

Once I had gathered sufficient information, I would work to transform the client's answers into a chronological life history and a legal argument that laid out why they met the criteria for refugee status and then third-country resettlement. This involved a process of resolving inconsistencies, conducting background research, deleting details deemed irrelevant, chronological reordering, and compiling evidentiary support. The testimony was focused on affirmatively arguing for a client's refugee claim as

70   CHAPTER 2

well as any additional reasons they should be considered for resettlement, because resettlement was only given to a small percentage of refugees— those who could prove particular vulnerability or their association with the occupying forces. Family members abroad who might perhaps sponsor or otherwise support a refugee when resettled were listed. The testimony also included some defensive moves: When applicable, military service was exhaustively catalogued to allay any fears of the applicant having committed war crimes, government employment and Baath Party membership was documented to make the relationship with the previous regime clear, and any ransoms paid to free oneself or a loved one from kidnapping were carefully described as coerced to avoid being interpreted as "material support" for terrorism. The humanitarian and human rights criteria for protection as well as the ways the state figured refugees, but especially Iraqis, as having possibly committed past harm or being a risk for future harm took up most of the testimony.

The testimony would be checked by a lawyer and then reread to the applicant to be sure no details were missed. Sometimes the applicants would bring evidence of their own to support their narrative, including proof of violence, such as threat letters, photos of injuries or destruction, as well as documentation of the effects of violence and displacement on their lives, such as medical or psychiatric reports. Only certain forms of violence and some kinds of injuries were deemed worthy of recognition within the resettlement process. There were those that conformed to refugee law—for example, persecution needed to be a specific threat on the basis of protected grounds in order to be considered; violence that could not be understood as specifically targeting the applicant directly was not considered sufficient. In chapter 4 I will discuss the forms of violence, need, and vulnerability that were recognized in the resettlement process. But here I begin with what the resettlement process might regard as excess but what we, following Mazen's guidance, might regard as what is most worthy of our listening.

While their narratives form a crucial aspect of the asylum process, refugees are frequently represented both implicitly and explicitly as imperfect, unreliable, or even fraudulent narrators of their own experiences. This double bind—in which narrative is both essential and suspect—pervades asylum and resettlement processes worldwide and reflects the hermeneutic of

WAR ARCHIVE 71

suspicion (Ricoeur 1977; Haas and Shuman 2018) that refugees face as they seek recognition and protection. Suspicion is wielded and weaponized in discourses applied to entire populations of people on the move when, despite their assertions about fleeing violence or persecution, they are scapegoated as "economic migrants," "security threats," or "potential terrorists." Suspicion also asserts itself in more intimate institutional encounters when refugees or asylum-seekers are compelled to repeatedly recount what are often some of the worst experiences of their lives to gatekeepers who, despite their best intentions, often regard them with distrust. Here the testimony serves another function in the resettlement process as adjudicators evaluate it for perceived inconsistencies and compare it to the oral accounts refugees offer in interviews as well as other evidence such as travel documents and reports. This was especially true for my Iraqi interlocutors, who had to prove themselves to be deserving victims while also defending against being perceived as terrorists, supporters of the previous regime, or both.

What follows is not Mazen's testimony but my compilation of a narrative he offered partly in the context of the testimony process and partly outside of it. In this chapter, I rely on my field notes, interview notes, and transcriptions as opposed to the final testimony because I am more interested in what Mazen wanted to tell and how his narrative exceeded the resettlement process than I am in its transformation into a legal argument. Mazen was glad to know that I was a researcher because he wanted his account to be heard and entered into the record. In this way, I think of Mazen as a subject of history in Trouillot's (2015, 23–24) sense; that the events he describes altered his life is clear, but it is not only the events themselves but his narration, his voice, that create the possibility for history even from within a bureaucratic process not intended to do anything of the sort. But this did not mean that it was necessarily easy for him to share it or that he did not have specific ideas about how he wanted his story told; because of ongoing safety and privacy concerns, we decided together to leave some details out and gloss over others. I focus on what Mazen brought to our conversations and intentionally include details that were excluded or de-emphasized in his final testimony and maintain, as much as possible, his voice.

The story recounted here is itself situated in particular locations, times, relationships, and processes of knowledge production, each replete with

72 CHAPTER 2

its own slippages, emphases, and silences. Testimonies are not only performative documents that seek to conform to the demands and dictates of refugee bureaucracies. The process of creating them involves dialogic encounters and intersubjective performances that produce relations and narratives that are related to, but do not conform to, the humanitarian conventions of the testimony. To view them only within the confines of demands of deservingness elides the ways that the encounters that produce the testimonies and, indeed, the testimonies themselves exceed and at times subvert what is demanded of them. It is tempting to imagine the testimony process as one in which the entire encounter is overdetermined by humanitarian logics and where the interviewer holds all the power—and there certainly is, of course, a power imbalance. But what I learned from taking dozens of testimonies and observing the work of the legal aid clinic for more than a year is that neither the presumption that refugees are powerless victims forced to give up their stories nor that they are cynical actors making up stories in order to get status had much explanatory power. I learned this early with Mazen, my first client, who had a story he wanted to tell that did not fit easily into the resettlement process but demanded wider forms of accountability. In this way, I began to see how what emerged in my legal aid work was not only testimonies that individual clients used to seek refugee status or resettlement but also stories not told in other settings, documents produced and collated in new ways, and connections drawn between individual experiences and the politics of imperial violence and humanitarianism. In short, an alternative archive of the war, one that emerges within the testimony process but cannot be captured by it. Here is one small part of that archive.

LISTENING TO A DIFFERENT KIND OF WAR STORY

Mazen is one of seven siblings from a Shia family from Baghdad. When he was nine years old, his father was conscripted into military service as part of the mass mobilization during the Iran-Iraq War. Shortly after, he was captured as a prisoner of war in Iran. The war, which lasted from 1980 to 1988, profoundly affected Iraqis' lives both during and after the conflict. One significant effect was the militarization of Iraqi society as Saddam

Hussein implemented massive conscription to prosecute the nearly decade-long war, which was fought on land, sea, and air.[3] By the war's end, one million Iraqis were mobilized. An estimated 250,000 Iraqis died during the war. A quarter of these casualties were Iraqi Kurds, many of them civilians, who were killed by the Iraqi military during the late 1980s as part of the Anfal campaign, which sought to brutally reassert control over the north of the country and suppress Kurdish dissent. The United States supported Saddam Hussein's prosecution of the war through a range of actions, including the provision of intelligence, funds, goods, and arms, including the sale of the materials for producing chemical and biological weapons, which Hussein subsequently used against Iraqi Kurds (Bonet 2022; Saleh 2020). As the war dragged on, the combination of massive arms and military expenditures with declining oil sales contributed to an increased national debt, which rose to eighty billion dollars by 1988 (Tripp 2007). Saddam Hussein's decision to invade Kuwait in 1990 was at least partly an attempt to relieve these burdens. After the war's end, some sixty thousand Iraqis remained detained inside Iran as prisoners of war while thousands of Iranian prisoners of war were also held in Iraqi jails. Although some were released in prisoner swaps at the end of the war, many, like Mazen's father, would be held for years afterward.

Left alone with six children, Mazen's mother, who had been pregnant when her husband was captured in 1982, did the best she could to support the family. As he got older, Mazen balanced studies with part-time work in order to contribute to the family's income. It was during one of these jobs, working in a small private pharmacy during the school holidays, that Mazen met his future wife, Zainab. His father's imprisonment also led Mazen to compete for a contract from the Department of Defense to become a military pharmacist, a position that, when he received it, guaranteed his income and his ability to support his mother and siblings. In 1998, Mazen's father was finally released and returned to his family, where he met his youngest son, then sixteen years old, for the first time.

After his graduation, Mazen worked as a pharmacist in a military hospital and ran a private pharmacy on the side. He and Zainab got engaged. Just five years after his father's release, war came again. The 2003 war would also have devastating effects for the family. When the Coalition Provisional Authority disbanded the armed forces, Mazen lost his job at

74   CHAPTER 2

the military hospital. Luckily, he was able to work in his private pharmacy and eventually found a job at a civilian hospital. His brother, who was just one year younger and a journalist for Iraqi National Television, also had to rebuild his career in the aftermath of the invasion when Iraqi national media were shuttered by the Coalition Provisional Authority as well. Ali was able to secure a job with Al Arabiya, a newly founded Saudi satellite news channel based in Dubai that targeted a pan-Arab audience. In this way, both brothers were more fortunate than many Iraqis who had worked for the expansive bureaucratic state and who found themselves unemployed in the aftermath of the occupation. They were able to continue working in their professions, albeit in different capacities. But as journalism became more and more dangerous in the aftermath of the invasion and occupation, Ali would not remain so lucky.

.   .   .   .   .

Ali's death took place around 8:30 p.m. on a spring night a year after the initial invasion. Along with a colleague from Al Arabiya and a driver, Ali had gone to report on the bombing of a hotel in Baghdad. They weren't alone: "There were about five cars from other TV stations, including global and national networks, such as CNN. Each press vehicle had 'TV' written in large capital letters on all four sides and on the top. This allows them to be identified as press at night and from the air." Mazen recounted this detail emphatically, repeating it several times during our conversation to ensure that I understood that his brother could not have been reasonably mistaken for anything other than a journalist.

Mazen did not directly witness his brother's killing, but others did. Many other journalists had also congregated to cover the story. In the days following the attack, the other journalists who had been present, many of whom were also Iraqis working for international news outlets and his brother's friends, came to the family's home in Baghdad to pay condolences and relay what they had witnessed, as did people working in the shops in the area. The only survivor from the Al Arabiya crew was the driver. He also visited the family's house to describe what he had experienced. The family's knowledge of Ali's death is largely constructed from these witness accounts.

From these witnesses, Mazen and his family learned that the US troops had set up a checkpoint in the neighborhood near the site of the attack. Assuming that I likely did not have firsthand experience of checkpoints, Mazen patiently described one to me, explaining how when the US troops would go out into the streets, they would set up temporary checkpoints, cordoning off areas in an effort to ensure their security by controlling others' movements. People learned to be extremely careful around these checkpoints, Mazen noted: "If anything threatens one of their vehicles, the rest of the [forces] will shoot randomly at anything that is moving."

On the night he was killed, Ali got out of the car and asked an American officer if he could interview him about the attack on the hotel. "The officer refused because he said that Al Arabiya and also Al Jazeera conduct interviews with terrorists and those who are in opposition to the American occupation," Mazen told me. "Because of this, according to the officer, the networks were supporting the terrorists. He then told my brother that he and his colleagues had to leave." According to witnesses, Ali then returned to the car, loaded the equipment, and prepared to leave.

At that moment, a man driving a white Volvo approached the checkpoint. Perhaps he hadn't seen the yellow tape indicating the new checkpoint until it was too late. As the car approached the checkpoint, the American troops opened fire, shooting the man in the Volvo many times and killing him. The white Volvo is present in all the reports—it is central to Mazen's account, the news reporting on the incident, and the US report. But despite the presence of the "white Volvo" as a specific, integral detail, the person inside the Volvo remains unnamed in Mazen's description and all subsequent reporting I read. I am haunted by the Volvo's driver. Who was he? How did those he knew learn about his fate, if they ever did? Mazen continued:

> Then, the troops shot the car of the Al Arabiya TV station where my brother and his colleagues had been loading their things and preparing to leave. We know that they were in the car because the back-windshield glass was broken by the shooting and there were witnesses to this. The same officer who told my brother to leave then ordered the two soldiers who were standing on the tank to jump down on the street. The two soldiers used a red laser light to aim at their heads and shot them. Each of the Al Arabiya employees, including my brother, had about three bullets in the head. They used the

76   CHAPTER 2

type of bullets that explode inside the body. After the shooting, the American troops refused to transfer them to the hospital.

When Mazen and his parents learned the news of the shooting, the family, along with their neighbors, piled into cars and traveled in a procession through the city at night to reach Ali in the hospital. Mazen recalled that they were all crying. To avoid further tragedy, the caravan flew white flags from the cars, a signal that they were not combatants. In Baghdad, ordinary people learned and employed the iconography of international humanitarian law as part of the new grammar of everyday life under occupation. Mazen described the family's anxious procession to the hospital, slowed on the way by searches of their cars at each military checkpoint they crossed. Once they reached the hospital where they thought Ali was being treated, a staff member told them that Ali had died. On hearing the news, Mazen's mother fainted. Shortly after, they learned with bittersweet relief that Mazen's brother's colleague, also named Ali, had died at the scene and that their Ali, who was on life support, had been transferred to another hospital. With intermingled sorrow and hope, the family rushed to the second hospital, which specialized in neurological problems. Mazen described the scene once they arrived:

> There was only one doctor there who was on rotation. At 6 a.m. a specialist came, and he wanted to do surgery. When he found that my brother had been shot with the type of bullet that explodes inside the body, he was not able to do anything. At that point my sister's husband, who is a plastic surgeon, said to my father and I that we must make the decision whether or not to shut off the oxygen. So, my sister's husband made that decision and we shut off the oxygen.

KILLING THE MESSENGER

As Mazen's account clearly shows, Iraq was a risky, even deadly, place to be a journalist during the 2003 invasion and subsequent occupation. More journalists and media support workers were killed in this conflict than in any other. Between 1994 and 2003, the Committee to Protect Journalists documented the killing of one journalist in Iraq. Between 2003 and 2022, that number jumps to 282 (CPJ n.d.). How and why were journalists and other media workers subject to so much violence, and what does this reveal about how war is fought and also understood? There are many answers to what is a complex question, but for the purposes of this chapter I propose we consider how the construction of Iraq as "dangerous" intersected with the US military's counterinsurgent aims as well as the impunity of necropolitical violence in the context of war. The portrayal of Iraq as dangerous was a tactic used by the occupying forces to dissuade journalists and other critical observers from traveling independently to and within Iraq at the same time as they themselves were the direct source of at least some of the danger, as we see from Mazen's account. This strategy was effective. By 2004, foreign journalists were either not traveling to Iraq at all, or they were reporting from the confinement of fortified bureaus in the few hotels that remained open or from embedded positions within the occupying forces where they were promised greater protection but had to run their stories by the military before publishing them.[4] The war in Iraq was the first time that the US military embedded a large number of journalists within its ranks. While a few journalists were embedded with US troops in the war in Afghanistan in 2001, around six hundred journalists were embedded with US and coalition troops in Iraq. Embedding was an elaborate military program, involving months of training for the journalists involved. It was also controversial; critics argued that journalists could be neither objective nor critical while they were literally "in bed" with the US forces.[5]

The prevalence of embedding journalists led to a paradoxical situation in which war coverage was ubiquitous, with journalists having seemingly unparalleled access to the battlefield, but coverage was almost always, quite literally, from the vantage point of the occupying forces. The inundation of coverage, which took many forms including twenty-four-hour live broadcasting of the invasion on cable news networks such as CNN and Fox News, is given material form in artist Rachel Khedoori's installation *The Iraq Book Project.* In the documentary exhibition, Khedoori compiled print news coverage that focused on Iraq from 2003 to 2009. Collected in identical books with no line or page breaks between the text, lined up on identical tables and filling an immense room, the artist attempts to interrogate what is known and recorded about the war. The effect is one of volume and weighty presence, which sits in stark tension to *The Guardian* reporter Maggie O'Kane's 2005 observation: "We no longer know what is going on, but we

78   CHAPTER 2

are pretending we do: any decent reporter knows that reporting from Baghdad does a disservice to the truth" (O'Kane 2005 in Gregory 2010).

During the invasion and occupation, media coverage became what Judith Butler (2016, 29) has called a "mode of military conduct."[6] But while it is important to focus on the content and perspective of media, especially given its counterinsurgent aims, it can be easy to forget that these imperial objectives were achieved through the risk to and loss of Iraqi lives. As Iraq became more dangerous for foreign reporters, the media came to rely more heavily on Iraqis to gather the coverage that would sustain the war's media machine. An increase in both occupying forces and the multiplying insurgent groups targeting journalists was accompanied by an intensified reliance on Iraqis to do the dangerous work of providing the on-the-ground war coverage, illustrating how differently Iraqi lives were valued during wartime. By 2005 the majority of journalists killed in Iraq were Iraqi, reflecting the unequal distribution of the risk of covering the war and the burden of knowledge-making both in alignment with and counter to US counterinsurgency in Iraq.

Ali and his colleague were far from the only journalists and media workers killed by the US forces. To remember only some of the most well-known examples: Tareq Ayyoub, a Jordanian working for the Qatar-based Al Jazeera, was killed when a US missile struck the Baghdad bureau offices of Al Jazeera on April 8, 2003 (CPJ [2005?]). The coalition forces claimed that they had been responding to fire from the location of the bureau and that they were acting within the "right of self-defense." Media reports at the time recounted that Al Jazeera had shared their bureau's location with the US forces months in advance and received assurances that they would not be targeted. After the attack, the Pentagon claimed that the building was a "known Al-Qaeda facility"[7] and claimed ignorance of the presence of the Al Jazeera bureau (CPJ [2005?]). Like Mazen and his family, Ayyoub's family does not believe his killing was an accident (Patel 2011). Later that same day, a US tank fired on the Palestine Hotel, a well-known Baghdad hotel then housing many civilian workers involved in the war, including journalists. Spanish cameraman José Couso and Ukrainian cameraman Taras Protsyuk, who both worked for Reuters, were killed and three other journalists were wounded. An investigation by US military authorities found that the tank unit was acting "within the

Rules of Engagement" and that the shelling had been a "proportionate and justifiably measured response" (CPJ 2008).

Perhaps the most well-known incident is the killing of a group of eleven civilians, including two Iraqi Reuters employees, Saeed Chmagh and Namir Nour-Eldeen, as well as the serious wounding of two children by US troops in New Baghdad in July 2007. Gunsight footage of the attack was leaked by Chelsea Manning in 2010 and then subsequently released by WikiLeaks, along with supporting documentation, still photos, a transcript, and analysis, under the title "Collateral Murder" (WikiLeaks, n.d.). It is worth taking a moment to consider WikiLeaks' founder Julian Assange's intention in choosing the name "Collateral Murder." "We want to knock out this 'collateral damage' euphemism," Assange stated, "and so when anyone uses it they will think collateral murder" (Tidy 2017, 97). The gunsight footage released by WikiLeaks places the viewer alongside the crew inside the Apache helicopter before, during, and after the killing. Watching it on www.wikileaks.com, viewers see what those who pulled the trigger saw and hear what they are saying as they do it.[8] In the crosshairs, Nour-Eldeen and Chmagh, alongside other civilians, appear as slightly pixelated black-and-white figures moving through a grayscale cityscape. On the "Collateral Murder" website, alongside the footage is the perspective from the other side of the sight lines. Still photos show the last pictures photojournalist Nour-Eldeen took: one just before the attack, then one in the first seconds of the attack that would take his life, and then finally one taken by US soldiers with Nour-Eldeen's camera after Nour-Eldeen had been gunned down. After the killings, Reuters demanded an investigation and sought the release of the video footage under the Freedom of Information Act. The results of the US military investigation concluded that the crew of the helicopter had acted within the rules of engagement and the law of armed conflict. The video was not released until it was leaked in 2010.[9]

"WE CAN DO NOTHING"

Mazen's account shares many commonalities with these other occurrences of the US military's violence against journalists, not least the failures and injustices of the response from US authorities. As Mazen notes:

80   CHAPTER 2

> There were many, many witnesses and much evidence, but because of the circumstances and the conditions of Iraq, we can do nothing. There was a law made by the ex-governor of Iraq, Paul Bremer, which says that the Iraqi courts cannot judge American soldiers. This law still exists. After two days, the American forces opened an investigation into the shooting of the Al Arabiya employees. After a period of a few weeks, an officer issued a statement saying that it was an accident. That was all.

As in other instances where civilians, including journalists, were killed by military personnel, the US military was the only body empowered to conduct the investigation into its own potential wrongdoing. A short investigation ruled the deaths collateral damage: a "regrettable" accident. This was not convincing to Mazen, his family, Al Arabiya, or for that matter to other Iraqi media workers. Al Arabiya pushed back against the designation of the killings as accidental by calling them "assassinations" in all their coverage. One week after Ali and his colleague had been killed, Colin Powell came to Iraq to hold a surprise press conference marking a year since the invasion. In lieu of asking questions, Najim Al-Rubaie, the editor of *Al Dustour* newspaper, read a prepared statement about the killings and the entire room of Iraqi reporters walked out in protest. "This was in response to the death of my brother and his colleague," Mazen told me. "It was considered a very big insult."

It is not surprising that other Iraqi journalists would be outraged by the killings and that they might fear that such a thing could happen to them. After all, Donald Rumsfeld had publicly accused both Al Jazeera and Al Arabiya of supporting the opposition and "terrorists." In 2003, after Al Arabiya headquarters in Doha broadcast a video showing Saddam Hussein speaking to the Iraqi people and urging them to rise up against the opposition, the US-created Iraqi Governing Council shut down the Al Arabiya bureau in Baghdad.[10] The US administration accused the network of fomenting violence and resistance to the occupation. Al Arabiya argued that the video, which showed that Saddam Hussein, whose whereabouts at that time were unknown, was still alive, was news. This, plus the other killings described above, show a pattern of US portrayal of Arab news media, especially Al Arabiya and Al Jazeera, as insurgent against the occupation and, as a result, as legitimate targets of counterterrorist violence.

While Mazen was interested in resettlement, his account also built a different kind of case, one that not only did not fit within the confines of the resettlement process but that also, in its demand for accountability, placed Mazen as a critic of the country most likely to consider him for resettlement. Just because he sought resettlement did not necessarily mean that he accepted the terms on which it was offered. Instead, Mazen delivered an argument that he had sutured together by piecing together details from the witnesses who relayed what they had seen to him and his family. It was his attempt to make sense of what had happened:

> There is evidence that the American troops targeted the reporters directly and that the killing of the man in the Volvo may have been an excuse to justify this. My brother was wearing clothes that said "TV" in large reflective letters and the Al Arabiya vehicle was also clearly marked. Also, the officer who ordered the shooting had been speaking to my brother directly only moments before. The media vehicles were on one side of the street and the Volvo was on the other. Of all the media cars, the Al Arabiya one was the only one shot. This old man was used as a way of hiding the killing of the reporters. The way that we know this is that the reporters were killed with a laser which assists the shooter to identify targets. The man who was driving was killed with random shooting and many bullets. The reporters were targeted and shot with very few bullets.

Despite the reliance on terms like "testimony," "case," and "evidence," in refugee legal aid questions of responsibility or justice were rarely raised explicitly. Yet here I was with Mazen, who used these very same terms to make a very different kind of case. Refugee law is intended to provide protection—an inherently unequal relation in which the protector can claim a kind of moral superiority—not restitution. In the context of advocating for resettlement, it was my job to identify violence from the state that Mazen had fled as well as in the country where he had sought asylum. Together, these forms of violence would make the case for why he had left and why he could not be protected in Egypt and therefore needed resettlement. There was no opening for considering unresolved violence committed by the same country that had appointed itself a country of rescue.

In this way, the resettlement process extended the impunity and lack of responsibility of the US military and civilian administrations in Iraq, if in a humanitarian register. Certainly, in Mazen's life these events and

82   CHAPTER 2

processes were connected. Following their investigation, the US military offered Mazen's family two thousand US dollars as compensation for Ali's death. So-called condolence payments became a feature of civilian death, injury, and loss of property in the war in Iraq. Although they were controversial within the military itself, condolence payments were seen as a key tool in counterinsurgency because, in the military imaginary, they would alleviate public anger in response to what the military saw as inevitable and incidental violence against civilians (Gilbert 2015; Gregory 2020). But the condolence payments, which were set at fixed amounts, not only did not have the intended effects but they served to make Iraqis feel that their lives held very little value to the occupying forces. Mazen told me how his family refused the payment that was offered to them: "First, it was too little, and second, we wanted answers to help us understand the reasons for his death." In a painful irony, after Ali's death, rumors circulated that the family had received a large sum of money in compensation from the US, and shortly after that, Mazen would be kidnapped and held for ransom. After his release, Mazen, his wife, and their young daughter fled to Egypt.

WARCHIVE

When Mazen and I began working together, I was not thinking in terms of a war archive. In fact, I was most focused on Mazen's own kidnapping, his family's subsequent flight to Egypt, and his situation in Cairo, especially his daughter's health concerns. These were the details that were most pertinent to his resettlement case. In the context of the resettlement process, his brother's killing was relegated to essential background that contextualized his own kidnapping. It was also challenging because the United States was at that time the country resettling the vast majority of Iraqi refugees from places like Cairo. But Mazen's account did not paint the US as a country of rescue but rather implicated it as an imperial power acting with violent impunity. Mazen's affect was not one of supplication and potential gratitude but clear-eyed anger at injustice unaddressed and unresolved. And he insisted on articulating this anger in a procedural context where anger and his critique of the US-led counterinsurgency could endanger his case. How would this play out in the resettlement process? How would the UNHCR and then, possibly, the Department of Homeland Security, read his testimony? And yet, I could not stop thinking about what had happened to Ali and his colleague.

I still was not thinking in terms of the archive when I became a more seasoned legal advocate, even as the documents and narratives I compiled, assembled, and wrote extended into the hundreds. Indeed, I am not trained in archival methods. And unlike more formal archives, the varied documents and narratives that accrue during refugee legal aid are not intended to remain as sources of knowledge to be read and interpreted by researchers. They are meant for the refugee bureaucracy of the UNHCR, the IOM, state security agencies, and resettlement organizations, all to be evaluated for veracity for the specific state-driven purposes of asylum, resettlement, and national security. In the legal aid process, at least at RLAP, they are used for advocacy, and then they are destroyed to retain privacy. This is understandable because they include privileged documents with ID numbers, scans of medical documentation, private photographs, and all kinds of personal information, including much that might put the applicant, their family members, and their community at risk if it were released. It is less clear, however, where the documents that states collect during asylum and resettlement process end up. We do know, however, that they are retained—that they are archived—because state agencies sometimes later redeploy them for criminal prosecution or to revoke the legal status of refugees years later.

The persistence of the materials collected in state asylum and resettlement processes and the ways those processes could come back to haunt refugees years later was one element that pushed me to begin to think about archives. Clearly, these materials were already being archived but in a manner and a place that people like Mazen and most researchers, including myself, could not access, never mind control their uses. This was driven home even more when, years after meeting Mazen, I came across the Freedom of Information Act request that the Committee to Protect Journalists filed in an effort to gain access to the US military investigation of the killings. The weighty stack of papers, partially redacted, includes the perspectives of many of the people involved that day but not, of course, of either Ali, the man in the white Volvo, or Ali's family. Here, as Saidiya

84   CHAPTER 2

Hartman (2008) reminds us, the archive is constitutively limited: in this case it is produced by those responsible for the killings and, while there are traces and moments within the archive where I catch glimpses of both Alis or the man in the Volvo—names, details, encounters—in the end these documents are limited in what they can tell us in any holistic way about the lives and deaths at stake.

Struggles over archives in war and archiving war were, and are, a recurring and unsettled theme in the history of imperial intervention in Iraq. Our consideration of a war archive must be set against the context of archives of imperial intervention in Iraq as well as the fate of Iraqi national archives during and after the invasion and occupation. As Omnia El Shakry notes, archives can be understood as both material sites and archival imaginaries—that is, what is understood as being archivable, what is appropriated, forgotten, or remembered. These imaginaries are infused with and constituted through regimes of power. Archival power, as Trouillot (2015, 99) describes it, can be understood as "the power to define what is and what is not a serious object of research and, therefore, of mention." In the context of Iraq, struggles over archival power continue today, shaping whose stories are told and who can access information and influencing what can be known and what remains unknowable. We see this in terms of scholarship in Iraq, where the years of the sanctions and conflict rendered certain forms of research, including archival research and ethnographic fieldwork, unattainable, especially for international scholars. We see this also in the preponderance of research on the British mandate archive—the colonial archive being the easiest for researchers to access and therefore more studied.

What has been missing is what Ma Vang (2021, 22) so cogently describes as a refugee archive. A refugee archive indexes refugee presence as well as refugees' "construction of history and production of knowledge to bring awareness to historical silencing." In the Iraq War, the effort to silence and obscure, as one part of imperial unknowing, was central to the prosecution of the war itself—linking Ali's killing because of his work producing counterhegemonic documentation of the war to Mazen's displacement in Cairo to the possible reconfiguring of Mazen's call for accountability into a testimony of protection and rescue within the refugee resettlement process. We can think of the refugee archive as bringing these threads together to create the possibility for writing a counterhistory of the Iraq War, one that is not simply an attempt to recover lost voices but that aims to disrupt dominant narratives of war, which are constructed through violence, seek their own self-absolution, and consistently silence and erase the voices and experiences of displaced Iraqis themselves. Counterhistory opposes not only the content of dominant narratives but also their forms and their methods (Hartman 2008, 12–13). It does not operate, however, entirely outside of dominant forms and methods of archiving and therefore cannot completely escape some of their violence. In the failure and contradiction illuminated from the simultaneous insideness and outsideness, counterhistory imperfectly but urgently shows the connections between past violence, present realities, and future possibilities.

WEAPONIZING ARCHIVES

The struggle over archives is not solely a symbolic one. It has played out in both the material and symbolic registers throughout the history of intervention in Iraq. As Alshaibi (2019) notes, archives became a very literal weapon in the US-led war in Iraq. Understanding the history of archives in the Iraq War and specifically how the archives themselves are conscripted into war helps to make sense of the many layers excavated by Mazen's narrative. It also renders clear how the struggle over who can, and should, tell the story of the Iraq War is ongoing.

Perhaps the most well-known story about archives in Iraq is the failure on the part of the occupying forces to protect them. In the immediate aftermath of the invasion, archives, museums, libraries, and other sites and objects were destroyed or stolen (Al-Tikriti 2007). The US military ignored pleas from local staff and others to protect sites of cultural, historical, and political significance, leaving them unguarded while other sites, such as the Ministry of Oil, were heavily guarded. The Iraqi National Library and Archives was looted and set on fire and looters stole or destroyed documents from throughout Iraq's history, including the Ottoman period, the monarchy, and Saddam Hussein's regime. Other important objects of cultural heritage from the rich archeological history of what is now Iraq also disappeared or were stolen.

86   CHAPTER 2

However, the United States did not simply stand by while others made off with Iraqi cultural heritage. It is telling that the largest collection of Iraqi archival documents, especially those from Saddam Hussein's regime, is held by the US Department of Defense. This appropriation of Iraqi archives precedes 2003; in 1991, Kurdish fighters seized a large trove of Baath Party documents, which they then passed onto the custody of the US military. During the 2003 invasion, the US military took some one hundred million pages of documents from Iraq (Damluji 2015). These documents remain classified and therefore inaccessible to Iraqis.

Another set of Baath Party records found themselves in the hands of Kanan Makiya, an Iraqi exile, professor, advocate of the invasion, and founder of the Iraq Memory Foundation, an organization funded by the US Department of Defense. In 1989, Makiya, a professor of Middle East studies at Brandeis University, wrote *Republic of Fear*, a book about the brutality of the Hussein regime. The book cemented Makiya's position as a leading expert and critic of Hussein and the Baath government, bringing him to the attention of the neoconservatives who were advocating regime change in Iraq. Makiya would become a leading Iraqi voice in the US media advocating a "humanitarian" rationale for invading Iraq and one of the principal Iraqi exiles who offered support and legitimacy to the neoconservatives' plans. When the US invaded in 2003, Makiya, who had advised the Bush administration that Iraqis would warmly welcome the American troops, watched the invasion live from the Oval Office with President Bush.

Following the invasion, Makiya returned to Iraq, and during his time there a US lieutenant pointed him to a cache of records at the regional Baath Party headquarters in Baghdad (Caswell 2011). The records comprised some seven million pages of documents from the Baath Party, including membership rolls, files from Saddam Hussein's secret police, and records of courts-martial. Makiya took the documents to his parents' home in the Green Zone, where he hid them until 2005. He eventually sent them to the United States on a US Navy carrier with the assistance of the US military, which scanned them for their own purposes before returning them to Makiya (Caswell 2011).

Makiya began to look for a US-based home for the archive. He first approached Harvard University, which was unwilling to take the documents because of their sensitive nature as well as questions about the ethics of their retrieval and possession. In 2008, Makiya entered into a five-year agreement with the Hoover Institution at Stanford University, a conservative think tank and library, to preserve and protect the records and make them digitally available to researchers at the Hoover Archives. The seizure of the archives by Makiya and the US military as well as their eventual placement at the Hoover Archives illustrates the political uses of archives during war. As Alshaibi (2019) notes, "In order to make the Iraqi documents 'speak' to the viciousness of Saddam Hussein, the Pentagon enlisted those best positioned to exploit this material to their advantage: a network that linked captured Iraqi records to American academics vis-à-vis an organization ostensibly focused on human rights." In this way, the archives became part of the war in important ways: The documentation of atrocities committed by Saddam Hussein became one means to justify the war during a moment when its failures were becoming more apparent.

When the removal of the archives and the subsequent agreement became publicly known, it precipitated a vociferous public debate over access to and ownership of these documents as well as about the acquisition, ownership, and protection of archives in the context of war and occupation more generally. Saad Bashir Eskander, the director of the Iraqi National Library and Archives, publicly demanded the archives' immediate repatriation. He was joined by professional archivist societies in both Canada and the United States that issued a joint statement arguing for the records' repatriation and stating that under international law, the removal of the records could be understood as an "act of pillage" (Caswell 2011).[11] Have these documents, many of which remain classified, become part of the United States' own warchive? When and where might they reappear? Are they used by the US intelligence apparatus when they seek to determine whether or not Iraqis pose a security threat as part of the resettlement process? Mazen's account and his insistence on telling it is part of this larger struggle over knowledge production in and about war. It is both a war archive and a refugee archive—and a necessary one in the face of imperial unknowing, which denies the connections between the imperial intervention of war and the refugee resettlement process.

These processes are connected in many ways, but in this chapter, I focus on how processes of war-making, state violence, and humanitarianism elide, obscure, appropriate, and seek to mold Iraqis' stories. But this is not just any story. Mazen's account is both a counterhistory and also creates an opening to think about where a refugee archive, grounded in refugee presence and narrative, might fit against the struggle for other forms of archiving and efforts to destroy or shape archives that took place as part of imperial intervention in Iraq and its aftermaths.

How are we to make sense of Mazen's effort to repurpose the resettlement process, and indeed my research, for justice for his brother? On the one hand, it illustrates how the disciplining of humanitarian bureaucracies is incomplete and partial. One might imagine that testimonies, produced as they are within humanitarian bureaucracies, would only produce accounts that either fit or fail to fit within the demands for narrativization and disclosure that are compelled in the resettlement process. Refugees do, as Liisa Malkki (1995a) documented in her research with Burundian refugees in Tanzania, learn to tell stories that are audible to humanitarian ears. But Mazen's account demonstrates that exactly the opposite also occurs and should not be read as his failure to tell a compelling humanitarian story. Mazen's narrative is one that neither fits nor fails within empire's constraints; rather, it subverts them for other purposes—for justice, for the love of family, for the desire to tell the truth—and in the process reveals knowledge that empire has been actively trying to hide.

3 Living in the Transit City

SEEKING REFUGE, REFUSING REFUGEENESS

"In the first place," Hannah Arendt (2008, 264) wrote, two years after fleeing Nazi-occupied France for exile in New York, "we don't like to be called 'refugees.'" The opening line of Arendt's 1943 essay on the struggles of Jews forced to flee Germany came to mind as I puzzled over Latif's objection to my consent form, mandated by my university's ethics review board. A fellow volunteer at the Resettlement Legal Aid Project (RLAP), Latif is one of the funniest people I have ever met. He is a former computer scientist from Baghdad whose greatest happiness seems to come from time spent with his much-adored wife and daughters. When he agreed to an interview, I prepared for the usual ethical and procedural concerns that come up in discussions of consent. But we didn't get that far. Latif objected to the title of my research project, which included the word "refugees." "I am not a refugee," he stated definitively. At first, I thought he was joking. Latif's gentle tricks regularly lightened the heaviness of our legal aid work. He was not joking. He repeated it again to make sure I understood: "I am not a refugee."

For Arendt, the situation of Jews forced to move from country to country seeking refuge, regarded alternately with suspicion and pity in each, exposed the ambivalence of the subject position of the refugee. As a

90   CHAPTER 3

political and legal category, refugee status confers deservingness and entitlement to protection for some (Yarris and Castañeda 2015), yet by definition it creates the conditions for others' exclusion by turning them into
"voluntary migrants," "illegal immigrants," or "failed refugees" by comparison. But Latif—and most Iraqis I met—were refugees, at least according
to the United Nations and the designation found in international law.
Latif's refusal, as well as Arendt's, reminds us how the term can be fraught
for those to whom it is applied, placing them outside the realm of citizenship and its ostensible entitlements and transforming them into victims
whose protection is contingent on recognition of their suffering (Fassin
2008; Giordano 2014; Ticktin 2011).

Latif's objection was striking because much of the work we did together
at RLAP involved assisting Iraqis to prove that they met the criteria for
refugee status, a prerequisite for resettlement. Latif's refusal of refugee
subjectivity, however, pointed to a larger ambivalence about the refugee
category.[1] In this chapter, I linger in the space between Latif's assertion
that he was not a refugee and other struggles over and claims to that very
same status in Cairo. My use of *space* here is not entirely metaphorical.
Indeed, space, place, and the material conditions of life in Cairo were all
instrumental in creating the circumstances in which Iraqis approached
the refugee category as well as how they were alternately recognized or not
recognized as refugees in different contexts. The preceding chapters provide a sense of why Iraqis left Iraq in the years following the US-led invasion and occupation. In this chapter, I turn to how they came to become,
more or less willingly, part of the large and diverse community of urban
refugees in Egypt, especially in its largest city, Cairo.

Just as they sought to reject imperial categorizations in Iraq, such as
the imposition of sectarian divisions, Iraqis also questioned and subverted
the ways they were defined bureaucratically and socially in Egypt.
Attention to their experiences of urban displacement is essential for
understanding both how they would experience the possibility of refugee
resettlement and how they resisted the transformation into passive
and voiceless victims that is often assumed to come with refugee status. To
this point, I also consider Iraqis' location among refugee populations in
Cairo as well as Cairo's place within the larger global refugee regime and
its racial ordering. Iraqis' self-presentations as well as their material

circumstances and social locations challenged humanitarian perceptions of refugees while also allowing some Iraqis to approach the category of refugee fluidly. But this was not an unencumbered fluidity, given the limitations of refugeeness as a category that provided contingent legal and material opportunities while also being significantly compromised both in Egypt and more globally.

REFUGEES IN EGYPT

In Egypt, as in other places, the state's response to refugees reflects shifting political alignments and relations over time. Currently, the vast majority of refugees, nearly 75 percent, seek asylum in countries in the Global South (UNHCR 2024), and in this regard Egypt is exemplary of the landscape of contemporary global displacement. But in other ways, the Egyptian state's relationship to the refugees within its territory reflects specific regional, historical, and contemporary political relations, many of them structured by imperial and anti-imperial politics as well as by regional histories of mobility and displacement. Egypt is both an Arab and an African capital, and regional politics have left their mark on refugees' experiences just as refugees themselves have influenced Egypt's politics. With a diaspora of more than nine million people, Egypt is often thought of as a country of emigration, but in recent decades it has also been host to one of the largest urban refugee populations in the world.[2] Egypt is also unusual in the Middle East as the only state in the region to have signed the 1951 Refugee Convention, the most important international legal instrument that determines states' obligations toward refugees.

In the twentieth century, Egypt's management of displaced populations has reflected and been shaped by the country's relations with imperial power. While Egypt is now thought of as a host for refugees from Africa or the Middle East, in the early-mid twentieth century, while still under the influence of the British, Egypt hosted diverse populations of European refugees.[3] After World War II, Egypt participated in the drafting of the 1951 Refugee Convention, although it refused to sign the final document (Fujibayashi 2022).[4] In the aftermath of the 1948 *Nakba*, the ethnic cleansing and expulsion of Palestinians was of great importance to Egypt,

92   CHAPTER 3

and the Convention's exclusive focus on European refugees did not address the concerns of Egypt or other Arab states about Palestinian displacement.[5] Following the 1952 revolution of the Free Officers' Movement that brought Nasser to power, Egypt played a foundational role in the forming of the Non-Aligned Movement, a key Third-Worldist initiative, and treated Palestinian refugees as near citizens of Egypt (El-Abed 2009).

Although Egypt did not ratify the Refugee Convention, it entered into a memorandum of understanding with the United Nations High Commissioner for Refugees (UNHCR) in 1954, which allowed the UNHCR to conduct refugee status determination for displaced people on its territory.[6] The memorandum of understanding also codified the Egyptian state's position as a country of "transit." Article two of the memorandum of understanding makes clear that refugees can remain in Egypt only until they can either repatriate or be resettled, a position that subsequent government representatives have repeated (Badawy 2010; Grabska 2006).

When Sadat, Nasser's successor, aligned with the US and made peace with Israel, Egypt was expelled from the Arab League and nearly ejected from the Non-Aligned Movement. Palestinians' situation in Egypt then deteriorated, and Egypt, which had previously refused to sign the 1951 Convention, ratified both that convention as well as the 1969 Organization of African Unity Convention. The definitions from the 1951 Convention would be those that my Iraqi interlocutors contended with most often as they variously refused and sought out refugee status.

Since Sadat signed the Camp David Accords, Egypt has become the second greatest recipient of US aid after Israel (Jadallah 2015) and a supporter of US interests in the region. The country has also come to play a central role in the management of refugees from both the Middle East and Africa for the Global North. These forms of migration management limit the mobility of refugees as well as Egyptians, sometimes with deadly consequences.[7] What's more, Egypt has in the twenty-first century become a key proxy in the US-led War on Terror. Egypt was notably one of the primary detention sites for the CIA practice of "extraordinary rendition," in which suspects are apprehended and then transferred, often secretly, to other countries for incarceration and often torture. This transnational practice can be directly connected to imperial unknowing and the war on Iraq.[8] For example, in 2001, the US captured Libyan national Ibn al-

Sheikh al-Libi in Afghanistan and rendered him to Egyptian custody, where, under threat of torture, he fabricated information about Iraq having sold biological and chemical weapons to al-Qaeda (see Isikoff 2008; Singh and Berry 2013). This story was subsequently used by the US administration, including forming a substantive part of Colin Powell's 2003 address to the United Nations Security Council justifying the invasion of Iraq. This might not seem, at first glance, like it is part of the same history of migration management; however, as Darryl Li (2019) has argued, the Global War on Terror has been significantly about the management of Muslim mobility and has developed, in response, a global network of carceral archipelagos. These specific regional histories deeply affected the lives of Iraqis in Cairo.

Egypt's ratification of the 1951 Convention as well as the 1954 memorandum of understanding with the UNHCR laid the groundwork for Iraqis in Egypt to be categorized as refugees, *al-laj'in*. By contrast, Syria and Jordan, both of which hosted much larger populations of displaced Iraqis, have not ratified the 1951 Convention and classified Iraqis not as refugees but as "guests," *al-duyūf*.[9] The category of *al-duyūf* evokes Arab genres of hospitality, which include obligations for both host and guest. Shahram Khosravi (2010, 127) writes that hospitality in the context of the nation-state is inherently ambivalent. Because hospitality always implies power relations between host and guest—the host opens their home to an outsider—it always includes a kernel of hostility and exclusion. Both Syria and Jordan have long-standing Palestinian refugee communities who have been instrumental in defining what it means to be a refugee and a citizen. The longevity of Palestinian displacement and states' responses to it have led countries such as Egypt, Jordan, Lebanon, and Syria to seek to categorize new populations of asylum-seekers, including Iraqis, as temporary and to attempt to designate themselves as "transit" countries regardless of how long displaced people live within their borders.

Beginning in 2007, the United Nations designated Iraqi exiles as prima facie refugees. Prima facie, Latin for "at first sight," is a relatively rare designation offered in certain dire situations of massive displacement. The UN applies this collective status to entire populations when it surmises that it would be neither necessary nor possible to individually determine refugee status for each displaced person, both because of the

94   CHAPTER 3

sheer numbers of people on the move and also because the UN determines that the conditions from which they fled are self-evidently such that most people would meet the legal requirements for refugee status. For the Iraqis who fled to Egypt in the early years of my fieldwork, this designation meant that unlike most asylum seekers, they did not initially have to undergo an individual asylum adjudication; by virtue of their presence in Egypt and registration with the UNHCR, they were given yellow cards and considered refugees. More frequently in Egypt and elsewhere, asylum-seekers undergo lengthy, individualized, and adversarial processes in which they must prove themselves to be refugees. Iraqis were, at least initially, freed of this burden, although they did have to go through such bureaucratic challenges to be considered for resettlement.

Perhaps even more unusual, not all Iraqis in Egypt needed to register with the UNHCR at all. Many took advantage of an Egyptian law designed to attract international students to the country's many private high schools and universities that allowed entire families to obtain temporary residency permits if a child was enrolled in a private school. Other Iraqis entered Egypt on a tourist visa, imagining their stay would be short, and only later registered with the UNHCR when they realized they were unable to return home. In other words, because Iraqis could arrive in Cairo on tourist visas and, if they could afford it, maintain residency by enrolling a child in private school, they did not always need to immediately register as refugees, even if their reason for coming to Egypt was in fact to escape violence and persecution.

In theory, one might imagine that prima facie status would therefore make it easier for Iraqis to enter the humanitarian category of the refugee by removing often adversarial and bureaucratic administrative hurdles. While this is partly true, it is not the whole story. Some Iraqis told me that they were initially unaware of the existence of the UNHCR, sometimes for years. But once Iraqis knew of the UNHCR, prima facie status certainly did make it easier for them to more fluidly enter and exit the category of "refugee," and this fluidity increased if they had the resources to maintain their residency in Cairo in other ways. Thus, for some Iraqis, refugeeness depended not only on institutional recognition or imposition but also partly on class status and assent, which changed over time and as their circumstances changed. Yet such assent was not always forthcoming, since

Iraqis chafed against the abjection they associated with displacement and expressed ambivalence about how the refugee category was adjudicated in the resettlement process. What's more, refugee status in Egypt comes with few material benefits—refugees are guaranteed few rights beyond a temporary residence permit and often receive little aid—and invokes the seemingly permanent connotations associated with the refugee category in the Middle East, where Palestinian displacement is paradigmatic. Iraqis simultaneously met the legal definition of "refugee," struggled for recognition and resettlement under that definition, and refused it.

Ultimately, in Egypt, what it means to be or not be a refugee unfolds in and through multiple overlapping and contradictory historical and contemporary relationships. As such, the refugee concept, as a contested but diagnostic social and political category, is a deeply relational and multiplicitous one that must be understood through the ways it is lived in everyday life. Its meaning emerges, yes, from how the category has been defined in law and reckoned in social theory, but what of the lived relations that come to constitute what it means to be a refugee at different moments and in different times? And what is created in the gaps between how the concept is defined in policies and peoples' lived experiences? Relatedness emerges through the processes and struggles by which lives come to be entangled with one another, even when those relationships are structured by violence, rejection, or indifference (Govindrajan 2018). The framings of international law and humanitarian discourse cannot contain or suppress the experiential and phenomenological dimensions of exile, which are lived in relationships that are made and remade across time and place. Tracing these forms of relationality provides a sense of the social and political meanings and material conditions invoked through the refugee concept and suggest that contestations over the term do not only happen in and through the humanitarian realm or the register of the nation-state but through other forms of relatedness.

ARRIVING IN EGYPT: CHOOSING FLIGHT AND EXPECTATIONS FOR EXILE

Before turning to the relationships forged in life in urban Cairo, we must understand why Iraqis came to Egypt in the first place. This is important

96 CHAPTER 3

because within the literature on refugees and migration more generally, practices of mobility have often been a neglected "black box" (Lindquist et al. 2012). This is especially so when it comes to South-South migration, which itself is underrepresented in the scholarship on migration and displacement (Fiddian-Qasmiyeh 2020). Additionally, Iraqis' reasons for traveling to Egypt and their expectations for their time there both defy common assumptions about refugees and provide crucial grounding for understanding their experiences of life in Egypt.

Legal and administrative definitions of displacement prioritize flight from threat over almost all else. This emphasis on *flight from* to the exclusion of *arrival to* has been institutionalized in policies and practices that seek to force refugees to (gratefully) accept asylum in the first "safe" place they arrive. In addition to creating a troubling designation of some countries as safe and others as unsafe, the binary between "forced" and "voluntary" migration imagines that the two can never coexist and erases, violently, how people often simultaneously escape in ways that chart specific "geographies of aspiration" (Watters 2019). This erasure also includes a willful misunderstanding of what displacement often looks like, both temporally and spatially. Although refugee journeys are often imagined as linear, one-way travel from flight to settlement elsewhere, this obscures the more multidimensional forms of mobility that emerge when escape intersects with other human commitments and relations. Some Iraqis came to Egypt for a short period of time to determine whether or not it was a suitable place to live before returning to bring family with them. Others came to Egypt, tried to return or travel elsewhere, but ultimately were either unsuccessful or found that return was not safe and came back to Egypt. Still others fled to Egypt and returned to Iraq for short periods for reasons that included saying their goodbyes to dying parents, selling assets to support their lives in exile, or retrieving paperwork necessary to enroll in school, among other reasons.

The majority of Iraqis arrived in Egypt during 2006–7 when sectarian violence in Iraq was at its height. Iraqis who had come earlier were often specifically threatened because of associations with the previous government or military or had been in Egypt for another reason and stayed on when return to Iraq became impossible. Following 2007, the conditions in Iraq improved somewhat, but Iraqis continued to experience violence and forced migration. However, beginning in 2007, the Egyptian government began to restrict entry visas for Iraqis, making it harder to choose Egypt as a destination and for Iraqis already in the country to come and go. Iraqis who were able to travel to Egypt after 2007 were likely enrolled in Egyptian educational institutions or had found another way to get an expensive and elusive visa.

The means by which Iraqis travelled to Egypt and the routes that they took depended on numerous factors including expediency, cost, and available modes of travel. At times, available transportation infrastructure was what made Egypt the destination. Many flew directly from Baghdad to Cairo. Others noted that at the time when they fled, planes were not flying from Baghdad to Cairo, so they were forced to travel first to Syria or Jordan, transfer, and then fly on to Cairo. Transfers in Syria or Jordan ranged from hours to months, as Iraqis sometimes had to wait for visas for onward travel, visited relatives or friends, or tested out the living situation in Syria or Jordan before travelling on to Cairo. A much smaller number of Iraqis took the arduous and lengthy journey over land to Jordan and then departed from the Port of Aqaba to travel to Egypt by sea, while others made the onward journey by land.

Iraqis who came to Egypt were overwhelmingly fleeing persecution, instability and insecurity. They described death threats, murders, kidnapping, detention, torture, home invasions, and generalized violence and insecurity as their reasons for coming to Egypt. This rationale accorded most closely with the legal category of a refugee as a person who is fleeing from persecution, not necessarily arriving somewhere. Personal threats or threats to a family member were frequently the impetus for leaving Iraq, but there were other aspects of war, occupation, and unrest that made their lives in Iraq difficult, including the loss of their jobs and livelihoods, lack of services and facilities, political instability, and a palpable sense that the country was changing politically, socially, economically, and even ecologically.

In some cases, travel infrastructure, visa rules, and other bordering techniques made travel to Egypt possible, while in other cases they made travel to Egypt the only possibility. Naza, for example, is a Kurdish woman who had lived in Baghdad before coming to Cairo. She had been among the first women to graduate from the police academy as part of a Baath

98   CHAPTER 3

Party initiative to encourage more women to go into the police and military. After the Coalition Provisional Authority disbanded the police, she eventually found a job working at the Egyptian embassy in Baghdad. When she realized she had to leave Iraq, her workplace happened to provide her with an escape route:

> I didn't want to come to Egypt, I just wanted to go out of Iraq by any means. Because my life there was so, so, so difficult. And because of the things that I saw in Iraq. I witnessed a lot of mess and killing and violence so I just decided that it's impossible for me to stay in Iraq forever. At that time, I just wanted to get out of Iraq, so I thought that any place will be better for me. I was working at the Egyptian embassy and it was easier for me to get the visa to Egypt, so I applied, and at that time the Egyptian visa was hard to get but they just sympathized with my situation because my husband had been killed in Iraq and they gave me the visa.

Naza's proximity to the Egyptian embassy as well as the sympathy that her situation aroused clearly gave her an advantage in terms of getting a visa to travel to Egypt. Likely because of her connections, she was given an unusual five-year visa for Egypt, which meant not only that she didn't need to apply to the UNHCR for refugee status but that she actually couldn't get refugee status without trading in her five-year visa for a six-month refugee residency. For Naza, Egypt was "not my choice. It was the only choice I had."

For other Iraqis, Egypt became a possibility when other destinations were closed off, as states in the region began to impose new rules to limit their ability to enter. Such limitations often used security rationales that explicitly targeted specific categories of Iraqis but ended up having much wider effects. When in August 2006 Suad's family finally decided to leave the country, they initially traveled to Jordan. Suad, her daughter, and her son piled into the car and made the drive from Baghdad to the Jordanian border. Most of the drive takes place along a desolate desert highway. Under normal conditions, the route takes about seven hours, but it took much longer during this time of proliferating checkpoints, banditry, and insecurity. When the family finally arrived at the Jordanian border after a full day of driving, they were stopped by the Jordanian authorities. Jordan had newly decided that no Iraqi men under the age of forty would be allowed inside the country, for security reasons. On the spot, the family was forced to make a decision. Suad and her daughter crossed the border, traveling onward to Amman. Her son would return to Baghdad, and they would figure out how to reunite from there. But by the time they arrived, the Iraqi side of the crossing was closed for the night. He spent the night alone and in limbo, sleeping in the car between the Iraqi and Jordanian borders, not allowed to enter either country. In the morning, he made the long drive back to Baghdad. In order not to be separated, the family then decided to go to Egypt instead.

Whereas Suad's family chose Egypt after exclusionary border policies forced them to quite literally reroute their plans, other Iraqis made their choice after comparing the situations in Syria, Jordan, Lebanon, and Egypt, often by asking friends and family who either had traveled to those countries already or who knew people who did. Points of comparison included cost of living, security, and feelings of comfort with the place and people. The reasons often blended into each other.

When I began to volunteer at RLAP, I quickly met and became friends with Shams. Shams worked at RLAP during the long months she waited for her resettlement case to go through. It didn't pay much, but at least it was something to do. Although she had a joyful personality and a sardonic wit, even a short conversation with Shams about her present circumstances would reveal that she was not happy in Egypt. Why then, I asked once, had she decided to come to Egypt, and why did she stay? Her answer revealed the type of comparative work that can go into a decision of where to seek asylum:

> Everything was closed or difficult. Jordan gives strict conditions for people to enter. You can get a visa to go to the US more easily in Egypt than in Jordan. Turkey is easier to go to, but life there is difficult because of the high standard of living. Staying in Egypt makes sense because I could get the visa, and the cost of living was possible, and I could enroll in a course at the university. When I think of these factors, I see that staying in Egypt is the better solution.

Although Shams fled because of a threat to her life, she nonetheless considered her options, limited as they were, before deciding to come to Egypt. In the end, the combination of educational opportunity, visa accessibility, the possibility for third-country resettlement to the US, and living conditions influenced her decision to travel to Egypt.

100 CHAPTER 3

But legacies of imperial war and authoritarianism also influenced Iraqis' choices of destination. In response to my questions about why they chose Egypt, Iraqis often mentioned that they had perceived it to be more secure than Syria or Jordan. Sometimes Egypt was explicitly referred to as "safe," but more frequently interlocutors referred to how Syria especially felt insecure because it was "close to Iraq" and "full of Iraqis." For example, Samar explained her decision to travel to Egypt with her husband and son in the following way: "Syria is too close. We went to Syria first but didn't feel safe because it was too close and there were Iraqi activities. So we went back to Iraq. And came here." Others told me that they had heard that militias operated in neighboring countries. While the problem associated with the "closeness" of Syria was mentioned explicitly by Samar, many more Iraqis simply referred to Syria euphemistically as being "too crowded" with Iraqis or, conversely, noted that Egypt was safer because it was farther away from Iraq.

Beyond, of course, the direct connection between the imperial violence of US invasion and Iraqi displacement described in earlier chapters, histories of earlier imperial interventions and the futures they portend influenced where Iraqis traveled. Saddam Hussein's authoritarian regime, first developed with US support, had cultivated practices of informing on and policing others. Similar processes of informing became common during the occupation and the civil war, when Iraq was cleaved along sectarian lines formalized by the US occupation. The threat of being informed on, especially for Iraqis who held high positions in the Baath Party and feared revenge or for Iraqis who worked with the occupation and feared being targeted by militias, created a sense of mistrust that followed Iraqis into exile. For those who had the means and ability to get to Egypt and those who felt themselves more vulnerable to "Iraqi activities," Egypt offered more distance from the imperial violence that trained its focus on Iraq and Iraqis. This was articulated most clearly by Sara, who explained to me why she came to Egypt in the following terms: "Syria, there are so many Iraqis there. Maybe there will be a war there with the Americans. There are so many Iraqis there. Wherever there are many Iraqis, there's a problem. It's possible to make war with them. Because the US says that there's always maybe a war."

I was and still am struck by the formulation of imperial war enfolded into Sara's statement. Her phrase "there's always maybe a war" resonates with US-based critiques of the "forever wars" but from the experience of a population that is the target of these never-ending wars, a people whom it is always "possible to make war with." For Sara, forever wars are a lived history, a possible threat of future wars, and a mobile threat in the sense that they are tied not only to territory but also to Iraqis as people interpolated as killable in imperial eyes. Of course, her prediction, made in conversation with me in 2009, resounds differently with the hindsight knowledge of the subsequent war in Syria, which has displaced millions of Syrians as well as a smaller number—but still in the hundreds of thousands—of Iraqis who had sought refuge there. This much more explicit concern reminds us that the reticence to live among other Iraqis emerges partly out of the lived aftermaths of US-led invasion and occupation and that imperial violence— and the sectarian violence and unrest it catalyzed—has long afterlives that reconfigure social relations, influence where people end up fleeing, and shape how they feel in exile.

Although it was mentioned relatively rarely, some Iraqis said that they had chosen to come to Egypt because they perceived the services or options for resettlement to a third country to be better there than in Syria or Jordan. This comes up in Shams's calculations when she talks about how it would be easier to "get the visa to go to the US" in Egypt than in Jordan. At the time of my fieldwork, Egypt was the site for the regional UNHCR office and there was an International Organization for Migration office processing US Direct Access resettlement cases as well. This infrastructure certainly made a difference in terms of access to resettlement, and a small number of Iraqis were aware of it and considered it while making decisions about where to go. Calculations that considered the humanitarian logic of scarcity of resettlement therefore also figured in Iraqis' decision-making, apparent in the evaluation that Syria in particular was "crowded" with Iraqis. For example, Karrar told me frankly that he had come to Egypt specifically seeking resettlement to the United States. He put it this way: "In Syria, there are many Iraqi people. About a million and more. Here in Egypt, the Iraqi people are fewer than in Syria. So, I have a chance for them to accept me [for resettlement]." Karrar, who was indeed in the resettlement process, had initially fled Iraq and traveled to Syria. He was eligible to be resettled to the United States because of a family member, his brother, who had worked with the American forces and

102   CHAPTER 3

had already been approved for resettlement, but he felt that he would have a better chance of being approved if he came to Egypt. As a result, he chose to relocate his family to Cairo and to apply for resettlement from there. Although rare, explicit discussion about humanitarian aid or third-country resettlement opportunities as a motivation for choosing one place of asylum over another demonstrates both the value that some Iraqis placed on these programs and also that, even before coming to Egypt, they had not imagined Egypt as a place where they would settle for a long time.

DISPLACED IN THE MEGACITY

Like refugees, the city is alternately in motion and immobile, propulsive and immobilizing. The traffic that snarls Cairo's streets is a testament to these conditions: lengthy periods of gridlock, honking, and sitting in fumes give way to occasional, exhilarating spurts of motion. Where urban planners imagined a street to have three lanes, Cairenes have reimagined it to have four or five. Crossing the road on foot requires bravery and more physical contact than feels comfortable to me. In stopped traffic, I gently touch a hood and make eye contact to make myself seen by the driver. When traffic picks up, wind brushes my skirt as cars begin to move around me. A kind stranger offers an arm when she sees that I'm hesitating to cross a particularly fast-moving street. I'm late to meet Shams for coffee.

The metro is similarly a play of movement and stuckness. With the thronging crowds of commuters and students, I rush down the stairs and make my way to the part of the platform dominated by women. Here in the middle is where the women's cars will stop. The Cairo Metro is one of only two underground metro systems in Africa. Opened in 1987, by 1989 two of the train cars were allocated for women only to protect against sexual harassment. In theory, women can ride in the other cars if they choose, but whenever I do, the proximity to male bodies makes me long for the crowded women's car. Woe to the man who inadvertently enters the women's only car: He is swiftly made aware of his mistake. I once saw one such unfortunate man spend the ride from one stop to the next with his head tucked all the way into his jacket collar until the subway finally came to a stop and he could emerge and, eyes still downcast, dart from the women's car into the adjacent mixed-gender car. At one pound a ride at that time, the metro was my preferred mode of transportation in Cairo. It's cheap, does not require the inevitable negotiation of a taxi ride, and fast, if cramped.

The metro, with only three lines, is of less use to Iraqis, most of whom lived in the outlying suburbs. They relied more often on the shared microbuses that travel the whole network of Cairo. Ancient white minivans with no seatbelts, these unregulated, private vans pick up at informal bus depots and drop passengers off all along their routes. Cheap, plentiful, and with available seating, microbuses offer some advantages over buses and the metro. Dangerous driving by an exhausted, possibly intoxicated driver is not one of them. The driver is usually accompanied by another person, often a young boy, who calls out the route to potential passengers and collects fares. Riders learn the hand signals by which they can indicate their destinations from a distance—for 6th of October City, the suburb where Shams lived and where the UNHCR office was located, the signal is five raised fingers on one hand and the thumb on the other. If an approaching microbus is heading the direction you indicate and there's space for you to ride, the driver will pull over and let you on. You pass your fare to the passenger sitting behind the driver, who makes change if necessary. It's an affordable collective experience, occasionally marred by breakdowns or crashes.

I arrive at Sadat Station and emerge from the underground at Tahrir Square, scanning the crowded street corner for Shams. If Cairo had a central hub, this would be it. During my time in the city, Tahrir Square figured as both transit point and destination in its own right. With its busy traffic circle, the central junction of the city's two metro lines, and microbus depots nearby, I would often end up there. It was where I met friends for tea and backgammon, attended talks and trainings at the downtown campus of the American University in Cairo, and also where refugees had to go for a residency stamp and Egyptians had to go for almost any imaginable kind of official paperwork, all of which involved making it through the Mugamma Building, a behemoth Farouk-era monument to centralized government planning that flanked the south side of the square. To get a sense of the Mugamma's scale, consider that behind its modernist façade thirty thousand civil servants are said to work and one hundred thousand people visit daily.

104   CHAPTER 3

In January 2011, Tahrir Square was bursting with people forging a very different relationship to the state and the city. Neither caught as frustrated supplicants in the state's bureaucratic labyrinth nor passing through in the snarl of foot and vehicular traffic, they filled the square and then the streets that radiated outwards from it, calling loudly for bread, freedom, justice, and an end to police violence and Hosni Mubarak's then thirty-year rule. Recently returned from a stint of fieldwork, I, like many in the Egyptian diaspora, did almost nothing but watch events in Egypt live on Al Jazeera and social media. Then, after eighteen days, the protestors achieved their aim—Mubarak stepped down.[10] It is not hyperbolic to say that the revolution changed Egypt, the region, and even the world, although in the years after 2011 it has become clear that those changes have not been the ones the youth in the square hoped and worked for (Mittermaier 2019; Hafez 2019).

But on the afternoon that I meet Shams downtown in the autumn of 2009, Hosni Mubarak had been in power nearly as long as I'd been alive. Egypt was ruled under a state of emergency law that gave the government, police, and military exceptional powers for that entire period. The popular uprisings that would bring down rulers around the region and would come to be called the Arab Spring still seemed unimaginable that afternoon. Tahrir Square loomed large but as a transit point and meeting hub, not yet an iconic site of revolution. Sitting at an outdoor café a couple of blocks from the square, drinking glasses of sugary black tea, Shams and I discussed her life in Cairo. When I asked Shams how she would describe her life, she said, "There's a proverb: 'Heaven without people is not wanted.' I am not in heaven and I am not with people." I looked around at the crowded café full of patrons, the street filled with pedestrians, and the line of cars stuck in traffic and thought about what she meant. What does it mean to be a refugee in one of the world's largest, most populous cities? How does the urban landscape—and the relations it enables and denies—come to shape what displacement means for Iraqis?

Within the framework of state sovereignty, territory, and citizenship, the refugee camp has come to be the paradigmatic image of the space, but not place, of displacement and of states' power to confine and immobilize people who are understood, in this framework, as being "out of place" (Malkki 1995b).[11] The labyrinthine bureaucratic monolith of the

Mugamma Building in Tahrir Square reminds us that the state is an inescapable part of the experience of being a refugee in Cairo. But it is decidedly not the only relationship that matters. Increasing scholarship on urban displacement offers one possible corrective to overly state-centric and camp-centric analyses of refugees.[12] It also reflects an almost commonplace reality: The world is increasingly urbanized and so is migration. The UNHCR estimates that some 60 percent of the world's refugees reside in cities (UNHCR 2018). In fact, the mass movement of displaced populations has been credited with increasing urban growth in many cities, especially in the Global South (UNHCR 2012). In the Middle East in particular, refugees, especially Palestinian refugees, have been central actors in the transformation of urban geographies (Peteet 2010; Doraï 2024; Allan 2013). Scholarship on refugees, however, has been slow to catch up to this reality, reflecting dominant normative framing of refugees in camps.

Until recently, the UNHCR has likewise been reluctant to confront the reality of urban displacement. The UNHCR released its first policy dealing with urban refugees in 1997, but while it "acknowledged refugees have a right to freedom of movement under international law . . . it implied that flows of refugees to cities were undesirable and reflected the priority of placing refugees in camps" (UNHCR 2012, 22). It wasn't until 2009 that the UNHCR released a new policy, titled "Refugee Protection and Solutions in Urban Areas," on the realities of protracted urban displacement. This policy came about largely as a result of and a response to Iraqi displacement after 2003, the vast majority of which was to capital cities in the Middle East and North Africa, including Damascus, Amman, Beirut, and Cairo.

Humanitarians whom I interviewed were often quick to point out that Egypt does not have any refugee camps. This remained true except for a period when a camp was set up in Salloum in western Egypt to house refugees who had fled violence and unrest in Libya beginning in 2011. Otherwise, nearly all refugees live in urban areas, the vast majority in Cairo and Alexandria. Cairo has the distinction of being the most populous city in the Middle East and, depending on how you count, the most populous city in Africa. At the time of my fieldwork, it was also host to one of the five largest urban refugee populations in the world, a diverse population of people on the move from various countries and with varying legal statuses. The heterogeneity of life in urban Cairo recalls Doreen Massey's (2005, 149)

106   CHAPTER 3

concept of "throwntogetherness"—which she describes as the relational politics of space that emerge in cities as different trajectories bring people together in conflict, negotiation, and collaboration. Spread out around the city and sprawling suburbs, Iraqis and other refugees lived among local populations and were often separated from one another as well as from the UNHCR and other humanitarian organizations. The majority of Iraqis in Egypt lived in three main areas, 6th of October City, Nasr City and Giza.[13]

As urban dwellers spread across these neighborhoods and further afield, Iraqis in Cairo were less legible to states and aid organizations, which created opportunities for them to define themselves outside the refugee regime. But this also made aid harder to access. Refugee services and humanitarian organizations were spread out around the larger urban area, requiring lengthy, costly, and sometimes dangerous travel to access them. Illegibility went both ways: Some Iraqis reported that they lived in Cairo for months or years unaware of the UNHCR, eventually learning that they might register as refugees by word of mouth. Refugees in Egypt receive quite limited aid, which meant that registration came with few benefits for those who had other means for establishing residency and could live off savings or other income. Some, like Latif, consciously chose never to register as refugees or waited to register until they decided to pursue resettlement. If Latif's refusal of the refugee category was adamant, the material conditions of life for Iraqis in Cairo created possibilities for a less stringent type of refusal, one that was more ambivalent and characterized by abstention or delay.

Unlike the camp, an ostensibly temporary place meant to separate refugees from other populations for the purpose of containing them, providing them with aid, and eventually, ideally, reincorporating them into the nation-state system, in Cairo, there is no clear physical boundary between citizens and noncitizens, refugees and Egyptians. Instead there are moments when Iraqis become legible as refugees and moments when they might blend into the city, unmarked as objects of humanitarianism. For African refugees like those from Sudan, Somalia, and Eritrea, racialization means that these moments of blending in are fewer. African refugees face significant anti-Black racism in Egypt. For many Iraqis, however, what marks them as different is their dialect of Arabic and their accents. Iraqi Arabic is different enough from Egyptian Arabic that it provides Iraqis with some (imperfect) opportunities to be impenetrable to Egyptians, and I also observed my Iraqi friends slip into Egyptian dialect when conversing with Egyptians. Egypt, historically the Hollywood of the Middle East, produced movies, TV shows, and music consumed by the entire region for many years such that the Egyptian accent is familiar to many in the region. Egyptians have a harder time with Iraqi Arabic. Until they speak, many Iraqis might well be Egyptians, and even once their accent is heard, they might, for better or worse, be conflated with tourists from the Arab Gulf states or foreign students or some other kind of foreigner. Haydar once explained to me, "When you use your accent, people start to recognize that maybe you have more money, maybe you are a tourist here, maybe you are from the Arab Gulf. Maybe, maybe, maybe . . . " Iraqis had mixed feelings about this partial experience of passing and the ways they were misrecognized. Many appreciated that they could move around the city relatively unencumbered and not be identifiable as refugees. But they also resented that, once the questions of "maybe, maybe, maybe" were raised and they were perceived as foreign, they were not recognized as people who had been forced to flee but instead as possibly wealthy foreigners who could be charged more for rent, food, and transportation.

Illegibility also had effects beyond Egypt. Camps are spatial devices for the containment of refugees—they render refugees potentially more legible and governable, although they do not guarantee their temporary nature or their visibility. However, the presence of displaced Iraqis in already highly cosmopolitan cities—Amman, Beirut, Cairo, and Damascus—spaces that neither marked them so explicitly as different from the rest of society nor that visibly contained them as a refugee camp would, enabled the near invisibility of Iraqi displacement in much discourse outside the region (Peteet 2010).

CONDITIONS OF DAILY LIFE IN CAIRO

When the Egyptian government ratified the 1951 Refugee Convention, it entered reservations to a number of articles, stating its intention not to accord refugees certain rights. Among the most important of these articles for refugees in Egypt are article 22, which asserts refugees' access to free primary education, and article 24, on refugees' right to employment. In practice, this has meant that refugees in Egypt are prohibited from attending public primary or secondary schools, and if they can afford it they must attend private schools, paying foreigner fees, often in foreign currency. There have been some exceptions; until 1978, Palestinian refugees were permitted to attend schools but in more recent years have been prohibited from attending public schools and also excluded from studying certain fields at the university level, including medicine, dentistry, pharmacology, and engineering (El Abed 2009). Sudanese students have been allowed to attend some public schools, but each pupil must have a valid residency permit. The refusal to allow refugees to work has been devastating, including for Iraqis. It forces refugees into the informal labor market and into reliance on limited humanitarian aid. For many Iraqis, the restriction meant that they did not work at all during their time in Egypt and instead subsisted on diminishing savings, occasional transfers from relatives, and sometimes aid.

Iraqis in Egypt occupied a conflicted and contradictory set of class positions. Their ambivalence about the refugee category was partly related to their perception of its association with both economic precaritization and abjection, or the loss of status and inclusion in a larger geopolitical order (Ferguson 1999). This experience of precaritization and abjection was felt by Iraqis at the same time as they were perceived by many Egyptians to be comparatively wealthy foreigners. Many of my interlocutors were highly educated, middle-class people from Baghdad. Some had studied, traveled, or worked in Europe or North America before their mobility was constrained by the sanctions imposed on Iraq in the 1990s. In Egypt they found themselves immobilized and living off savings, pensions, and support from family abroad. As the years passed, these sources dwindled or became harder to access, leading to a slow-moving precaritization, as Janna, a woman in her mid-thirties from Baghdad, described it: "In the beginning of my stay in Egypt we traveled by taxi. Since then, my financial situation has gotten worse, and I have been forced to use the microbus. In the beginning we used to have the best of everything in food. Now we have food but not like before. So, for example, with a chicken. Previously we had it for one meal, now we will divide it in two. Now we eat everything. Not just the best."

Although this experience of economic decline was almost universal, some Iraqis I met were destitute, surviving on the charity of acquaintances, friends, or mosques, while others were wealthy by any standard, having traveled to Egypt with significant resources and continuing business or other financial pursuits from exile. Most were, like Janna, somewhere in the middle. They had worked in many fields, including as doctors, teachers, pharmacists, dentists, businesspeople, government employees, and members of the military. In Egypt, where life was "not like before," their standard of living had in many cases radically deteriorated.

These class dimensions were not lost on expat and national staff humanitarians, Egyptians, and refugees from other nationalities, leading one humanitarian to somewhat dismissively describe Iraqis to me as "five-star refugees." Among the humanitarians I interviewed, the question of Iraqis' "expectations" was most often raised as a problem. One Iraqi physician, who worked as a humanitarian and thus uneasily navigated both the roles of aid provider and refugee, described the situation this way:

> When people come to Cairo, because they are getting the visa and paying the fees for the tickets and everything, they expect that life in Cairo will be much easier than anywhere else. And this is wrong. Because they are refugees and there should be someone to help them. The fact is that because you are a refugee you will lose a lot of your rights. Because you will have certain rights written by someone else for you. We can't expect more than what is written, and sometimes we have to expect less than what is written. And these people can't understand it. Because they come from a high social level and now they are living as a refugee in another country. So, they expect the same level that they lived in or more, and this is totally wrong. Now you secured your life, which is the best for you, and you are getting your safety.

Humanitarians' anxiety over Iraqis' expectations reflected the ways that Iraqis refused and rejected the loss of rights, status, and resources that humanitarians associated with refugeeness. They were unwilling to accept abjection and to perform gratefulness for the gift of their safety to the satisfaction of humanitarian expectations. They chafed against the many losses of the wars and displacement: of their jobs, their savings, their homes, their ways of living. A second dimension to this was the economic struggles facing many Egyptians as well as refugees of other nationalities, a fact that Iraqis often acknowledged in conversations. Indeed, some

110   CHAPTER 3

Iraqis had more economic resources than many Egyptians who also struggled to find work, feed their families, access health care, and send children
to school. The same physician described it this way:

> Like when I am going to talk as an Iraqi refugee to UNHCR, I will expect
> that they will serve me in a way that will make me live better than the
> Egyptians. And this will never happen. You should live in the same way that
> the Egyptians live in Cairo. They can't provide you with more. Many Iraqi
> refugees are living in the same way and maybe better than Egyptians in
> Egypt. But they are looking for better. And I just wonder, what is the better
> that they can give you that is better than Egyptians living in Cairo?

Cairo is a city of striking inequality. US aid is touted by the US government as promoting democracy and the "free market" with the twin goals
of keeping Egypt a beacon of "stability" in order to support the US foreign
policy goal of normalizing Israel and integrating Egypt into the regional
security architecture and US-dominated global capitalist system (Jadallah
2015). The result has been "stability" through decades of dictatorship and
increasing privatization, policing, militarization, and a decline in the standard of living of ordinary Egyptians. Living "in the same way" as Egyptians
during the contemporary period of their displacement would have meant
a significant drop in the standard of living that the mostly middle-class
Iraqis would have experienced in Iraq prior to the war where, despite
living in a politically repressive state, they had access to free public education, health care, employment, and other services. Iraqis did not experience their exile in Cairo as one of privilege. They were, after all, undergoing
significant personal socioeconomic decline while at the same time being
mistaken for wealthy Gulf tourists and often charged more for everything.
Simultaneously, they were being blamed, by their presence, for raising the
cost of necessities and rent for already struggling Egyptians. Of course,
the imposition of free market "shock therapy" and disaster capitalism on
Iraq during the US-led occupation, notably also under the premise of promoting democracy and the free market, destroyed the institutions and
systems that Iraqis remembered nostalgically from exile in Cairo (Klein
2010). Although Egypt was held up in imperial eyes as an ally and Iraq
under Saddam Hussein as an enemy, there was a kinship and a relatedness
to the processes to which both societies were subjected. And these rela-

LIVING IN THE TRANSIT CITY   111

tions as well as other histories of connection affected relationships between individual Egyptians and Iraqis in Cairo.

EATING AT YOUR UNCLE'S HOUSE

"*Inta mnein* (Where are you from)?" the taxi driver asks as he peers at us in his rearview mirror, prayer beads and SpongeBob SquarePants air freshener bouncing as he deftly winds through downtown Cairo. It's evening and Haydar and I are heading to meet some colleagues and friends for tea and backgammon after a long day in the office that was long enough that we've indulgently decided to take a taxi. "I'm from Iraq," Haydar offers. I'm tired from a day almost entirely spent talking. Haydar's day probably included more talking than mine, but he's in a good mood and willing to chat. "*Ahlan wa-sahlan* (Welcome)!!" the driver enthuses "*Ahsan nas! Menawar Misr* (The best people! Welcome to Egypt)!! Iraq is a beautiful country," he says. "Are you from Baghdad?" "Yes," Haydar replies. "Ah, Baghdad!" sighs the driver. "What neighborhood?" Haydar responds in vague terms. The driver is clearly excited: "I lived there for seven years and worked in Baghdad that whole time. Beautiful city. Terrible what the US has done, terrible. Saddam Hussein was a great man." I bristle a little. I have seen this conversation before and have a sense of what might be coming. No topic is off limits to Cairene taxi drivers, it seems. "Why did you leave?" the driver asks. Mercifully, the driver is genuinely asking the open-ended question and does not, as has happened on some other occasions, use it as an opportunity to launch into a monologue about how Iraqis should have stayed to defend Saddam and fight the Americans. "The war," Haydar says simply but definitively, closing off conversation. The driver gets the hint and shifts to me: "*Inti mnein* (Where are you from)?"

As is clear from our taxi ride, Iraqis and Egyptians are not strangers to one another. In the 1970s and especially the 1980s, millions of Egyptians, including our taxi driver, traveled to Iraq as migrant laborers. They comprised the largest part of a growing population of Egyptian workers who traveled to work in oil-rich countries in the region beginning in the 1950s but accelerating in the 1960s when the Egyptian government relaxed

112   CHAPTER 3

stringent exit visa regulations before dropping them entirely in the 1970s as part of Anwar al-Sadat's program of *infitah* (opening) (LaTowsky 1984). But it was during the eight-year Iran-Iraq War, when the vast majority of the Iraqi working population was conscripted into the military, that up to seven million Egyptians came to make up the bulk of Iraq's wartime labor force.[14] They took up diverse posts in government, agriculture, private businesses, services, and a small number of Egyptians volunteered to serve in the Iraqi Army. A small group of farmers *(fellahin)* from different regions in Egypt participated in a bilateral resettlement scheme in which they settled and cultivated planned agricultural villages in Iraq. Of these migrant farmers, Saddam Hussein said, "The Egyptian peasant in Iraq is not a migrant. He is a citizen who has changed his place of residence. The sons of the Nile will embrace the river-basins of the Tigris and the Euphrates with all the affection we hold for the Nile itself" (Solh 1985). Egyptians' travel to Iraq and their lives once there were facilitated by Iraqi government policies borne out of a confluence of pan-Arab solidarity and political and economic expediency. Egyptians did not require work permits, could access schools and health care, and could apply for Iraqi citizenship. The Egyptian state benefitted too. The remittances these workers sent back to their families made up a substantial part of the Egyptian economy; in 1988, Egypt received some 3.8 billion dollars in remittances (Feiler 1991). It was not all positive, however. At the end of the Iran-Iraq War, newspapers reported attacks and harassment of Egyptian migrant workers by Iraqis returning from the war. As word of the attacks spread, thousands of Egyptian migrant workers fled the country (Cowell and Times 1989). In my daily life and especially when I am out with Iraqi friends I meet many of these former migrant workers in Cairo, and most report fond memories of their time in Baghdad, recalling favorite streets, neighborhoods, and restaurants. Many left by the 1990–91 war with Kuwait. The years of sanctions and wars that forced Iraqis out of their country have also mostly ended Egyptian labor migration there.

An urban legend circulating in Egypt gives a sense of the connections Egyptian migrants felt to Iraq: "A popular tale that speaks to migrants' close association with the country tells of an Egyptian worker who was arbitrarily blamed by a wealthy Iraqi for dirtying the latter's brand-new car. The Iraqi proceeded to beat the Egyptian until, by chance, Saddam

Hussein—who just happened to be driving by—intervened, sending the Iraqi to prison and handing the Egyptian a match to set the car alight" (Carroll 2013).

Urban legends, no matter how dubious, can reveal a lot about how their tellers and listeners view the world: In this one, the autocrat's brutality and sovereign power are both acknowledged—but in this tale, his power is wielded to protect the poor Egyptian migrant worker over the wealthy Iraqi. While many Egyptians are aware of and acknowledge the violence of the Baath government, many, including many who never traveled to Iraq for work, express admiration for Saddam Hussein. Part of this is related to Hussein's reported fondness for Egypt; not only did Saddam Hussein speak glowingly about Egypt and Egyptians, but he himself lived in exile in Egypt for four years in the 1960s. Many Egyptians I met also reported admiring Hussein's Baath Party pan-Arab ideology and public willingness to speak out against US empire. How these sentiments related to the Iraqis living in their midst is more contradictory. But this and related tales were also shared by Iraqis, who told the story as a complaint about their treatment in Egypt. Iraqis too drew on the history of Egyptian labor migration to Iraq, especially in a rhetoric of protest about their reception in Egypt. In a blog post on the "Iraqi Voices" section of the website accompanying the short documentary *Iraqis in Egypt,* Kifah N. Abdullah (2008) unfavorably compares the treatment Iraqis received in Egypt with that Egyptians received in Iraq. He writes: "Now we are here in Egypt, where many of us know by name the Egyptians we knew in the years they spent in our country. But here we Iraqis are not allowed to work, or have any of the privileges Egyptians enjoyed in Iraq. It is a bitter pill for us to swallow."

This history of relatedness had significant, if ambivalent, implications for Iraqis' experiences of life in Cairo and also of Cairenes' experiences of the Iraqis in their midst. Some Egyptians who had traveled there felt a strong sense of connection to Iraq, which led to them feeling a sense of welcoming and obligation toward Iraqis. Others felt strongly and expressed that Iraqis should have stayed and fought; like much of the world, they too had been consuming news of the war and occupation for years, and many Egyptians I met had strong opinions about it. Others, like the taxi driver, expressed some mix of both. During my fieldwork, I witnessed many small daily encounters between Egyptians and Iraqis. Some

114   CHAPTER 3

were mundane, like a taxi ride, while others, like an interview with local staff at the UNHCR or International Organization for Migration office, were more consequential. Some of these relations happened outside of humanitarian framings, while others were very much central to the vernacularization of humanitarian concepts and practices in Egypt (Merry 2006). I also listened to many opinions about Egyptians from Iraqis and many opinions about Iraqis from Egyptians. In both cases, this was uncomfortable, if instructive, terrain. Being half Egyptian and fiercely loving my Egyptian family and friends, I felt a certain defensiveness or shame when Iraqis spoke poorly about their interactions with Egyptians. At the same time, as I developed strong bonds with the Iraqis whom I came to know, introducing them to my family and friends, I felt similarly uncomfortable when Egyptians spoke ill of Iraqis.

Daily and ongoing forms of relatedness between Iraqis and Egyptians were ambivalent and transcended the historical and geopolitical. They also very much emerged, as we shall see, from everyday forms of relation, especially economic ones, although these were often fraught. Some Iraqis, especially those studying in high schools or universities, forged close and lasting friendships with Egyptian classmates. Others reported having almost no contact with Egyptians beyond cursory interactions in shops, offices, and while moving around the city. However diverse and varied they were, Iraqis' relationships with Egyptians, and their place in Egypt more generally, were influenced by mutual (mis)imaginings of one another, built on historical and contemporary knowledge including firsthand experience, stories, and official and public discourse. All of this certainly influenced what it meant and how it felt to live in exile in a place that was both known and strange, among people who felt that they too knew you. As Shams put it when she described how she felt in Egypt: "When you are in your home, it is different than living in your uncle's home. It is different to eat in your home than in your uncle's home. Even though he is your uncle, and you are related."

CITY OF REFUGEES

In addition to the complex sense of distant relatedness that Iraqis experienced vis-à-vis Egyptians and Egypt, Iraqis in Cairo were also joining a large and diverse population of urban refugees. Egypt has long been a place of refuge for people fleeing violence and persecution, especially from Africa, the Middle East, and Europe. Like with Iraqis, these displacements index the ongoing presence and history of imperial and other geopolitical relationships. However, the traces of these earlier migrations also shape the experiences of those that come after them: in their descendants who remain in Egypt, among communities who have moved on or returned but remember or memorialize their time in Egypt, in the humanitarian, cultural, and national architectures that they built or were built to manage and serve them, in the possibilities for mobility and official efforts to foreclose mobilities, and in the policies and administrative attitudes that are then applied to subsequent refugee communities.

In Egypt and especially in the metropolitan areas of Cairo and Alexandria, displaced people are not sequestered by nationality but come into contact with refugees from other countries not only in daily life but also and especially through their interactions with the humanitarian apparatus in Egypt. Refugees of any one nationality in Cairo are not understood or governed in isolation but imagined and managed in relation to other refugee populations, including those that came before them and those that will come after them. These understandings extend to refugee populations themselves; Iraqis cultivated a shifting sense of distinction from and solidarity with other refugee and migrant populations in Egypt.

It was not a coincidence that Iraqi displacement was often referred to as "the largest refugee crisis in the region since 1948" (Fargues et al. 2008) or that Palestinian displacement—in particular the numbers of people displaced as well as its enduring quality—often came up in conversations I had with Iraqis and humanitarians. Since the Nakba, or "catastrophe," as Palestinians call their 1948 ethnic cleansing from Palestine, Palestinian refugees have come to be seen as the paradigmatic example of what it means to be a refugee in Egypt and in the region more broadly. Palestinians never fled to Egypt in the numbers that they did to Jordan, Lebanon, Syria, the West Bank, or Gaza, and the United Nations Relief and Works Agency has never had a presence in Egypt (El-Abed 2009). However, although the population itself has been relatively small, around seventy-five thousand people, their experience as well as the status of the Palestinian refugees in the Middle East more generally looms large in

116   CHAPTER 3

terms of what it means to be a refugee in the Middle East, both in popular imaginations as well as in how governments reckon with displaced populations. Palestinian refugees began fleeing to Egypt in the 1930s, with large displacements in 1948, 1967, and 1990–91 (Zohry and Harrell-Bond 2003). Most Palestinian refugees in Egypt throughout this period have neither been registered with nor received assistance from any UN agency. Beginning in 1954, policies under President Nasser treated Palestinians similarly to Egyptian nationals. They could access state services, attend schools and universities for free, and were permitted to work.[15] The government changed its laws to strike the word "foreign" from any descriptions of Palestinians (El-Abed 2005). This is sometimes referred to as the "golden age" for Palestinian refugees. However, in the late 1970s, after the signing of the Camp David Accords with Israel and the assassination of the Egyptian minister of culture by a militant Palestinian faction in Cyprus, Egyptian policies toward Palestinians changed. Starting in 1978, Palestinians in Egypt were stripped of many of the rights they had gained. They could no longer access free education, residency permits, or employment, and they had to attend universities as foreign students paying in foreign currency. Laws were amended to designate Palestinians as "foreigners" once more.

Ironically, although Palestinian displacement was frequently invoked by humanitarians and refugees in my fieldwork, Palestinians were often rendered invisible within the humanitarian landscape in Egypt, subject to a "protection gap" where they were caught between policies, protections, and institutions that are either ineffectual or exclude them (Gabiam 2006). The small number of Palestinian Iraqis in Egypt especially fell through this legal and humanitarian gap. In Iraq, Palestinians had received somewhat favorable treatment under Saddam Hussein, whose government had rejected the United Nations Relief and Works Agency and instead provided housing and services to Palestinians directly. Following the overthrow of the Baath government, Palestinians became the target of resentment, reprisals, and threats, forcing many of them to flee (Gabiam 2006). Many Iraqi Palestinians, as stateless refugees doubly displaced, had a hard time gaining asylum outside Iraq. The few who made it to Egypt found themselves unable to gain recognition or receive services.

LIVING IN THE TRANSIT CITY   117

One other moment of refugee history in Egypt, which occurred just before the vast majority of Iraqis came to Egypt, profoundly affected the landscape of displacement in Cairo. In September 2005, Sudanese refugees held a three-month sit-in at a park directly across from the UNHCR office, which was then located in Mohandisin, a bustling, upscale neighborhood of shops, restaurants, and apartment blocks not far from downtown. Sudanese represent one of the largest and longest standing refugee populations in Egypt. In late 2004, in anticipation of a forthcoming peace deal, the UNHCR suspended refugee status determination and resettlement procedures for Sudanese in Egypt. If peace were to return to Sudan, the logic went, Sudanese in Egypt would no longer require protection and could return. But Sudanese refugees in Egypt experienced the suspension as the stripping away of their legal status, access to humanitarian protection, and resettlement prospects.

What began as a small improvised gathering at the UNHCR gate transformed into a highly visible encampment of thousands of Sudanese in Egypt. Together, drawing on international refugee law, they demanded to be included in conversations about their legal status and solutions to their displacement. The protesters demanded "radical solutions" to their plight, rejecting "compulsory involuntary repatriation" (FMRS 2006, 62) and local integration, instead requesting third-country resettlement (Moulin and Nyers 2007). On December 30, Egyptian police and security forces, allegedly at the request of the UNHCR, violently evicted people from the park, killing at least twenty-eight, injuring hundreds, and detaining hundreds more (FMRS 2006).

The Sudanese protesters sought to be recognized as both a population of care and concern and as political actors. They addressed the UNHCR, which, in administering refugee status determination and resettlement, had come to be almost a surrogate state (Kagan 2011). Collectively, they reappropriated the UN's own language of durable solutions to demand that they be included in discussions about their status and any solutions to their situation. The crackdown on the sit-in illustrates the extreme violence that a policy of transit can provoke—in addition to the structural violence of social, economic, and political marginalization, transit can become a threat to life itself. In response to the protest and the violent police crackdown, the UNHCR moved its office from Mohandisin to a

118   CHAPTER 3

fortified compound in 6th of October City, more than an hour by car from downtown Cairo. The violence with which the sit-in was disbanded would have long-lasting effects for the Sudanese community in Egypt and also for the architecture of refugee governance in Cairo.

SECURITY AND INSECURITY

One clear way that imperial relations and histories affected Iraqis' daily lives in Egypt was how they were understood by the Egyptian state, and sometimes by one another, as dangerous and untrustworthy. When I began my fieldwork, I was puzzled to note that most national and ethnic communities had community-based organizations in Cairo, but Iraqis did not. When I asked about it, Iraqi interlocutors regularly told me that there was no Iraqi community in Egypt.

There was a kind of unsayable and unknowable nature to the "security" problems that Iraqis faced in Egypt. Haydar, for example, described them to me by saying, "You know, there are also security problems for Iraqi refugees here. For reasons that nobody knows about, and I shouldn't talk about it. But . . . " He trailed off for a moment. "We don't know why there are restrictions for a lot of things for Iraqis here." Security here had multiple valences. The Egyptian state conceived of Iraqis as a security threat, perhaps riffing off of the perception by Western states, rooted in the Islamophobia and anti-Arab racism of the Global War on Terror, that Iraqis were in some way more dangerous than other refugees. The result, however, was that Iraqis experienced a different form of "security problem," namely a persistent feeling of insecurity in Egypt.

Government officials occasionally described Iraqis as a security threat and evoked sectarian difference, including through fears of "Shia proselytizing" (Abdelaaty 2021). This was despite the actual ethnic and religious diversity of Iraqis in Egypt. Iraqis often told me that Egyptians—official and ordinary civilians alike—often asked them about their sectarian affiliation. Iraqi friends told me that they found this reproduction in exile of the imposed primacy of sectarian identity—the very violence that forced them to lose so much—upsetting and alienating. When I began my fieldwork, I received the advice more than once not to ask people about their

LIVING IN THE TRANSIT CITY 119

sectarian identity for exactly this reason. Iraqis rejected not only the reproduction of the violence they had fled and the reduction of their identity but also the reification of categories that, they argued, had not been determinative of their lives prior to the war and occupation.

In Egypt, Iraqis noticed that when they congregated, problems ensued, so they stopped congregating. Some Iraqis told me that when they first came to Egypt, they had tried to organize social events and one Iraqi man had even made some efforts to start a community-based organization, but he had been detained by state security. I heard similar stories about Iraqis who had tried to collect mutual aid donations for needy Iraqis during Ramadan but found themselves facing questions from the authorities. Others had sought the necessary permits for starting organizations, but they were never approved. There was an inchoate feeling of being surveilled that I experienced through the stories, embodied comportment, and social relations—including with me—of my Iraqi interlocutors. Haydar spoke about calls he received on his cell phone from unknown numbers and of experiences of feeling like he was being followed.

Earlier experiences of living under authoritarianism in Iraq and living through the rupture that accompanied the "cartographic violence" (Peteet 2010) of remapping Iraq along sectarian lines combined with the experience of being surveilled and rendered as security threats in Egypt to create an isolating and anxiety-provoking experience of displacement. Iraqis' relations to one another in Egypt were shaped by these histories, just as at times their choice to come to Egypt was based on a desire to be away from other Iraqis. As Haydar explained, "Between Iraqi refugees themselves, not with Egyptians, the problem is, these people survived from sectarian divisions. They suffered a lot during their life. There is mistrust between them. There is a kind of prejudgmental idea about their tribe and sect."

In Cairo, the possibility of third-country resettlement, and in particular its scarcity and opacity in a context where so many rights were denied, only contributed to feelings of mistrust. Later in our conversation, when I asked him about other challenges Iraqis in Egypt faced, Haydar told me how resettlement created suspicion even among friends:

A lot of Iraqis now don't want other Iraqis to know what they are doing. Because they want to push the competition away from them. If there is an

120   CHAPTER 3

opportunity for only two people to have something and you are one of them, you are never going to tell anyone. Like you can find a lot of people who are really friends and one of them is going to leave for resettlement and never tell the other. They are afraid of envying each other for what they have. They are afraid and they do not believe that their life is going to get better until they will be in it. He will never believe he is going to the United States until he is there. So I think mistrust keeps breaking the social network between them. But still there is a social network between Iraqi people. And by the fact that everyone is dealing with a lot of problems. A lot of problems. Because everyone is frustrated with his life or her life. No one wants to sit with the sad man and hear sad stories. Because everyone has sad stories. They want to cheer up, and they want to relax sometimes. And this pushes them away from each other.

Haydar's answer to my question points partly to the scarcity of resettlement. He notes how, with relatively few available places, Iraqis who were in the process sometimes were afraid that they would be envied and possibly undermined by jealous others. Throughout my fieldwork, I heard Iraqis describe multiple instances of friends who suddenly disappeared, only for them to discover later that they had been resettled. Haydar provides two possible explanations for this: One is that they were avoiding dealing with the consequences of envy, not an unreasonable concern. I occasionally heard gossip and rumors that so-and-so had told a false story about a medical concern, so-and-so had lied about their military service or position in the Baath Party, so-and-so had lied about being a single mother. Haydar wasn't so worried about it—"The UNHCR isn't stupid," he said—but other friends were worried, afraid that they may have lost the opportunity to someone who may not, in their eyes, have deserved it. I heard rumors and could never know whether they were true or reflected anxieties of "why them and not me?"—or both. While the veracity of such claims is itself unknowable, it is nonetheless important to reflect on the social fallout of the categories imposed through the resettlement process, which I will discuss more in subsequent chapters. Haydar's second reason was a different kind of protection—that Iraqis might not, given the scarcity and difficulty of the resettlement process itself, be able to publicly or even privately affirm that they were going to travel. A potential third reason, which Haydar did not mention during this conversation, is that Iraqis whose resettlement was as a result of their work with the US in Iraq might be unwilling or afraid to admit so publicly. Indeed, some Iraqis told me that because the US resettled the most refugees, and because of the well-known special resettlement programs for Iraqis who worked with the US, anyone who was resettled was potentially suspected of having worked with the occupation in some way.

To say that Iraqis mistrusted one another in Egypt was not to say that they did not maintain an identification with Iraq and a nationally defined sense of "being Iraqi." They absolutely did, in affective and material ways. It also does not mean that there weren't friendships, relations, and forms of mutual aid and care forged in Cairo that lightened the experience of being there. As Hayder said, there was still a "social network" even if it was fragile and ruptured in places. Um Muhammad, for instance, who had worked for women's rights in Iraq, endeavored to build relations with other Iraqi women and especially to support women who were struggling financially and socially in Egypt. She said: "We have a community here. We support each other. We teach each other and give advice: how to cook a certain meal, how to deal with a baby . . . but it's not the same as it was in Iraq. It's not the same relations that we had in Iraq. There are limits."

Shams's articulation that she was not in heaven and not with people seemed to hint at the loss of relations that Um Muhammad described above. Many Iraqis imagined Egypt as a place of transit even before they arrived. Some, such as Karrar and Shams, conceived of Egypt as a stop on an onward journey elsewhere; the vast majority of the Iraqis I met at least initially imagined and hoped that their time in Egypt would be relatively short and that they would return to Iraq when the situation improved. While the Egyptian state identifies itself as a transit state to avoid long-term responsibility for refugees, Iraqis experienced the existential state of transit as an expectation of movement, both in space and time. Ironically, they also experienced it as an unfolding process of temporal and spatial immobilization; over time they came to realize that exile had not, as they had hoped, been a brief interlude before they could return home or travel elsewhere. Iraqis most frequently described their existence in Egypt as not life at all but a space between a previous life and an unknown, uncertain future life. They described Egypt as "transit," "a station," or "a temporary place." As transit extended into the future with no tangible possibility of forward movement, it took on characteristics of what Bridget Haas (2017,

76) describes as "existential limbo." Several interlocutors described their condition as "between earth and sky," evoking a suspended horizon, the fuzzy in-betweenness where sky melts into land. Mariam, a single woman whom I met during my work at RLAP, described this existential suspension to me. "I don't have stability," she said. "Every day we are waiting for life to return. When will it come?" Within this context of never-ending temporariness and under the weight of imperial histories, Iraqis made and remade categories and relations of refugeeness both within and outside the registers of humanitarianism.

4 Negotiating Humanitarian "Solutions" to Displacement

IRAQIS' EXPERIENCES OF THE REFUGEE
RESETTLEMENT PROCESS IN CAIRO

Saif had invited me to accompany him to his interview with the United Nations High Commissioner for Refugees (UNHCR). Knowing we had to arrive before the office opened to secure a spot in line, we left central Cairo early, when the morning sun was bright but the haze had not yet descended on the city. We traveled in fits and starts through heavy traffic along the desert road that leads from Cairo to 6th of October City, the suburb where the UNHCR is located. Saif, a single Iraqi man in his forties who had lived as a refugee in Egypt for almost four years, hoped that this interview would be a step toward his resettlement (*'i'adat tawtīn*) in another country, such as the United States.

The UNHCR compound, set on a residential street, truly looks like a compound. Its shuttered windows are set in walls painted the color of the surrounding desert. The facade is designed so that the building is unidentifiable when you approach it from either side—only from directly in front does it become clear where you are. The heavy metal sliding door studded with a bulletproof glass window evokes a sense of fortification and imprisonment. The first time I visited, I remember being shocked by how the organization whose mandate it is to protect refugees seemed, with its physical presence, to be protecting itself from them. Saif and I arrived

124 CHAPTER 4

before 8:30 a.m. The UNHCR was still closed, but a diverse group of about twenty people was already waiting in line. Others gathered in the small park across the street, and more people were arriving all the time. Uniformed security personnel milled around in front.

We joined the line. After we had waited awhile, a guard emerged, yelling, "Appointments! Appointments!" A new line formed. Those with appointments came forward, showed their UNHCR identification cards and appointment slips, and waited to enter. Shuttered windows opened, revealing workers behind glass, and we filed forward. Only those with appointments, like Saif, were allowed to enter. Our bags were searched and the men were passed over with a metal detector. Once we were cleared, a guard opened a second heavy metal door and we were inside. We stepped from the securitized entrance into the waiting area. Slowly, the courtyard filled with people waiting, uncertain when they would be called.

I had been happy when Saif asked me to accompany him because I knew he struggled with these appointments, finding it extremely difficult to speak of the violence he had experienced. It had taken several months before he would tell me concretely what had happened to him in Iraq or about his life in Egypt. In our meetings he pushed his psychiatric reports across the table or brought me short letters on crumpled pieces of paper, each one providing a bit more information than the last. The slow unfolding of Saif's narrative and his extreme reluctance to tell his story were worrying in the context of the resettlement process, in which it was essential for a refugee to be able to prove their vulnerability and to establish their credibility by conveying their story to multiple, often skeptical gatekeepers. In the days before the interview, we had spent hours together practicing, with me trying to guess the questions they might ask and Saif gamely practicing answers.

Every available bit of shade in the UNHCR courtyard was occupied by people waiting their turn; only children ran around in the full sun, undeterred from their playing by the heat. Other than the gaggle of children, which grew as new friendships were instantly made, people mostly kept to themselves. But there were little moments of sociality. People shifted over to make space for others on a bench. Someone offered to share with us the snacks they had wisely thought to pack. As we waited, I saw that Saif was nervous—closing his eyes, sighing, and fidgeting in his seat. I realized I was nervous too. Would Saif be able to recount his testimony to the UNHCR officer, a stranger, in the short time allotted for his interview? Was this even a resettlement interview?

Like many Iraqis I met in Egypt, Saif had come to hope that resettlement might allow him to reclaim an imaginable future from the prolonged stasis of urban displacement. But the moment at the UNHCR threshold was freighted with ambivalence and uncertainty. The uncertainty can be partially attributed to the opacity of resettlement bureaucracy specifically (Thomson 2012) and the government of displaced people more generally (Biehl 2015), which often is achieved through the weaponization of time.[1] But more can be gleaned from attending to the institutional encounters and relationships that compose the process of seeking resettlement. Following Iraqis' experiences with the resettlement process in Cairo renders visible, alongside uncertainty, something else: a profound affect, practice, and position of ambivalence about the humanitarian categories and solutions applied to displacement.

My attunement to ambivalence emerges from juxtaposing two recent theoretical interventions in anthropology. The first is Georgina Ramsay's (2020) call to attend to the situated histories and relations that produce uncertainty in displacement rather than ascribing uncertainty to "refugeeness" in general. The appeal to situatedness draws our attention to the histories (imperial intervention in and displacement from Iraq) and the terrain (urban Cairo in this case) on which resettlement selection occurs. Likewise, transnational so-called solutions to displacement, such as resettlement, take on particular meanings based on the conditions from which refugees approach them, meanings that exceed the humanitarian logics that seem, on the surface, to govern resettlement.

Such meanings are fraught with ambivalence for those seeking resettlement.[2] While I initially worried about Saif's ability to perform in his UNHCR interview, I eventually came to understand that this was only part of the story. Saif sought resettlement despite his doubts, some of which emerged from the demands of the lengthy, uncertain, and bureaucratic process. His other doubts, however, were related to the idea of resettlement itself. What would resettlement mean for him? Would it really improve his life? He had asked me these questions several times, knowing

126   CHAPTER 4

that I lived in the United States. I didn't know how to answer him. Many other Iraqis also sought resettlement while refusing the requirements that they inhabit particular subject positions, express gratitude, and narrate trauma and difficult experiences in specific ways. Others were ambivalent about resettlement as a putative solution to displacement; still others conceptualized the problem of displacement itself much differently from states and humanitarian organizations. The resettlement process often denies, ignores, presumes, or renders problematic refugees' desires, yet it looks very different when those desires and aspirations are taken seriously.

UNSETTLING RESETTLEMENT

According to the UNHCR—the intergovernmental organization tasked with global refugee protection—resettlement is one of three "durable solutions" to displacement alongside voluntary repatriation and local integration. The UNHCR (2011, 3) defines *resettlement* as "the selection and transfer of refugees from a state in which they have sought protection to a third state that has agreed to admit them ... with permanent residence status." Although the use of resettlement has changed over time, the UNHCR currently describes it as the durable solution of last resort, to be used for the most urgent cases or the most intractable refugee situations. Of the millions of refugees living in urban or encamped displacement worldwide, less than 1 percent are resettled each year, typically those individuals designated by states and the UNHCR as most vulnerable.

In this chapter, I focus on Iraqis' experiences of undergoing humanitarian resettlement through the UNHCR, looking especially at their experiences of navigating humanitarian bureaucracies, living in the uncertainty of the resettlement process, and their ambivalence about the categories of deservingness that they had to navigate for recognition. While I briefly describe it here, in chapter 5 I will turn more fully to how Iraqis experienced the Direct Access Program that was created by the passage of the Refugee Crisis in Iraq Act in the United States. In practice these two programs were not completely distinct—and Iraqis did not treat them as such, reflecting an additional way that they refused imperial categories—but

I treat them separately because they had different subjective effects for Iraqis and, I contend, do different epistemic work in the world.

Working with the Resettlement Legal Aid Project (RLAP) provided access to an otherwise opaque bureaucratic process. But because the process includes so many actors and stages, many of them intentionally opaque, even resettlement workers and adjudicators cannot penetrate the black box of resettlement bureaucracy (Thomson 2012); there were aspects of the process, such as security clearances and resettlement interviews, that I could never observe firsthand. This multiplicity and opacity is central to what made resettlement so difficult to navigate for Iraqis. To supplement my work at RLAP, I also interviewed Iraqis who were unaffiliated with the office, uninterested in resettlement, or not registered as refugees at all.

Most studies of resettlement begin after the process is complete, thereby excluding the vast majority of refugees whose lives may be substantively affected even if they are never resettled (El-Shaarawi 2021). Centering Iraqis in Cairo thereby unsettles the conversation about how humanitarian solutions to conflict and displacement are enacted and how refugees themselves experience, negotiate, and contest them. Seeing resettlement from the position of sitting with Saif at the threshold, if you will, shows how resettlement reflects and produces forms of existential uncertainty, extending imperial unknowing from war into the humanitarian realm and exposing resettlement as part of a continuous process of imperial intervention.

Unlike the asylum process, in which people approach or cross borders on their own before requesting international protection, the resettlement process occurs largely at a distance, giving resettling states greater control throughout the entire procedure. States, often assisted by the UNHCR, select people who have typically undergone asylum processes in another country and offer them residence and, often, eventual citizenship.[3] While asylum is a right under the 1951 Geneva Convention Relating to the Status of Refugees and under many national laws, resettlement is discretionary, depending on the benevolence of states and the coordination of the UNHCR, governments, and NGOs. Resettlement through the UN is, in a sense, a sign that asylum has failed, that the country in which the refugee sought refuge is unable or unwilling to offer the humanitarian

128   CHAPTER 4

protection that they need. In practice, resettlement both fails to step into that breach and also has many more meanings than that. The resettlement process is a complex, transnational assemblage of laws, guidelines, practices, and relationships, and this assemblage in turn creates heterogeneous and plural local processes (Sandvik 2011). Many states do not offer refugee resettlement programs at all. Of those that do, the US has historically accepted the largest number of cases, followed by Canada, Australia, the UK, and Scandinavian countries.[4]

In many of these countries, refugee resettlement programs have recently become the subject of contentious public debates. Such debates focus on legal and moral obligations to refugees as well as possible risks, costs, and benefits to the receiving state (van Selm 2018). Like much of the existing scholarship on resettlement, these discussions often exclude refugees' own perspectives and take refugees' arrival in the resettlement state as their starting point. Combined, these tendencies foreground the state's analytical gaze, reflecting the enduring conception of the refugee as a problem for the "national order of things" (Malkki 1995a, 1995b), one that is solved only when the refugee is reincorporated into a state through integration, repatriation, or resettlement. These discussions also obscure how many refugees live with these hybrid transnational and local selection processes for years, possibly decades, of their lives (Garnier et al. 2018).

If resettlement programs are presented by the UNHCR, states, and humanitarians as a solution to displacement, the question becomes: a solution for whom? What kind of a solution? For a country like Egypt, resettlement moves refugees off its territory, providing a mechanism for enacting its role as a place where refuge is always, in theory, temporary. For so-called resettlement states, resettlement schemes present an opportunity to project a favorable image and to engage in what states call "burden sharing"; resettlement programs bolster a state's claims to humanitarianism and its posture as a "country of refuge." States such as Australia and the United States have simultaneously hardened and militarized borders, punishing and excluding asylum-seekers who travel to these states on their own, while touting their resettlement programs—operated from "countries of first asylum" such as Egypt—as the correct way to seek protection. For states, refugee resettlement can also solve other kinds of political problems. For example, the United States hailed resettled refugees from Communist states during the Cold War as "voting with their feet"—embodied examples of the superiority of the American way of life. Yến Lê Espiritu (2014) argues that the resettlement of refugees in the US in the aftermath of the Vietnam War, which was the largest refugee resettlement program in American history, allowed the United States to transmute the difficult memories of a war lost into hopeful stories of refugees whose lives were saved in the aftermath.

If resettlement can be a solution for states, refugees' experiences of resettlement complicate its designation as a durable solution for displaced people themselves. For refugees, resettlement can have many complex and contradictory meanings as well; it can be a way to reunite family, continue careers or education, build livelihoods, and/or escape from unlivable and insecure presents, among many other reasons. Recent ethnographies of post-resettlement life show how some refugees encounter ongoing or renewed feelings of displacement in their new places of residence (Besteman 2016; Ong 2003; Ramsay 2017; Tang 2015). In her ethnography of Iraqis' experiences of resettlement in the United States, Sally Wesley Bonet (2022) has shown how, contrary to the protection they were promised and expected, Iraqis were folded into positions of exploitable labor. Such studies provide crucial insight into whether resettlement fulfills its promise as a solution to displacement for those who are selected. But they cannot elucidate the experiences of a much larger population of refugees—about 99 percent of them—who engage with the resettlement process in diverse ways, sometimes for years, but who may never actually be resettled.[5] In the time and space before resettlement, resettlement represents a possibility and a process of becoming, but one that has unclear boundaries and ambivalences. From contexts of prolonged displacement in camps or cities, refugees often envision resettlement as a solution to problems of prolonged immobilization, the denial of rights, and political exclusion (Horst 2006; Jansen 2008).[6] Given the scarcity of resettlement, these longings, as Cindy Horst (2006) illustrates, can be painful, even debilitating.

For Iraqis in Cairo, the stakes of resettlement were at once intimate—emerging from personal and shared hopes for what life might be in the aftermath of war and displacement—and geopolitical—implicated in violent relations of occupation, war, and dispossession. They also involved

130   CHAPTER 4

complicated imaginings of what a future elsewhere might entail. As a form of humanitarian governance (Garnier et al. 2018), the resettlement process evoked much suffering but held out the possibility of protection and citizenship. For Iraqis, however, the meanings of resettlement exceeded a humanitarian frame; resettlement could offer citizenship or protection but might also represent other things, such as a compromise, an escape route, or a form of reparations. These meanings introduce an existential ambivalence into dominant portrayals of resettlement as humanitarian protection for vulnerable refugees and a solution to the "problem" of displacement. Such ambivalence is twofold. First, Iraqis experienced ambivalence about the process of seeking resettlement, a process that claims to identify and protect vulnerability but, at least in the short term, seemed to exacerbate it. Second, Iraqis were ambivalent about resettlement itself. If resettlement is often imagined as an inherent humanitarian good that all refugees desire, Iraqis' orientations to it reflect a more complicated relationship with resettlement as a possible solution to conflict and displacement.

RESETTLING IRAQIS

In the aftermath of the invasion and occupation of Iraq, Iraqis would come to be among the most resettled populations in the world, although only a small proportion of all displaced Iraqis would be resettled.[7] Syria, Jordan, Lebanon, and Egypt initially allowed Iraqis entry and provisional leave to remain, but governments were uniformly reluctant to offer them legal status and rights, emphasizing that Iraqis were "temporary guests" (Sadek 2010). Yet efforts to designate displacement as temporary—an ambition shared by host governments and most Iraqis—were challenged by the unfolding realization that the decisive victory promised by the Bush and Blair administrations was not to come. As the political and social geography of Iraq fractured, it became clear that many displaced Iraqis would be unable to return in the foreseeable future.

Resettlement was, however, more than a humanitarian response to the perceived intractability of Iraqi displacement. It reflected political and epistemological struggles over the meaning of the war, occupation, and displacement. After the 9/11 attacks, the US government suspended resettlement entirely, even though there were no refugees among the perpetrators. When the program resumed, Iraqis were subject to additional security measures, illustrating how refugees, especially from the Middle East, are caught between discourses and practices that alternately portray them as at risk or a risk. Yet, in addition to a humanitarian politics of care and control, other geopolitics were at play. When it became clear several years into the war that Iraqis were fleeing en masse, the US initially refused to acknowledge the exodus (Libal and Harding 2007) because it exposed the failures of the war and occupation administration.

By 2006 it became impossible to ignore the deteriorating situation in Iraq, especially in Baghdad, as well as the millions of people displaced within Iraq and neighboring countries. Stories emerged about Iraqis who worked with the occupation forces, most famously as interpreters, and who were then targeted with death threats, kidnappings, and executions by militias accusing them of collaboration (Johnson 2013). Under pressure from media coverage, scholarship, political advocacy, and activism, the US government eventually took up the case of these "Iraqi allies." Advocates' and politicians' arguments for their resettlement touted a US "special obligation" to Iraqi refugees, but they often also included a more instrumental concern: that the occupying forces might lose the Iraqis on whom they depended for their linguistic, cultural, and logistical skills. The same logics of securitization that justified excluding Iraqis as refugees became arguments for including them; proponents of resettlement argued that the refugee crisis would "destabilize the region" and that interminably displaced Iraqis might be vulnerable to terrorist recruitment (Berman 2011).

The 2007 Refugee Crisis in Iraq Act created resettlement slots specifically for those who were persecuted for helping the US government or US-based media or NGOs in Iraq.[8] Nicknamed the Direct Access Program, it allowed Iraqis to bypass the United Nations for US resettlement, though the process remained bureaucratically challenging, adversarial, and lengthy. Designated a processing site for the Direct Access Program, Cairo came to have two main streams of resettlement for Iraqis in Egypt: one for "Iraqi allies" and another for humanitarian cases through the UNHCR. These streams operated according to different logics, though they

132   CHAPTER 4

occasionally overlapped. The Refugee Crisis in Iraq Act mobilized patriotic language to argue, as some had claimed about refugees from the Vietnam War (Walzer 1983), that Iraqis who had been employed by the US forces were aligned, either through shared work or shared values, with Americans—they were not Americans but neither were they wholly Other.[9]

By contrast, resettlement through the UNHCR is governed by humanitarian logics and is intended to offer a durable solution to refugees who are unable to either return home or settle more permanently in the country where they have sought asylum. Because there are always more refugees who fit this categorization than places willing to accept them, the UNHCR allocates its scarce resettlement spots to refugees whom they designate as most vulnerable. This is especially so in places like Egypt where humanitarians frequently told me that "local integration" was unfeasible because of policies that render life impossible for refugees. The UNHCR writes that "priority attention should be given to those refugees with acute legal and physical protection needs and, in particular to the most vulnerable such as women-at-risk and unaccompanied children" (UNHCR 2004, 63). The *UNHCR Resettlement Handbook* of the Department of International Protection, which UNHCR staff use to guide their practices around resettlement, lists eight resettlement priorities: (1) legal and physical protection needs, (2) survivors of violence and torture, (3) medical needs, (4) women at risk, (5) family reunification, (6) children and adolescents, (7) older refugees, and (8) refugees who lack prospects for local integration (UNHCR 2011). Here, eligibility hinges not on service to the occupation in Iraq but on being identified as the right kind of "morally legitimate suffering body" (Ticktin 2011, 3), echoing tropes of vulnerability used to categorize populations in humanitarian settings (Feldman and Ticktin 2010). Despite such resonances, the use of these categories is not best understood as an example of the historical shift from rights-based to humanitarian care–based forms of governing, as documented in asylum systems (Fassin 2005; Ticktin 2006). This is so because resettlement is not conceptualized as a right. Instead, the UNHCR uses these criteria to distribute scarce resettlement slots and, in some cases, to dissuade states from implementing discriminatory resettlement policies, such as selecting refugees based on religious, racial, or ethnic identities that the resettlement state considers desirable (Berman 2011).

NEGOTIATING "SOLUTIONS" TO DISPLACEMENT   133

If on paper the two separate programs were governed by different logics, the two streams sometimes converged. In Cairo, Iraqis often interacted with both simultaneously or perhaps first tried one, then the other, while sometimes exploring other potential modes of travel. In everyday speech, Iraqis referred to the US program as "Direct Access," but when describing the UNHCR program, they talked about "being resettled as a refugee."

"HERE THERE IS NO FUTURE"

> In Iraq, we say work makes you tired in two ways, physically
> and mentally. Physically, you will heal from it. Mentally, you
> keep thinking and even if you rest for twenty-four hours, it
> keeps happening. Here there is no future and this makes
> people tired (*ta'ab*). The people who passed away suddenly
> here in Egypt, they were thinking and tired, and it is because
> of lack of control of the future. The strange future is a very
> difficult thing for people. It makes you tired. People are
> thinking, "What will happen to us? Will they kick us out of
> Egypt?" and other matters, over and over.
>
> ABU NASIM

We were sitting on white plastic lawn chairs in the otherwise bare room that used to be Abu Nasim's dining room. The late afternoon sun cast long, uninterrupted shadows on the floor, emphasizing the room's emptiness. Abu Nasim laughed wryly as he reminisced about how, when they'd first come to Egypt, his wife, Um Nasim, had insisted that they purchase new furniture to furnish the flat. He had resisted, saying that they would only be in Egypt for a few months, so why the unnecessary expense for what he was sure would be a temporary situation? They had brought as much of their savings to Egypt as they could get in cash on short notice, but that was all the money they had. It could be better spent elsewhere. His resistance turned into a quarrel and then, eventually, into new furniture for the flat they had rented in 6th of October City. "She was right," he conceded. "Okay, we spent a bit of money, but it felt like we hadn't had such a big reduction in our standard of living. It made it feel a bit more like home." The bitter irony of their current living situation combined with Abu Nasim's playful admission that his wife had been right all along was too much and we all laughed. Um Nasim's laugh trickled in from the kitchen where she was making Iraqi tea, spiced with cardamom. After being in Cairo for four years, the family had finally been approved for resettlement to the United States. In anticipation, they had sold the furniture that for those years had helped them feel not quite so much like temporary visitors, refugees, in Egypt. But now, months had passed since their resettlement acceptance. No travel date had been set. So, with their bags already packed and their landlord impatiently waiting for notice, we sat on temporary furniture as Abu Nasim narrated how the unpredictability of the future could make you sick. Even kill you.

Early in my fieldwork in Cairo, I noticed a pattern, almost a motif: In my conversations with Iraqis, they regularly told me that uncertainty about the future was the most important cause of their ill health and suffering. I kept asking questions about mental health and, in return, I nearly always received answers about uncertainty and its embodied effects. Iraqis used many adjectives to describe the troubling future: strange, as Abu Nasim did here, but also uncertain, unknown, or unstable. Sometimes the future was negated entirely, as when Shams told me, "For me, time has stopped here." I came to realize that to take Iraqis' experiences of exile seriously, I would have to understand what uncertainty meant to them in this context, why its effects were so deleterious, and how it related to the resettlement process.

Indeed, they were not alone. Scholarly accounts of displacement and refugees draw heavily on concepts related to uncertainty. Increasingly, displacement is understood as a problem of uncertainty (Griffiths 2014; Horst and Grabska 2015), a rupture in everyday life and relations (Das 2006) that holds people in a kind of social and political liminality and renders the future unknowable (Brun 2015). But scholars have also questioned the relationship between displacement and uncertainty. On the one hand, glossing displacement as universally uncertain fails to account for historical and local specificities that generate uncertainty (Schiltz et al. 2019). On the other hand, attributing uncertainty as an exceptional condition of refugees elides how it may be a shared condition of life under late capitalism (Ramsay 2020). But if uncertainty is a common theme in the scholarship on displacement, in some ways it remains an elusive or ambiguous subject. On the one hand, to simply accept uncertainty as a condition associated with displacement seems as though it risks slipping into state-centered narratives that posit refugees as the pathological foil of citizenship.[10] On the other hand, and more generally, is not uncertainty, particularly of the future, a near-inherent part of human experience? What renders uncertainty, and by extension temporality, so salient to a person that it becomes the defining feature of their existence, at least for a time, and the cause of ill health and suffering? This conundrum requires an attention to uncertainty in context in Cairo and, in particular, to the specificities that render uncertainty existentially threatening.

While the experience of displacement involves geographical dislocation, it may force a reordering of temporal relations as well, especially over the long term. These changes have important implications for refugees' mental health and well-being. We should take Abu Nasim's sentiment that the uncertain future can kill seriously. As Coker (2004, 17) notes, drawing on Becker (1997), "In the refugee experience, the future, present, and even the past become the unknown terrain that must be relearned." For Coker, this relearning occurs on the terrain of the body and is expressed through what she terms "illness talk." The stories refugees tell about illness may reflect their efforts to address and make sense out of the disordering and dislocating experience of exile (Becker 1997). Embodied expressions of illness may thus both reflect responses to political and social injustices or traumatic experience (Jenkins 1991) as well as being a way in which refugees seek to remake their worlds in conditions of disjuncture or at least to make sense of them. But they can also reflect and recount experiences of suffering as the future one has imagined spirals out of control.

The institutions that manage and govern refugees have their own temporal rhythms and orientations. Refugees' subjective experiences of time in displacement are not separate from institutional rhythms but intersect with them as refugees navigate the constellations of care and control that structure part, but not all, of their lives in exile. This contemporary moment, characterized by the erosion of asylum, proliferating nationalism, and record numbers of people on the move, brings into relief a temporal tension inherent in the framing of the refugee protection

136   CHAPTER 4

regime. Refugee status as a legal and humanitarian category is intended to be temporary. The legal and categorical architecture of the refugee regime is organized around this temporariness, but in practice, displacement is increasingly protracted, with refugees living in exile for an average of about twenty years. The refugee regime's traditional "solutions" to displacement—repatriation, integration in a country of asylum, or resettlement in a third country (Milner and Loescher 2011)—often take years to materialize or are entirely foreclosed. Some refugees live in exile for generations, waiting for the opportunity to return home or begin their lives anew in another place (Feldman 2018). In countries of first asylum, whether in cities, rural areas, or camps, refugees are often unable to exercise the rights accorded to them by international law. At the same time, anti-immigrant and antirefugee rhetoric scapegoats refugees in racialized terms as burdens, security threats, or invaders.

Humanitarianism, writ large, has been described as "present-focused" with a crisis orientation that makes it challenging to deal with the longue durée (Feldman 2018). Humanitarian action typically focuses on needs that can be identified and addressed in the present rather than planning for long-term change. The humanitarian horizon is short and limited by mandates, temporary funding streams, a crisis orientation, and the pull of the next emergency. Indeed, both of the UN refugee agencies (UNHCR and the United Nations Relief and Works Agency) were provisionally created in the mid-twentieth century as temporary agencies with the idea that the problem they were designed to address would go away and they would no longer be necessary. When refugee situations stretch on over time, as so many of them now do, challenges emerge from the discordance between categories and orientations and the situation humanitarians, legal advocates, and adjudicators face. As I mentioned above, the legal category of a refugee is marked by an assumed temporariness that is belied by the actual lived experience of displacement as significantly lengthy, if not protracted. Legally, the refugee category is focused on the past: Past persecution (and to a lesser extent fear of future persecution) is central to the construction of the refugee as a legal status. Third-country resettlement processes are also imbued with these two temporal orientations but add another. In order to be resettled, a refugee must be in need of exceptional protection from their present conditions in exile as well

NEGOTIATING "SOLUTIONS" TO DISPLACEMENT   137

meeting the legal definition of a refugee. Both the past and the present must be a threat.

SABR, OR GOING THROUGH THE RESETTLEMENT PROCESS

While the formal description of resettlement as a process of "selection and transfer" implies that refugees passively undergo the process, in practice it required them to spend time, perform labor, and draw on ample resources of *sabr* (patience). *Sabr* involved, paradoxically, both sustained labor and the appearance of patient waiting in a context of prolonged uncertainty. This was true for Mariam and her nephew, Ahmed. Ahmed lived with multiple disabilities, and Mariam, a single woman, had taken on his care after his parents died. When Mariam fled in 2006, it was her first time traveling outside Iraq. Despite her fear about the journey, she never questioned whether Ahmed would accompany her. "If I was married and had a son, would I just throw him in the street?" she asked me a bit reproachfully.

Sitting in the sweltering RLAP office one afternoon, I asked Mariam how she spent her days. She sighed, gestured around her, and said, "One day at the UN, one day at the hospital, one day at the embassy, one day at the clinic." Mariam's week was filled with the work of pursuing resettlement, and her visit to RLAP to check on her case was just one stop on her weekly circuit. I knew from accompanying other Iraqi friends to appointments that each of these visits could take the full day, often including more than an hour of travel each way and then waiting, sometimes outdoors, for hours to be seen. Her three years in Egypt had been difficult. Over tea, Mariam recounted what had led her to seek assistance from RLAP. "I felt like I was in a jail, a prisoner," she said, describing what she called a "nervous breakdown." She had been seeking resettlement alone. "I tried to write lots of letters with the help of my friends. But no one answered them." Paradoxically, it was perhaps her breakdown, caused by the combination of the stress of her persistent yet fruitless pursuit of resettlement on top of caring for Ahmed alone with little support and no income, that put her on the road to resettlement. When she finally approached RLAP

138   CHAPTER 4

for help, she mentioned her mental health challenges to her legal advocate who, concerned about her but also seeing a possibility for her to demonstrate a need for resettlement, referred Mariam to psychiatric care.

Her psychiatrist ultimately referred Mariam to the UNHCR for consideration for resettlement, identifying her as a "woman at risk," one of the categories of resettlement priority. The mechanics of selecting people for resettlement were frequently bound up with care, such that health care became part of the resettlement process because certain trusted professionals could forward cases to the UNHCR while refugees' own requests, like Mariam's, were ignored. Iraqis found themselves in a bind; their agency was necessary, but it had to be imperceptible to adjudicators, who viewed it as invalidating or possibly an indication of fraud. In any case, tremendous fortitude, patience, and labor—alongside often enduring a significantly worsening situation—were necessary to be identified as vulnerable enough to need resettlement.

.   .   .   .   .

Najla, Mohammed, and their two children waited over a year before the UNHCR referred their resettlement case to the US. Although they were never allowed to see their file, Najla and Mohammed learned that they were selected for resettlement under the category "survivor of violence and/or torture," one of the typologies of vulnerability that could prompt resettlement. Mohammed had been kidnapped and brutally tortured in Iraq, and their case was deemed eligible because of his ongoing psychological suffering in Cairo, suffering that, according to the *UNHCR Resettlement Handbook*, necessitated complex treatment, placing him in danger of further illness and disability if he remained in Egypt.

When their legal advocate heard about Mohammed's ordeal, he had referred Mohammed to Al-Nadeem Centre for victims of torture, where Mohammed received psychiatric treatment free of charge. After assessment and treatment, Mohammed's psychiatrist agreed to write a report diagnosing Mohammed with complex post-traumatic stress disorder attributable to the torture he had suffered. Mohammed's legal advocate attached the report to the testimony he had prepared and then forwarded the file on to the UNHCR for consideration.

After some time, the UNHCR called Mohammed for an interview. This was not always the case—many times a case file would get sent off and nothing would happen—but RLAP tried to prescreen its clients to ensure that they maintained credibility with the UNHCR for only sending them "good cases." Mohammed and his family then went through three interviews over a span of months at the UNHCR alone: one for registration, one to determine if they qualified for refugee status, and one to determine whether they needed resettlement. Each interview took all day; refugees were told to arrive before the office opened and to stay until they finished their interview. The interviews varied dramatically in length, as did the reported kindness and attention of the officers. Refugees frequently did not know the purpose of an interview, even after it was completed.

If the UNHCR deemed that a refugee needed resettlement, it referred their file to a resettlement country. The process by which the country was selected was opaque to refugees and somewhat to RLAP as well, although UNHCR staff told me that they made referral decisions based on the fit between the circumstances of the case and the criteria of specific state-resettlement programs. Referrals to the US were transferred to the International Organization for Migration (IOM), to which the US outsourced the early administrative stages of resettlement. UNHCR referrals to other countries, such as Canada, were transferred to that country's embassy.

Najla and Mohammed made it through the UNHCR interviews and learned that their case was referred to the US. After many more months of waiting, they would have more interviews. They next had two interviews with the IOM before a final one with officers from the US Department of Homeland Security (DHS). DHS officers travel from country to country on "circuit rides," conducting interviews and making resettlement decisions. While NGO and UNHCR staff tended to simply call the visiting adjudicators "DHS," Iraqis in Cairo referred to this traveling band of American interviewers as "the jury" (*al-mohalifeen*), referencing how officers decided applicants' fates. The jury arrived in Cairo several times a year, setting up shop briefly inside the IOM, interviewing many refugees, and issuing acceptances and rejections. Officers relied on interpreters to interview refugees who couldn't speak English. Iraqis blamed these interpreters, often Egyptian staff, for all manner of interpretation errors owing

140   CHAPTER 4

to differences between Egyptian and Iraqi Arabic. Since the interviews were not recorded or conducted with an advocate present, it was impossible to review or document any errors or misunderstandings.

After the interviews, months might pass before a refugee learned if they were accepted. If accepted, they would undergo security and medical checks—these too could take months and might also result in exclusion. Security screenings for US resettlement were universally the most dreaded. Every family member's file wound its way through a labyrinth of classified biometric and biographical checks, traversing multiple law enforcement and intelligence agencies. One family member's clearance could be held up for months or years with no explanation. Occasionally this delayed the entire family, while in other cases those with clearances traveled ahead, forced to choose between either leaving behind the unapproved family member or perhaps giving up resettlement altogether. "*Mowatna,* security checks! (Security checks have killed us!)" people often said. Once cleared, families received a brief cultural orientation followed by a travel date. They never knew how long the entire process would take and little information was provided to them throughout. At almost any stage in the process, they could be excluded. Sometimes exclusion came in the form of a rejection notice, but sometimes no response came at all, creating tremendous anxiety about whether people were still under consideration.

When Najla and Mohammed were interviewed by *al-mohalifeen,* or the traveling DHS officers, Mohammed was so overcome with anxiety that he could not recount his torture in Iraq. Najla described how Mohammed had become silent, unable to answer the officer's questions. Najla had tried to intervene—she knew the family's story well—but the officer prohibited her from answering for Mohammed. The outcome was affected neither by his psychiatric reports indicating his diagnosis of PTSD nor by the fact that the UNHCR had referred the family for resettlement specifically because of Mohammed's kidnapping and resulting psychiatric disorder. Privileging testimony-based, evidentiary forms of trauma in humanitarian settings (Fassin 2010; Lynch 2013), the interviewer refused to allow Najla to recount the events, insisting that Mohammed narrate his persecution in his own voice. Mohammed could not do so, and the family was later rejected for failing to demonstrate persecution.

In our conversation on the balcony of their Giza apartment after their interview, I watched Mohammed, a normally eloquent and cheerful man, struggle to verbalize what had happened during the interview, becoming increasingly anxious and finally giving up. By that time we had become good friends, yet even in this less threatening context, Mohammed struggled to speak—not about the persecution itself but about his efforts to recount it during the interview. This powerfully demonstrated the existential challenges of expressing violence and suffering when so much is at stake.

Mohammed and Najla's experience highlights resettlement as a complex bureaucratic process in which refugees must navigate multiple institutions—institutions that, although ostensibly working together, may have different goals, structures, and idiosyncrasies. While the UNHCR identified Najla and her family as vulnerable, the DHS officer did not define vulnerability in the same way. Mohammed's inability to recount his persecution raised questions about his credibility for the DHS interviewer, who perhaps felt that if Mohammed had actually experienced the events described in his file, he should have been able to speak about them. Paradoxically, the manifestation of the very vulnerability, namely psychological trauma, that led to Mohammed's identification as requiring exceptional humanitarian protection impeded his ability to pass the next stage of the process, rendering both him and his testimony suspect. Refugees' experiences are often reduced to individualized, psychologized, and episodic trauma (Zarowsky 2004), but Mohammed's experience illustrates that proving one's trauma was not a single encounter but several, recurring and changing. The successful response in one encounter could be unsuccessful in a subsequent one, yet inconsistency across contexts, such as between interviews or between interviews and documentation, was often grounds for denial.

Ultimately, however, the UNHCR did not accept the US rejection as the final word. On learning of the family's rejection, it re-referred the family's case to the Canadian program, which, after many more months of waiting and another round of interviews and security checks, finally accepted them. Najla, Mohammed, and their children now live in Canada, where they have become citizens. In 2010, Mariam's case was referred by the UNHCR for resettlement to Australia as a "woman at risk." Australia, frequently in the news for its draconian asylum policies, has long specialized

142   CHAPTER 4

in resettling refugee women and children at risk. Imagining her future, Mariam said, "When the UNHCR told me that I would travel, I felt like all the doors of the prison opened. I could travel. I could see the world."

AMBIVALENT DESIRES

"I could travel. I could see the world." Mariam's words paint resettlement not only as an instance of rescuing vulnerable lives at risk but also as an object of desire, adventure, and freedom. By definition, refugees travel, but their mobility is often separated analytically and politico-juridically from that of other travelers—expats, tourists, immigrants, pilgrims. As forced migrants fleeing persecution, refugees are, at least theoretically, allowed to cross borders without permission and to make certain claims to protection when they arrive. In practice, these legal rights have been eroded worldwide, but their moral force, while contested, continues to structure debates about inclusion and exclusion. To be forced against one's will to flee is the key way that refugees are distinguished from other categories of people on the move. Yet this emphasis on compulsion bleeds into other aspects of refugee governance, and refugees' desires and choices are often disregarded or rendered suspect.

In the refugee system, where resettlement is construed as a scarce and benevolent form of protection, desiring resettlement turned refugees into untrustworthy subjects. The *UNHCR Resettlement Handbook* is clear that in adjudication processes, "a distinction should be drawn between a refugee's need for resettlement and the possible desire of that person for this durable solution" (UNHCR 2004, 64).[11] In conversations with humanitarians and adjudicators, I noticed that they almost always assumed that all refugees wanted to be resettled and that it was therefore their responsibility to determine who was truly in need of it. Vulnerability could only be identified by others, specifically trained humanitarians or adjudicators, and one could not be vulnerable and desirous at the same time.

This imputation of desire not only revealed Iraqis' attitudes to resettlement but also reflected how humanitarians and adjudicators themselves construed residence and citizenship in "resettlement countries" as desirable. Assumptions about resettlement's desirability, regardless of how

NEGOTIATING "SOLUTIONS" TO DISPLACEMENT 143

those assumptions related to refugees' motivations for pursuing it, raise the specter of colonial and neocolonial hierarchies that render some states and citizenships desirable (Danewid 2017). When humanitarians framed resettlement as desirable, they rarely acknowledged the unequal and exploitative relations of force that created such geopolitical inequalities in the first place. In this way, resettlement seemed to naturalize global inequalities that were in fact created through imperial intervention. My Iraqi interlocutors had a different view—some may have held dreams of freedom and prosperity associated with imaginations of life elsewhere. Indeed, heterogeneous aspirations for other places and futures can be escape routes from unviable pasts and unsatisfactory presents that result from particular local and geopolitical power relations (Piot 2010). But many Iraqis also spoke to me about how before imperial intervention took them away, the Iraq of the past had many of the conditions of life that they sought in resettlement, such as a robust public education system and a strong health care system.[12]

In conversations, humanitarians and adjudicators tended to assume that all refugees wanted to be resettled. This imputation of desire did not necessarily reflect Iraqis' attitudes to resettlement, but it did reflect how humanitarians and adjudicators construed residence and citizenship in "resettlement countries" as desirable objects. Humanitarians also ascribed their own meanings to resettlement that were not always in accordance with those described by refugees or with formal resettlement criteria. For example, one Egyptian humanitarian, Lina, who had on many occasions referred refugees to the UNHCR for resettlement, said while bemoaning the scarcity of resettlement: "If I could, I would send the good ones abroad." Lina's framing of resettlement as something she wished to give "the good ones" certainly reflected particular notions of deservingness (Willen 2012) in this context, but it also reflected one of the multiple meanings of resettlement in Cairo as well as an oblique acknowledgment of the challenges of life in Cairo for refugees and Egyptians alike. In the view of humanitarians, many of whom, like Lina, were Egyptian national staff, resettlement represented not only protection but access to mobility, residence, and citizenship that they themselves could not access. From this point of view, gatekeeping around resettlement was not only related to nationalist, securitarian, or exclusionary concerns; when practiced by

144 CHAPTER 4

Egyptian national humanitarian staff, it represented the control of a particular aspiration for a future that they themselves might desire but from which they were just as likely as refugees to be excluded.[13] But Mariam's response to her impending resettlement reminds us that even if refugees desired resettlement, the content and meaning of those desires cannot be taken for granted.

Although humanitarians themselves saw resettlement as desirable, they frequently saw—or imputed—desire as a discrediting attribute in refugees. Hassan, who had fled after his house had been used as a watchtower by American troops, found himself unable to gain consideration for resettlement. Despite resettlement submission categories for elderly people and for severe medical need as well as Hassan's repeated efforts, extensive documentation, and clear disability, Hassan was neither receiving the care he needed in Egypt nor being referred for resettlement.

Hassan, like many seeking resettlement, carried a clear plastic folder with him to appointments and meetings. These folders—reminiscent of what Erica James (2010) has called "trauma portfolios"—contained the documentary evidence of lives: identity documents; diplomas; military service papers; marriage, birth, and death certificates; medical and psychological reports, including diagnostic images, prescriptions, and appointment records; and evidence of violence, such as death threats or newspaper reports of attacks. Refugees understand that their accounts of suffering are considered credible to the extent that they are supported by the expertise that such documents signify (Thomson 2018). Documents, however, are double edged. They themselves could become suspect if refugees were imagined as transparently using them to pursue resettlement. And documents do not stand in for a refugee's oral testimony—they must be animated by refugees' own voices, as was the case for Mohammed and Najla.

Having perceived that his account alone was insufficient, whenever Hassan spoke about his health conditions, he qualified them by speaking of his ability to provide proof: "I have a slipped disc. Very simple movements can hurt me. I do not have reports to prove it. I have an ulcer, but the reports are in Baghdad." Despite having reports to document several other afflictions, he was unsuccessful in convincing the UNHCR of his vulnerability for resettlement: "I went to the UNHCR to tell them about my problems here. They took all my reports and all my letters from the doctors. I told them that I cannot live in Egypt medically or socially. I wanted to give the UNHCR my complaint, but they did not want to take it."

Hassan had learned the vocabulary of the resettlement process, specifically speaking about his inability to "live in Egypt medically or socially," echoing the language of the *UNHCR Resettlement Handbook*, which prioritizes refugees who have medical needs that impair their ability to live in the country where they have sought asylum but which might be ameliorated with care or support available abroad.[14] But although Hassan appeared to fit the UNHCR criteria, his repeated efforts to seek recognition seemed to render him illegitimate or undeserving. Hassan's listing of his afflictions and the accounting of the evidence for each was seen as too transparent of a request for resettlement in a context where to seek resettlement was to arouse suspicion as to whether or not one truly "needed" it.

The opacity of the resettlement process means that I cannot say for sure why Hassan's visible, documented, and articulated suffering was never sufficient for resettlement, despite the fact that one of the resettlement categories was "the elderly." He never received a reply to his many inquiries, which left him uncertain whether he had been excluded or if there remained a chance that he might be considered. It may be that Hassan's vulnerability was too mundane—despite having fled as a refugee, his afflictions in Cairo were not the spectacular wounds of war or torture that adjudicators sometimes demand that refugees show to prove their persecution. Instead, Hassan's vulnerability was perhaps read as the nonexceptional afflictions of aging. Perhaps the adjudicators were also making calculations that slipped in from other logics of migration. Were they wondering if Hassan, despite or perhaps because of his vulnerability, might be a burden on the state that resettled him? Were they perhaps assuming that at his age such a transition might be too difficult? I can't know. What I do know from conversations with adjudicators and humanitarians is that these labor market–based assumptions about integration certainly infused the resettlement process, despite being carefully absent from formal criteria based on vulnerability and need. It is certainly true that in the US, the country that resettled the most Iraqis, resettled refugees are offered very few benefits in a welfare state hollowed out by decades of neoliberal policies. Refugees are expected to be economically "self-sufficient" in a matter of months and not to be a "burden" on the state, a process Sally Wesley Bonet (2022) has described as "meaningless citizenship." The irony is that Iraqis were explicitly selected for resettlement based on their vulnerability and need for assistance only to be thrust into positions of precaritized labor after resettlement.

Resettlement provides access to juridical citizenship in the Global North at the same time that perceived desire for such citizenship rendered refugees ineligible. Aspiration for better educational or employment opportunities or even for cross-border mobility through resettlement contradicts or troubles the humanitarian impulse undergirding resettlement where legitimacy stems from a focus on "life in crisis" (Redfield 2013, 20) or saving "short, violent, and hungry lives" (Chua 2014). What is more, assumptions about the value of citizenship in the Global North, based on colonial and other geopolitical hierarchies that naturalize some states as "resettlement countries" while others are "asylum countries," influence the relationships that make up the resettlement process at the same time that the resettlement process reproduces such hierarchies.

Many Iraqis certainly desired resettlement, but they also expressed considerable ambivalence. Seeking resettlement was a difficult and adversarial process that imposed existential costs on refugees and reinforced a sense of uncertainty while they waited. For some, it was simply not worth it. Moreover, for some Iraqis, there was a painful irony in seeking resettlement in the US, the country that had the largest resettlement program but had also been responsible for leading the invasion and occupation that made them into refugees. Some Iraqis wanted to be resettled "anywhere but America." Their logic was similar to that of the US Direct Access Program, in which resettlement was offered as redress to Iraqis who had been persecuted because of their work with the Americans, but the conclusions were different: Iraqis blamed the US for their displacement, but for some, it was unclear why they should then be expected to gratefully move there. Resettlement was not a salve for the violence and loss they had experienced. But others argued that they were owed resettlement, either for the harm they had suffered while working with the US-led occupation or for the violence that they had experienced; the loss of loved ones, livelihoods, and homes; and the destruction of their country. Here, resettlement was reparative.

Ultimately, refugees were not allowed to specify or request which country they would be referred to. That was up to the UNHCR and resettlement state, meaning that Iraqis might be sent to the US regardless of how they felt about it. As recipients of humanitarian protection, especially the scarce good that is resettlement, refugees were expected to gratefully move wherever they were accepted.

Perhaps the discordance between assumptions of resettlement's desirability and Iraqis' desires and aspirations explains why, after undergoing the entire resettlement process with its many steps and hurdles, refugees occasionally, when it was finally time to travel, simply didn't show up at the airport. Several humanitarian interlocutors reported this occurrence, which they found mystifying. People would simply disappear or exit from the process at the last moment. The refusal to travel represented a rupture in resettlement as a process of regulating mobility, and it broke down resettlement's affective charge as a desirable humanitarian gift. By not showing up, this small number of Iraqis refused to take on the role of grateful refugee.[15] While rare, these moments of refusal draw attention to the failure of the bureaucratic process, a failure that perhaps resulted from how refugees' desires were considered threatening or irrelevant to the process of interpellating them as future citizens of a resettlement country. Moreover, these moments of refusal call into question the authority of those who distribute and adjudicate (Simpson 2014), and they illustrate how uncertainty in this context is not unidirectional (Cabot 2013). These moments of exit reveal profound, if rare, ambivalences about the possibility of resettlement to address the existential questions of an uncertain future.

THE AMBIVALENCE OF SOLUTIONS

Resettlement discourse and practice construe refugees as (ideally) passive objects who receive the beneficence of states and humanitarian organizations. Discursively, this passivity is reflected in how resettlement is represented as "selection and transfer" instead of active movement, as benevolence instead of rights, as protection instead of aspiration. Passivity is also enacted through disciplinary practices, such as not telling refugees

148   CHAPTER 4

the purpose of interviews, ignoring queries, or making them wait hours for appointments. In Cairo, it is also enforced through the material infrastructures of resettlement.

The day that Saif asked me to accompany him to the UNHCR office, he also asked me to sit in on his interview for support. He nearly succeeded in having me accompany him, but, in a move that suggested perhaps this was a resettlement interview after all, I was unceremoniously ejected by the UNHCR interviewer. I would have to wait in the courtyard, nervous and uncertain once again, to hear from Saif how it went. In this chapter, I have attempted to render visible some of the moments of existential and epistemological uncertainty that characterized the resettlement process in Cairo. I have done this not only to illustrate the lack of bureaucratic transparency or to argue for the value of paying attention to moments of indeterminacy in ethnographic practice and representation, though both are of course important, but also because it became clear to me that uncertainty was central to the lived experience of navigating resettlement and to the ways that resettlement functioned to construct citizenship in resettlement countries as scarce.

Waiting, Bourdieu reminds us, is a technique of power. Who is made to wait (and to wonder, I might add) and how they experience waiting is indicative of the intimate relationship between power and temporality (Bourdieu 1997). As long as refugees in Cairo hoped they might be resettled, they were less likely to pursue other forms of mobility. Not knowing where they were in the process kept them in place, waiting and hoping. Some aspects of indeterminacy emerged from the explicit suspicion with which refugees' agency was regarded, while other aspects were structural, rendering the process uncertain for the gatekeepers themselves. As Iraqis moved through the resettlement process, they navigated multiple governments as well as intergovernmental and nongovernmental organizations. Najla and Mohammed's eventual resettlement in Canada is one example of how these multiple sovereignties allowed refugees (and humanitarian organizations) some room to maneuver. Yet these same inconsistencies and obscurities contributed to the indeterminacy of seeking resettlement, holding Saif and others in place as they waited.

The violence with which the Sudanese protesters' dreams for resettlement were dispersed in Cairo in 2005 dramatically illustrates how the undocile refugee is constructed as a threat. There are also more subtle signs that refugees' aspirations and desires are considered not only problematic but also dangerous. When Iraqis refer to resettlement adjudicators as *al-mohalifeen*, they reference how a jury decides not only one's fate but also one's guilt or innocence. Iraqis were well aware by the questions they were asked in interviews and the myriad security checks they endured that they walked a knife's edge of deserving or dangerous, innocent or guilty. If displacement can be construed as the loss of an imaginable or navigable future (Ramsay 2020), then this edge illustrates how a future can be simultaneously promised and withheld.

What are the existential stakes of upholding and simultaneously withholding something as a solution? For Iraqis in Cairo, solutions to displacement, especially resettlement, were inseparable both from conditions of exile, especially the understanding of Egypt as a place of transit, and the conflict that precipitated it. Indeed, these relations, as well as the existential costs of going through the prolonged and uncertain resettlement process itself, are essential for understanding how resettlement was simultaneously desired and refused. Exiting the process at the last minute is perhaps the most extreme sign of this ambivalence. It illustrates that resettlement, with its promise of citizenship in a new country, is not so easily construed as a solution to displacement for Iraqis but not so easily dismissed either.

Until now, I have focused primarily on the local, everyday encounters that made up the resettlement process in Cairo as an alternative to state-centric views of resettlement. But in order to understand this transnational process that includes both cross-border mobility and imaginaries of elsewhere, it is also crucial to view resettlement in global perspective. Despite the relatively small number of people admitted under them, resettlement schemes have recently been central to public contestations over belonging, citizenship, and exclusion. Take for example recent challenges to the US refugee resettlement program that threaten to hobble the world's largest program of this kind.[16] Why is a humanitarian program that ultimately benefits such a small number of the millions of displaced people worldwide the subject of such controversy? Is resettlement truly exceptional in both the refugee protection regime, where by offering the prospect of naturalization it seems to offer more than a humanitarian

150   CHAPTER 4

"minimal biopolitics," and the border regime, where selective filtering increasingly seems to allow only certain people entry, specifically those whose labor can be exploited, and even then in temporary and precarious situations (e.g., Razsa and Kurnik 2014)?

Resettlement does not exist in isolation but in a complex field of humanitarian and migration politics. With the ongoing trend toward border fortification (Andersson 2014) and a decline in the legitimacy of asylum (Gibney 2004), resettlement is one of the few means by which refugees can gain formal admittance to countries in the Global North. For those few refugees who are resettled, resettlement often comes with rights and opportunities that may be denied in contexts of first asylum, such as the right to work, access public education, and citizenship. Yet as we saw with Mariam, who was eventually resettled to Australia, liberal states see no contradiction in excluding large numbers of asylum-seekers while seeking to maintain their humanitarian face by resettling small numbers of "vulnerable" people. Such programs are often accompanied, as they were for Iraqis, by increased support for aid programs designed to keep the larger proportion of a refugee population in place in the host country (Agier 2011). This is gatekeeping on a global scale: a select few are allowed in, while the vast majority become a different kind of humanitarian subject, maintained at a distance.

However, this level of analysis only illuminates one view of resettlement, and it is one that privileges, if critically, the logics of western liberal states and therefore reproduces one of the key assumptions of much refugee discourse—that refugees are victims who must be rescued, most often through humanitarian means. It is this assumption and the erasure of refugees' agency that underpins part of the flawed and incomplete distinction between refugees and migrants. Resettlement, which takes as its primary aim the rescuing of the most vulnerable refugees, represents the apex of this humanitarian hierarchy of deservingness.

When we look closer, we see how the scarcity of resettlement is maintained through everyday forms of gatekeeping, in moments such as Saif and others not knowing why they had been called to the UNHCR office, Mohammed being rejected for being unable to narrate his persecution to the satisfaction of his interviewer, and Hassan's ambiguous discreditation. We also see how refugees nonetheless act within a system that demands their passivity, showing both the cracks and fissures in the system itself as well as what resettlement and the resettlement process mean to refugees. From this vantage point, resettlement is more than simply the outcome of 1 percent of the global refugee population becoming citizens of the Global North. It is about what that citizenship, or at least the imagination of it, means—for Mariam, it meant the promise of care for her nephew as well as freedom for herself. For Najla and Mohammed, it meant opportunities for their children to go to school. For Saif, it was an escape from an intolerable present situation—a leap of faith and a hope for something better. The ability to move, to travel, is an emancipatory narrative that does not fit well with the imperative for refugee travel to be "forced migration" or "selection and transfer."

Ironically, while resettled refugees travel from Global South to Global North, the logic of vulnerability that justified their mobility often does not. Georgina Ramsay (2017) documented how refugees in Australia felt that violence against them had continued after resettlement. In the US, people are often selected for resettlement because of medical and psychological vulnerabilities for which they cannot access care once they arrive. Instead, the US resettlement program strives for refugees to achieve "self-sufficiency" in a matter of months, complicating and challenging refugees' experiences of refuge (see Besteman 2016; Gowayed 2022). Vulnerability as an axis of inclusion, as described above, is in many ways the opposite of definitions of citizenship that are based on one's capacity to participate in public life or in the market.[17] The denial of agency that is so central to the resettlement process in Cairo is in many ways the opposite of the agency that will be demanded of refugees once, or if, they are resettled.

In Cairo, however, the humanitarian logic of vulnerability justifies the scarcity of resettlement, reinforcing and justifying the limitation of mobility to, residence in, and citizenship in the Global North through a humanitarian idiom. While the resettlement process is far from the "border spectacles" described by De Genova and colleagues (2017), it can be considered part of the larger architecture that keeps most refugees far from the borders of the richest states. In Cairo, Iraqis waited for months or years before eventually being resettled or, in some cases, returning to Iraq. Not knowing where they were in the process or, indeed, whether they were in the process, kept Iraqis stuck in Cairo, waiting. At the same time, Iraqis' endurance in the face of impenetrable and obfuscating bureaucracies and their negotiation of the resettlement program provides a window not only into how geographies of inclusion (and exclusion) are constructed but also how they are taken up, challenged, and reappropriated in contexts where other opportunities for mobility are foreclosed.

5 Allies and Enemies

RESETTLEMENT AND THE CONDITIONALITY
OF IRAQIS' RELATIONS WITH US EMPIRE

Almost three years after I had waited outside the UNHCR office with Saif, I found myself back in Cairo at yet another humanitarian threshold. I was here to meet Karrar, a friend and interlocutor who had invited me to a protest that he and other refugees had organized in front of the office of the International Organization for Migration (IOM). As I stepped out of a taxi on the corniche road that separates the Cairo office of the IOM from the Nile, I saw a handful of people standing across the street holding handmade placards. The protesters were few and restrained—a far cry from the multitudinous energy of Tahrir Square. Yet it did seem to me that the revolution—embodied but not contained by Tahrir Square—had inspired Karrar and his compatriots to organize.

For me, that moment in Egypt felt like the threshold between a past order that I had known and, unimaginatively, had thought would continue and a future yet to be enacted. It was the spring of 2012. The massive protests of January 2011, which had captured the attention of Egyptians and, indeed, the entire world, were over. But the streets of downtown Cairo still bore the marks of the uprising and its repression. Layers of revolutionary graffiti covered buildings and concrete blast walls separated neighborhoods. These barriers, designed to control peoples'

154   CHAPTER 5

movements, were also soon adorned with art and slogans. Occasional protests took place, but there was neither the massive turnout of the uprising's early days nor a return to Cairo's prerevolution twenty-four-hour social and economic life. Instead, I found the streets often filled with an eerie emptiness. The 2013 coup that would bring the military back into power had not yet happened and, although there were signs that the revolution had faltered, the outcome did not yet seem sure.

The uprisings that swept the region also changed the landscape of displacement in Cairo. By 2012, it was Syrians, not Iraqis, who became the largest new population of arrivals in Egypt as they fled the violence of the Syrian Civil War.[1] Mohamed Morsi, the first democratically elected president of Egypt and a member of the previously outlawed Muslim Brotherhood Party, took a more generous approach to the new arrivals than that of the prerevolution government. Syrian children were permitted to attend public schools free of charge and Syrian refugees of all ages could access public hospitals (Norman 2017).[2] At the same time, international programs and funding for Iraqi refugees dried up and were replaced by programs and funding for Syrians. During the height of the revolution, resettlement interviews were put on hold, which led to cascading delays in travel. Those of my Iraqi friends who remained in Egypt were dismayed to find themselves left behind in the uncertainty of postrevolution Egypt while the short attention span of humanitarian relief and funding moved on to the newest crisis.

This feeling of being left behind was exacerbated because by 2012 many Iraqis had left Egypt. Some departed through formal resettlement programs, others by returning to Iraq, still others by leaving for another country in the region, or, less frequently, by traveling on their own by air or sea to seek asylum in Europe or North America. To still be in Egypt was especially frustrating for Iraqis like Karrar who had been waiting in the resettlement process for years, always anticipating the possibility of traveling but finding it perpetually deferred.

As I walked over to greet him, Karrar handed me a printed sheet of paper that summed up the protestors' demands. I read the petition, which was carefully typed up in both English and Arabic and addressed to the director of the IOM in Cairo.[3] The first item on the numbered list of demands was for the IOM "to consider and deal with us seriously, and to contact the related departments in the United States of America to find appropriate solutions for us, whether positively or negatively." As the overseas processing entity for the US government, the IOM was the intermediary through which refugees hoping to be resettled encountered the US government.[4] The nature of this encounter was made clear in the petition's second demand, which stated: "Stop inhumane treatment and do not close the doors of the humanitarian organization with iron. Stop responding to phone calls in which your employees are treating us in ways that are not related to humanitarian or human rights." As if that wasn't clear enough, Karrar also attached a photo that he had taken, which he titled *Bab IOM* (*Door of the IOM*), depicting the locked metal security cage that controls refugees' access to the IOM. In the photo, one unnamed refugee stands at the outside of the closed gate, looking in.

To understand why he had organized the protest outside the IOM office, it is helpful to know a bit more about Karrar's experience with resettlement. In 2008, more than two years after Karrar moved to Cairo, the US government passed the Refugee Crisis in Iraq Act. This act mandated the resettlement of "Iraqi allies" who had been threatened as a result of their work with the US occupation. It also allowed some Iraqis and Afghans, two of the largest populations displaced by the United States' ongoing Global War on Terror, to approach the US resettlement program "directly" (although ironically through the IOM as the US government intermediary) as opposed to having to go through the United Nations High Commissioner for Refugees (UNHCR) first. As a result, the program was dubbed the Direct Access Program. Egypt, and more specifically the Cairo office of the International Organization for Migration, was one of the program's initial processing sites.

When word spread to Cairo about the new resettlement program, Karrar thought he might fit. After all, he had periodically shared information about militia activity with the US military, hoping they would do something about the violence unraveling his Baghdad neighborhood. Rumors had spread that Karrar was sympathetic to, and maybe even working with, the occupying forces. His brother was in fact employed by the Americans and, even though no one in the family spoke about it openly with outsiders, surely people knew. But when Karrar approached the IOM in early 2008 to apply for Direct Access, he was asked for a letter

156   CHAPTER 5

of recommendation and the email address of a US citizen who had been his direct supervisor. When he couldn't provide that, Karrar was turned away.

Nearly a year passed, during which Karrar registered with the UNHCR hoping he would have more luck with the humanitarian resettlement program. The UNHCR never called. During this time, Karrar's brother, who had worked full time as an interpreter with the American forces, was resettled to the United States. He then applied for Karrar and his family to join him under a provision in the law that allowed for family reunification. This process began in late 2008 and represented Karrar's second attempt to be resettled under the Direct Access Program, this time as kin of an "Iraqi ally."

When he organized the protest outside of the IOM, Karrar had been formally in the resettlement process for nearly five years but still had not received a final travel date. Everything was complete except for the family's security clearances, without which they could not be resettled. While waiting for his security clearance to come through, Karrar's medical checks kept expiring, meaning that he had had to repeat the medical tests, a prerequisite for resettlement, four times. I knew how frustrating this had been for Karrar so I was not surprised to read item eleven on the petition: "Regarding the medical examination, we strongly demand making it valid for a full year instead of six months," as well as item four: "We demand to know an immediate answer about the reason for the delay in many cases for more than three or four years. We also demand to know the real situation of our cases and stop telling us about the subject of the security checks because it has become an unacceptable excuse!" Privately, Karrar later speculated to me that the reason for the delay in his and other Iraqis' cases was "because they caught two Iraqis in Kentucky who were terrorists, so they are making more security checks now."

Karrar's experience with resettlement sheds some light on how Iraqis navigated a resettlement program that figured them simultaneously as possible allies and enemies. While states often justify refugee resettlement programs using the rhetoric of humanitarianism or international "burdensharing," some resettlement programs, like the Direct Access Program, are premised on much more intimate, entangled, and explicit relations of violence, collaboration, and obligation between the resettlement state and refugees. Edward Kennedy, one of the senators who spearheaded the Refugee Crisis in Iraq Act, argued that "America has a special obligation to keep faith with the Iraqis who now have a bull's-eye on their backs because of their association with our government."[5] It is clear from the protest and petition that Karrar would agree that the US has obligations to Iraqis in the aftermath of war. It is also clear that, in the view of the small assembly outside the IOM gate, these obligations were not being fulfilled. What is less obvious is how Iraqis understood and struggled over their relationships to US empire and specifically what they believed the US owed them through the resettlement process and beyond. What is the nature of obligation that emerges in the aftermath of imperial war? And who gets to decide what these debts are and how they are carried out?

In this chapter, I consider how Iraqis navigated the ally/enemy binary imposed on them in the context of US imperial intervention. I argue that the Refugee Crisis in Iraq Act—the motivations for the law, its discursive text, and its bureaucratic implementation as the Direct Access Program—is colored by the intersection of militarization, the racialization of Arabs and Muslims, and the instrumentalization of refugees in the context of imperial war. Scholars of Islamophobia and anti-Arab racism have documented how empire constructs and divides Muslims and Arabs as either "good" or "bad" and that these designations shift depending on "whether one supports or opposes US policy and empire" (Kumar 2021, 12).[6] In keeping with this good/bad binary, the US resettlement program sought to identify "true allies" from those who are imagined instead as enemies. The desire to know, identify, and classify Iraqis resonates with histories of imperial desires for mastery (Daulatzai 2021; Singh 2018). It also corresponds with the security logics, discourses, and practices associated with counterterrorism, to the extent that these are predicated on the assumed potential in all imperial subjects to become insurgent (Rubaii 2018). Even when Iraqis are recognized as "allies," they are nonetheless understood and treated as threatening. Counterterrorism thus desires to know but always acknowledges the possibility that a threat might be lurking undiscovered, acknowledging the limits of imperial mastery but also justifying never-ending efforts to uncover potential threats that might menace imperial projects. This is evident in the interminable security checks that refugees are subjected to for resettlement and in the ways that

158   CHAPTER 5

refugees continue to be identified as possible enemies after resettlement and even after they have been naturalized as US citizens.

Important recent scholarship has described the racialization of Muslim and Arab refugees in the United States (Gowayed 2020; Nojan 2022). For Iraqis, this racialization began even before they came to the US, first when they were conscripted into work with the occupation while simultaneously being treated as threats and then second when they underwent the bureaucratic process of seeking to be resettled under the Direct Access Program, where they were also treated as possible threats to national security.[7] How did Iraqis themselves understand and experience this process of being construed simultaneously as possible allies and possible enemies of empire? The Direct Access Program is built on and reinforces very specific ideas of US obligation towards a small number of Iraqis who collaborated with US empire and were threatened as a result. In doing so, the categories of ally and enemy became guiding principles for separating good from bad refugees, militarizing, racializing, and masculinizing refugee resettlement in the process. Even within this process, Iraqis repurposed and reappropriated their associations with US empire and the obligations that they argued emerged as a result. Their critiques unsettle binaries and demand different forms of accountability, leading us perhaps to an anti-imperial understanding of obligation.

A DIFFERENT KIND OF WAR STORY II: COLLABORATION WITH EMPIRE

The experiences of Iraqis who worked with the US occupation are often interpreted as allyship, a framing that implies a reciprocal relationship with mutual benefit. But a first step toward thinking about obligation through an anti-imperial lens might involve refusing to unquestioningly accept the definition of *ally* put forth by the occupation and instead to investigate the complex and often fraught relationships that imperial war produces. Iraqi knowledge and labor were essential to the occupation of Iraq. This is not such an unusual fact; imperialism relies, to different degrees, on forms of coercion, co-optation, and collaboration with colonized people (Said 1994). However, the form of these relations and what they mean materially, politically, and ethically to the people who engage in them under varying degrees of coercion, pragmatism, and ideological identification are not predetermined but rather unfold in the context of specific histories and places.

Collaboration is a fraught and ambivalent concept. Increasingly, in art and scholarship collaboration is valorized as ethical practice, especially when it involves decentering the power of the researcher or artist and elevating marginalized communities and individuals whose contributions have gone unrecognized. But it also carries with it negative valences; *collaborator* can be synonymous with *traitor* or with identification and support of oppressive regimes, as in the figure of the Nazi collaborator. In contexts of conflict and repression, collaboration is often presented as the opposite of resistance. However, the collaboration/resistance binary does not accurately represent the nuanced relationships and agency of people who are subject to occupation. Moreover, it fails to consider how collaboration may at times be a form of resistance in itself or that people may collaborate at some point and then resist at another (Githuku 2018). In a meditation on photographic collaboration, Azoulay (2016, 188) places collaboration within the context of other forms of being together and defines it as "the negative form of collectivity—it describes a mode of working together without implying a collective." This more capacious definition of collaboration leaves room for a range of affective economies and power relations, including violent, hostile, and exploitative ones.

The most famous example of collaboration in the Iraq War is undoubtedly the role that Iraqi exiles, most notably Ahmed Chalabi and Kanan Makiya, played in promoting US- and UK-led regime change as a means to overthrow Saddam Hussein's dictatorship.[8] While collaboration between exiles and governments in justifying and carrying out war are certainly worthy of analysis, I will put these high-profile examples aside for now to instead consider the postinvasion experiences of Iraqis who were living in Iraq at the time of the war and who came to work with the occupation in a wide range of capacities. Such labor did not necessarily imply ideological support for the invasion and occupation (although it may have), but it inevitably produced intimate and complex forms of entanglement with empire.

160   CHAPTER 5

The structural conditions and experiences of this work varied tremendously. Iraqis worked in a wide range of formal and informal capacities with many of the organizations and institutions that participated in the invasion and occupation: US and other coalition militaries, the Coalition Provisional Authority, the US government, intergovernmental organizations such as the United Nations, humanitarian and human rights organizations, private military contractors, subcontractors, and international media outlets, among others. Much of their work was through contracts of widely varying levels of formality, on a spectrum ranging from the kinds of informal, contractless assistance that Karrar provided, to Iraqi businesspeople who won official subcontracts that they then managed, to Iraqis who were directly employed. In including many more forms of collaboration and labor than would be considered "allyship" by the Direct Access Program, I intentionally recuperate relations with empire that interlocutors such as Karrar described to me to broaden the frame of collaboration.

In this broader framework, "working with the Americans" could entail working directly for an American employer or with American coworkers, or it could involve more complicated hierarchies of contracts and supervision that might mean that an Iraqi worker would never actually work directly with American people. Remuneration varied significantly as did the safety of the work itself and the extent of risk or exposure associated with it. While much of this work would not qualify Iraqis to be considered "allies" for the purposes of US resettlement, in the eyes of many Iraqis and certainly for militias, work with any of these organizations counted as "working with the Americans." Faisal, for example, owned a small construction company that had done occasional maintenance and repair work for the UN mission in Baghdad even before the 2003 invasion. Following the invasion, the presence of US forces around the Canal Hotel, where the UN was headquartered, brought Faisal into contact with the Americans. In an interview, he told me, "American Forces were surrounding the United Nations, so people thought that we were working for the Americans when we worked with the UN. As a result, I was known in the area as someone who worked with Americans even before I started to work directly with the American military."

But his UN contacts led to US contacts and soon Faisal was working with the Americans directly. When, in the first months after the invasion, the Americans set up an office near the Canal Hotel, a UN employee who knew Faisal's work recommended him to the Americans, who were looking for someone they could trust to help them set up the office: "The Americans asked me to do the maintenance for their office. They paid me without a contract and without a check. They would ask me to do a job, and after I did it, they would pay me in cash directly. I did many jobs such as cleaning, painting, and installing air conditioners, lamps, and fans. This was my first business with the Americans and it opened the door to my future work with them." Soon, an American colleague offered Faisal work with the US military at Camp Eagle, in Baghdad's Sadr City. "They liked my work," Faisal explained. When I asked him why he had agreed to work at the base, he simply explained that "they said I would find better jobs there." Each job led to a new one—repair work turned into constructing bathrooms, which turned into rebuilding a damaged hangar—and soon Faisal was doing regular renovation and construction work in the camp.

Although Faisal worked directly with the American military, the labor of collaboration could take many forms. In Egypt, I met translators and interpreters, service workers, doctors, pharmacists, media personnel, entrepreneurs, construction workers, equipment operators, and bureaucrats, all of whom had labored with the occupation in some way. Shams worked on programming and campaigning for women's rights for a US-based NGO that promotes economic self-sufficiency, education, and skill building for women in conflict-affected areas. Abu Nasim is an engineer who was hired by a US-based private contractor to rebuild public infrastructure that had been destroyed during the invasion. Lina, who spoke fluent British-inflected English, did interpretation and translation work for a UK-based media company.

THE POLITICAL ECONOMY OF COLLABORATION

The labor market created by the war in Iraq was paradigmatic of this era of global capitalism in which vast global supply chains were managed by a complex assemblage of state actors, corporate actors, and constantly shifting subcontractors. Understanding the public/private, outsourced, and

162   CHAPTER 5

globalized nature of the occupation's labor economy is essential both for making sense of Iraqis' relationships to the occupation and for reckoning with questions of accountability and responsibility in the war's aftermath. It is also important for understanding how the US, as an empire, waged war during the early years of the Global War on Terror (GWOT).

Politicians and reporters often focus on troop numbers as an index of the human presence and impact of war. However, in Iraq, laboring alongside uniformed personnel was what reporter Sarah Stillman calls an "invisible army" who did, and still do, much of the support, technical, service, and infrastructure work of war and occupation (Stillman 2011). Many members of this "invisible army" were Iraqis or migrant laborers from around the world. Although these people support and participate in the work of the government and the military, in the GWOT many were, and still are today, employed by private contractors. The outsourcing of the GWOT contributed to imperial unknowing in two interrelated ways. First, the outsourcing of war from military to private actors, even if those private actors were paid with public funds and engaged in work on behalf of the government, meant that much of war moved into an unaccountable and opaque private and corporate realm, rendering it impenetrable to public scrutiny (Coburn 2018a, 2018b). Second, and relatedly, the use of private contractors overseas as opposed to, for example, a conscripted military contributed to the global nature of the war by bringing in employees from around the world and further exacerbating the distance many Americans had from the effects of the war on Iraqis and Iraq. This constructed divide between the military and "civilian" public in the United States has been central to depoliticizing and suppressing opposition to the war among Americans (El-Haj 2022).

Although private actors have always been part of the economy of war, contractors were a particularly strong presence in the wars in Iraq and Afghanistan. Multinational corporations with ties to oil extraction and previous US wars, such as Fluor, Bechtel, Halliburton, and KBR, received massive US Department of Defense contracts for goods and services and then subcontracted with a dizzying number of smaller companies to complete the work. Contractors cooked, cleaned, and did other service work in the Green Zone and on military bases. They engaged in reconstruction work. They were hired mercenaries and guards, including infamously as guards in Abu Ghraib prison.[9] At various points throughout the occupation, there were more contractors in Iraq than uniformed personnel (Li 2015a). This was especially true near the end of and after the formal occupation, as contractors allowed the government to publicly cite reduced troop numbers while maintaining a military presence (Peltier 2020). Thousands of contractors continue to work for the US military in Iraq to this day.

For private contractors, war was an opportunity to profit in a context where there was little accountability and regulation. These companies, many of which received exclusive, noncompetitive, and indefinite contracts for billions of dollars, made fortunes rebuilding, or claiming to rebuild, schools, roads, water systems, and other infrastructure that the US-led intervention had destroyed. Their profits were funded by public money, both US and Iraqi. Under the Coalition Provisional Authority, about twenty billion dollars of the funds from the Development Fund for Iraq—the fund created by United Nations executive order in 2003 to hold Iraqi oil revenue in trust—was flown in cash on cargo planes from the Federal Reserve Bank in New York, where it was being held, to Baghdad. Audits conducted in 2004 revealed that around $11.7 billion disappeared and has not been accounted for to this day (Quadri 2022). To make accountability even more difficult, no one seemed to be keeping track of the contractors. Pentagon officials admitted that they were unable to even provide an estimate of the number of contractors they had hired directly. As Zaynab Quadri (2022, 525) argues, the unprecedented use of contractors in the Iraq War "diluted the US government's onus of responsibility by obscuring the extent and nature of the war behind the proprietary details of contractors' work in Iraq." The Nisour Square massacre in Baghdad in 2007, in which Blackwater Security Consulting employees killed seventeen Iraqi civilians and injured twenty, is just one of the most egregious examples of the abuses committed by private contractors in Iraq.[10] Contractors have also been accused of fraud, human trafficking, sexual harassment and abuse, workplace safety violations, environmental damage, and negligence (NBC News 2004). With rare exceptions, contractors have not been held responsible for any of these abuses.

War was not only privatized but outsourced. Many contractors recruited and hired employees from other countries, described in military-speak as

164   CHAPTER 5

third-country nationals or TCNs, to work in Iraq providing support to the occupation. TCNs traveled from many countries to work in Iraq. Their routes to Iraq were not always voluntary; some were hired under false pretenses, forced to take on personal and family debt to pay the exorbitant fees charged by some recruiting firms, and had their passports confiscated by their employers, rendering them unable to leave dangerous or exploitative work conditions. TCNs faced similar and different risks than Iraqi workers, alongside whom many of them labored.

However, employers often saw TCNs as an alternative to Iraqi workers. As Darryl Li (2015b, 2015a) has documented, the proportion of TCNs in both military and nonmilitary operations increased as the occupation wore on, while the proportion of Iraqi workers decreased. Counterinsurgency logic as well as neoliberal economic practices contributed to this trend. Not only were TCNs even more easily exploitable labor than Iraqis, but, more importantly, Iraqi workers were always implicitly or explicitly deemed a security threat. In his book on the Coalition Provisional Authority, *Imperial Life in the Emerald City,* Rajiv Chandrasekaran (2006, 10–11) tellingly described how all the food service workers in the Green Zone were South Asian migrant laborers: "Halliburton had hired dozens of Pakistanis and Indians to cook, and serve, and clean, but no Iraqis. Nobody ever explained why, but everyone knew. They could poison the food." From the perspective of the US military, the relationship between TCNs, Iraqi workers, and the goals of occupation and counterinsurgency were less clear cut. On the one hand, some felt, as Chandrasekaran reported, that Iraqi workers represented a threat. However, others felt that hiring TCNs represented a missed opportunity to bring Iraqis into the project of occupation as a counterinsurgency strategy in itself.

Much of the reporting on Iraqis who collaborated with the occupation, especially in explicit counterinsurgency operations, has focused on interpreters, who were referred to with the misnomer *translators* by Iraqis and much English-language reporting and as *terps* by US military personnel. In Iraq, *translator* became a loanword with multiple connotations including, as Entisar noted in chapter 1, *traitor.* It is perhaps not surprising that translators were among the most threatened of the many Iraqis who worked with the occupying forces. It is also unsurprising that their plight was the most documented in the press since international reporting also depends heavily on interpreters and local fixers. The occupation relied on interpreters whose skills in translating spoken language between occupation forces and Iraqis, often in crucial moments, were essential. Their skills were not only linguistic, of course. Interpreters smoothed relations, helped the occupiers avoid cultural and contextual blunders, identified contacts, and gathered information, among other tasks. The nature of their work as intermediaries between occupiers and local communities forced many of them to be seen in public with the occupying forces, putting them at significant risk.[11] Some interpreters took to wearing masks or other disguises to avoid being identified.

Part of the US military's cultural turn was a recognition of their woeful lack of linguistic and cultural preparedness for war and, especially, long-term occupation; reliance on Iraqis to provide this knowledge was one, but not the only, strategy the military used to counteract this deficit and to attempt to produce the military as "cultural insiders" in Iraq (Stone 2022). This epistemological work was imagined by the US as relational; the move to understand the war as counterinsurgency meant that military objectives moved from a focus on precision killing to one of building relationships with civilians and addressing social and political problems as a means of disempowering resistance forces. This reflected a perhaps not-incorrect understanding that insurgent groups sought support from disenfranchised residents of poorer neighborhoods but also a concomitant total unawareness that foreign military occupation might itself be a cause of legitimate resistance (Gregory 2008a). If the military saw counterinsurgency as "armed social work," as it was occasionally described (Gregory 2008b), it is not surprising that relationships were at the center of this work; trust, communication, listening, negotiation, and persuasion were skills that were central to counterinsurgency doctrine, training, and practice. The ability to come anywhere close to these ideals of cultural intimacy was dependent on Iraqi labor, knowledge, and willingness to participate.

However, these relations at times exceeded and at other times undermined the goals of counterinsurgency. The relationships that the military cultivated with their Iraqi employees were at times intimate, if always deeply hierarchal and unequal in terms of risk. Some of these relationships endured beyond the duration of wartime employment, while others

166   CHAPTER 5

were much more fleeting. At times, these relationships were described by Iraqis and Americans alike in kinship terms, particularly in the masculinized idiom of brotherhood. Campbell (2016) carefully analyzes how the work of interpretation was structured by gendered power relations, relations that affected the working conditions of Iraqi interpreters as well as their experiences after resettlement. Women interpreters experienced forms of sexualization while men were more likely to be represented in accordance with the War on Terror caricature of Iraqi masculinity as violent, potentially terrorist, and misogynist.[12] If men were more likely to be seen as possibly dangerous, they were also more likely to be imagined through the militarized fictive-kin relation of brotherhood while women were seen as objects of aid. When Americans appealed for the resettlement of Iraqis with whom they had worked in Iraq, they often invoked this metaphor of brotherhood.[13] Brotherhood was based on the shared project of rebuilding Iraq as well as the quotidian experience of working alongside one another (Campbell 2016, 121–23). A few of the Iraqi men I met during fieldwork described close, enduring relations with former employers or coworkers, similar to those described by Campbell. However, I also heard many stories that implied distance—of relationships that were instrumental, fleeting, or exploitative. Of emails and letters unanswered and of promises unkept.

In a context of counterinsurgency, where engagement with local populations is central to the prosecution of war, the relational work of collaboration writ large might be understood through the metaphor of translation. Translation here can be understood as mediation on unequal terrain that both communicates across difference and creates it (Asad 1986; Campbell 2016; Giordano 2014). Iraqis provided vital threads of connection between military, nongovernmental, media, and other occupation institutions and local populations, often working within their own communities in intimate settings such as homes and neighborhoods. Indeed, in ways that are rarely acknowledged or perceived, they alter the course and outcome of war (Baker 2010). Merry reminds us that

> translators are both powerful and vulnerable. They work in a field of conflict and contradiction, able to manipulate others who have less knowledge than they do but still subject to exploitation by those who installed them. As knowledge brokers, translators channel the flow of information but they are

often distrusted, because their ultimate loyalties are ambiguous and they may be double agents. They are powerful in that they have mastered both of the discourses of the interchange, but they are vulnerable to charges of disloyalty or double-dealing. (Merry 2006, 40)

In this analysis, Merry agrees with Frantz Fanon's (2008) discussion of cultural interpretation under colonialism, where he notes that the colonized subject's command of the language of the colonizer both brings tremendous power and causes loss. Fanon notes the racializing power of the command and deployment of the colonizer's language—the use of the language of colonization brings the colonized subject closer to, but never reaching, whiteness. When deployed in the service of powerful institutions like colonial governments, militaries, and state bureaucracies, translation renders others legible and categorizable to those in power. In the process, translators gain limited power and privilege yet are also caught in the middle—subject to accusations of betrayal from both sides. Iraqis who worked with the occupation certainly experienced both this distrust and vulnerability.

THE DANGERS OF COLLABORATION

During the years of the occupation, Iraqis who were seen to be collaborating with the occupation faced death threats, kidnapping, extortion, and murder. The militias fighting against the occupation saw Iraqis who worked with the Americans, formally or informally, as enemy forces, accusing them of being traitors and collaborating against their country. At times threats and violence came from known militias, at times from neighbors and former colleagues or friends, and at times they were anonymous.

It is difficult to know how many Iraqis were threatened, killed, or injured while working for the occupation. The US government never kept track of how many Iraqis it employed directly, but it seems clear that they number into the tens of thousands. It also did not keep records of how many of its Iraqi employees were killed or injured (Arango 2011). Private contractors likewise may or may not have kept records of their Iraqi employees and of any deaths or injuries. Snapshots of information provide

168 CHAPTER 5

a partial sense of the much larger toll the war economy had on the lives of the Iraqis who worked within it. For example, in 2005 Iraqi interpreters made up about 40 percent of the deaths reported by private contractors to the US Department of Labor (Twu 2009, 729). However, private contractors faced very little regulation and oversight, and not all deaths or injuries were reported. Take for example Titan Corp, a San Diego defense contractor whose internal database was leaked and then published by ProPublica, allowing us a glimpse into the numbers of Iraqis who worked for US contractors as well as the risks inherent in the job.[14] Between March 2003 and March 2008, Titan hired more than eight thousand Iraqi interpreters; at least 360 of these interpreters were killed and more than 1200 were injured (Miller 2009).

Faisal told me how the first threat he received came in the form of a handwritten note left outside of his house some months after he began working at Camp Eagle. "It said: 'You are working with the US Army. You must leave this work or else.' At first, I was in denial about the threat and was afraid to take it too seriously. But to be safe, my wife and the boys went to live with my wife's aunt and I went to live with my sister." It was hard to be apart, made worse by Faisal's worry about his family's safety and his family's concern for his well-being. In an effort to avoid being tracked, Faisal borrowed a friend's car and started taking a different route from his sister's home to work every day. This made it especially concerning when he left the house one morning to find another note on the hood of the borrowed car. This time, the message was more ominous: "This is Judgment Day and you will be punished for your work for the Americans." At this point, Faisal was terrified. "I started to feel like someone was watching me every time I entered and exited my sister's home. Because of my fear, after this threat I stopped going to work on a regular basis. I told my boss about the threat and tried to avoid going to work as much as possible." Faisal's boss was sympathetic but said there was nothing he could do. Faisal began to think seriously about leaving Iraq.

The dangers of collaboration were not confined to the person who did the work but extended to kin and friends. Yousef is from a working-class family in Baghdad. His father worked as a driver and Yousef, to support his family, left his studies and went to work as an electrician. In the 1990s, one of his brothers was accused of joining an opposition party and was forced to flee Iraq. He fled to Syria and eventually received refugee status in the United States. During the 2003 invasion and occupation, Yousef's brother took a relatively lucrative job with the US Department of Defense as a contractor, returning to Iraq to provide technical support to the US Army. His brother had not been particularly enthusiastic about the war, Yousef told me, but he had been struggling financially in the US and had needed the money. Yousef described the ambivalence he felt having his brother close by after so many years of separation but not being able to see him because it was dangerous for him to leave the base. Despite being worried about his brother and not being able to see him much, Yousef told me that he felt a lot of comfort in being able to call his brother occasionally to check in and ask his advice during that turbulent and unsettling period. Despite the danger, Yousef remembered how he once traveled to visit him at a posting and another time, his brother was able to leave work to visit his parents. For his foray off the base, Yousef's brother wore a disguise and took other precautions to avoid being seen.

In 2006, Yousef was kidnapped and held for five days. "For me it was as though it was five years. They insulted me and my family. They tortured me and put my head in water. They told me that I was an agent [for the Americans]. They said, 'Your brother is working with Americans.' Their first and last goal was money." The kidnappers demanded a ransom of twenty thousand dollars. It was all the money that Yousef had and more. "I sold everything I had. I refused to let my brother help me because I know he is in a difficult financial situation." Yousef recounted what had happened after his family had paid the ransom:

> They took me out and put me in a car, and I thought for sure that they would kill me. I was blindfolded and they put something over my head. They threw me out of the car while it was moving. . . . For six months afterwards, I was not able to sleep. They tried everything and I do not know why. I am a peaceful person. When I remember, I cannot control my nerves. . . . After this, I knew that I did not have any life here.

Shortly after the kidnapping, Yousef left Iraq for Egypt. While Iraqis who worked with the occupation were treated as threats by their employers, they themselves were subject to violence for their collaboration, especially as resistance to the occupation turned into an armed insurgency.

170   CHAPTER 5

While most Americans stayed inside the heavily fortified Green Zone or military bases and only ventured into the "red zone"—that is, the rest of Baghdad—in armed convoys, many of the Iraqis who worked alongside them had to commute, unprotected, into and out of these sites on a daily basis. Some, like Faisal, took great pains to protect themselves and their families by changing routes, driving different vehicles, and even moving between multiple houses to try to keep their work a secret. They were denied the same level of protection to which their American coworkers had access. The risks of collaboration extended beyond the person who worked directly with the occupation to their family members, such as Yousef, who believed he had been kidnapped as a result of his brother's work with the US military.

THE DIRECT ACCESS PROGRAM: THE MORAL OBLIGATION TO RESETTLE "ALLIES"

On June 11, 2008, an Iraqi man, pseudonymously named Ibrahim to protect him from reprisals, testified before a joint session of the US Congress alongside Kirk Johnson, the founder of The List Project to Resettle Iraqi Allies, and Christopher Nugent, senior counsel at Holland & Knight, one of several law firms that had been working with The List Project to offer pro bono legal assistance for Iraqis who had worked with the US forces in Iraq and were seeking resettlement in the US. Ibrahim, listed only as "an Iraqi Citizen," was one of a small number of Iraqis who at that point had been resettled to the United States under the newly passed Refugee Crisis in Iraq Act.[15]

Kirk Johnson, who spoke alongside Ibrahim at the hearing, is an American from Chicago who had worked for the United States Agency for International Development (USAID) in Iraq during the early days of the occupation. He began The List Project in 2007 after an Iraqi former colleague received death threats and reached out to Johnson for assistance (Johnson 2013). The List Project began as a list of US-affiliated Iraqis who were threatened as a result of their collaboration. Over time, it grew to become a full-fledged advocacy project to resettle Iraqi allies. This campaigning, alongside advocacy from other organizations, journalists, and individual Americans who had worked in the occupation, laid the groundwork for the laws that resulted in the Refugee Crisis in Iraq Act.

The act included provisions for the resettlement of Iraqi allies who had been forced into hiding or exile as a result of their association with the American forces. The act's sponsors and the advocates who worked for it described the need for the legislation in terms of moral obligation and American values. In a cable to Condoleezza Rice, Ryan Crocker, the US ambassador to Iraq, argued for the need to "reward Iraqis working for the United States for their sacrifice, loyalty, and dedication" (Twu 2009). Under the act, only certain Iraqis were eligible for resettlement:

> Iraqis who were employed by, or worked for or directly with the United States Government, in Iraq; Iraqis who were employed in Iraq by a media or nongovernmental organization based in the United States; or an organization or entity that has received a grant from, or entered into a cooperative agreement or contract with the United States Government; spouses, children, sons, daughters, siblings, and parents of the primary applicant; and Iraqis who are members of a religious or minority community and have close family members ... in the United States. (*National Defense Authorization Act for Fiscal Year 2008* 2008)[16]

Even with these strictures, under the law, thousands of Iraqis should have been eligible for resettlement. But in summer 2008, despite the new law, resettlement was moving slowly, which is what brought The List Project before the US Congress. Ibrahim, who began working with USAID in Baghdad in 2003 before being forced to flee Iraq after receiving death threats, was asked to speak in the name of US Iraqi allies. It is worth quoting from Ibrahim's testimony at length:

> I literally risked my life every day for the American government, and I risked the lives of the Iraqi staff who worked with me to bring anything that our American colleagues needed from outside the Green Zone. In the simple things, we wanted to remind them of their homes back in the states, such as low-fat yogurt with apricots sometimes.
>
> Soon after I joined USAID, my country became classified as one big dangerous threat zone. High walls separated the American citizens from the rest of the country, yet there was one problem for Iraqis who worked for the Americans. We were not American citizens.

172   CHAPTER 5

We lived on one side of the wall and worked on another side. Outside those walls the violence grew worse. Outside the Green Zone, we were hated by the Iraqis, who no longer considered us Iraqis. Inside the Green Zone, no one understood that, according to Islamic culture, Iraqis like me were worse than infidels.

In a divided country, the only thing that unified everyone in Iraq was hatred of those individuals who worked for the United States, who were viewed as collaborators. . . .

When the first Iraqis were killed because they worked for the United States . . . [we] asked the United States to stop exposing us to needless dangers. For example, our identity was never protected. Our photos and names were available on USAID Web sites, which anyone could access.

Soon, our photos, names and addresses were more public to the Iraqis than the U.S. effort to reconstruct Iraq. When we asked if there was a plan to protect Iraqis working for the United States, we discovered that it's very clear that there was nothing in place to protect us.

We suggested simple ways to improve the situation, but nothing was done. This led us to believe that our lives were worthless in the eyes of those who were supposedly trying to win the hearts and minds of Iraqis. We didn't mean anything to the Americans.

But we meant something to the terrorists. Killing a supposed collaborator sent a clear message about who really controlled the land. Sadly, like so many other Iraqis who worked for the Americans, my life became a horror movie.

It started when I had a serious health emergency. My family had to take me out of the emergency room, afraid of militiamen who enter the emergency room and kill people, if they identified me.

Then my own mother, 67 years old, was beaten in the street, because her son worked for the Americans. In another incident, an Iraqi policeman threatened me, and I was assaulted by an Iraqi policeman. I reported all these incidents. Nothing happened to protect me.

Eventually, I was sentenced in a very direct way. I received a death letter, telling me I was the target of JAM, Jaish al-Mahdi, the al-Mahdi militia. I had to run away.

At that time networks existed that smuggled many of my former colleagues to Sweden. I heard that Sweden was providing sanctuary to Iraqis who worked for the U.S. government. I decided to take the same dangerous trip that many of my colleagues took when their lives were at stake.

The smugglers took me on a dangerous trip to India, and along the way the smugglers treated me brutally. Unfortunately, I was arrested by the Indian immigration authorities and deported to Syria. There I saw the Iraqi refugees suffering from humiliation and lack of basic human needs.

ALLIES AND ENEMIES   173

> I could not stay, so I continued my journey out of the Middle East through the smuggler network. They decided to take me to Egypt. Unfortunately, the Egyptian police did not allow the smugglers to succeed. I had no option but to hide in the slums of Cairo. I lost all hope and wished to die, so I could save myself from further suffering.
>
> Eventually, I registered with, and I'm still under the protection of, the United Nations High Commission for Refugees, UNHCR. Nevertheless, the Egyptian authorities arrested me, because I had illegally entered their country. I spent three weeks in jail, where I was tortured and beaten and humiliated.
>
> UNHCR came to my rescue by protesting that if the Egyptian authorities deported me to Iraq, I would be killed. Even though I was released from my prison, my life had become nothing but a serious of hardships. Every day I questioned God's wisdom and wondered [how] a person like me, who lost everything and was rejected by his own country and people, should live. (CSCE 2015)

I linger on Ibrahim's testimony because, like Karrar's petition, it reveals the constraints and possibilities for Iraqis to speak directly to the US government, which at various points was their occupier, their employer, and their humanitarian protector. I also share Ibrahim's testimony because much of what has been produced about the experiences of Iraqis who worked with the occupation and about the Direct Access Program has been written not by Iraqis but by members of the US military, other Americans who worked with the occupation, or US journalists.

Unlike Karrar's petition, which is written from outside the territorial boundaries of the US and at the periphery of the IOM, Ibrahim speaks from within the halls of the US Congress. Ibrahim's account is constrained and limited by the venue as well as by the purpose, process, and practices of the hearing; as a resettled Iraqi who is now an employee of The List Project, he tells his story in order to urge the US government to resettle other Iraqis like himself. But his account, like that of Mazen's in chapter 2, is not completely contained by its venue or the expectations of its audience. It is not one of supplication. He reveals intimacies, like the recognition of his American colleagues as people far from home who might be comforted by a familiar flavor of yogurt. He reveals the negligence of his US employers who made no effort to protect his identity and then refused to improve the situation when he and others raised

174 CHAPTER 5

concerns. He brazenly critiques the US reconstruction efforts when he says: "Our photos, names, and addresses [on the USAID website] were more public to the Iraqis than the US effort to reconstruct Iraq," and when he points out the irony that "our lives were worthless in the eyes of those who were supposedly trying to win the hearts and minds of Iraqis."

Ibrahim goes on to narrate for the US lawmakers the circuitous, clandestine route he took to seek safety outside of Iraq, a route that eventually landed him in Egypt, where he was detained and at risk of deportation. Earlier, I described the double burden of suspicion that Iraqis faced, but Ibrahim's testimony illuminates a third element of suspicion that Iraqis who worked for the US faced: "From the US Forces, to whom they represented potential threats to American security; from fellow Iraqis, some of whom saw their work with US Forces as a betrayal to Iraq; and, not least of all, from each other" (Campbell 2016, 3). Or, as Ibrahim succinctly put it in his testimony: "In a divided country, the only thing that unified everyone in Iraq was hatred of those individuals who worked for the United States, who were viewed as collaborators."

Why was resettlement moving so slowly, despite the millions of Iraqis displaced and the many reports in the press detailing how Iraqis who had collaborated with the occupation were being threatened, kidnapped, and murdered? One reason was the sheer difficulty of getting one of the allocated visas. The burden of proof was onerous. In order to be eligible, applicants had to have worked with the US forces for at least twelve months, have received a favorable written recommendation from a general or flag officer from the US unit that the applicant worked for, have passed a background check, and not be otherwise inadmissible. For many Iraqis, this was an incredibly difficult standard to meet. Iraqis also had to prove they were facing an "ongoing serious threat" as a result of their employment. This latter requirement essentially forced them to prove that they were refugees even though not all of them were actually classified as such. They also had to undergo significant security vetting, including extensive biometric and health screening. Many of them had already been subject to polygraphs, fingerprinting, and other security measures in order to work with the US, leading Johnson to call them "the most documented refugees on earth" in his testimony.

In its implementation, the US Department of State and the IOM defined who was eligible for the "reward" of resettlement even more specifically. In Egypt, Iraqis had to have a functional email address for their direct supervisor in Iraq. As part of my work at Resettlement Legal Aid Project (RLAP), I came to have a working knowledge of how US military and government email addresses were constructed, trying to reverse engineer email addresses from the names Iraqis remembered, their letters of reference and commendation, their ranks and the locations where they worked, and their photos. Many Iraqis who worked with the US appealed directly to former employers or colleagues; those who maintained close relationships and had access to email addresses went directly to the IOM and often did not need to seek assistance from RLAP. Many of the Iraqis who had worked with the occupation who approached our office did not have email addresses. They sometimes had badges, photos of themselves with US military, letters of commendation, and of course their own accounts. Faisal, for example, showed me photos of him standing and smiling in a row with uniformed servicemen. These were not enough for resettlement. They remembered names, like "Captain John" or "Mister Ryan" and stories of kind and supportive, or exploitative, bosses and colleagues. But when they had left their work and fled Iraq before the law had been passed, they could not have imagined that they would need to bring evidence with them or obtain an email address to prove that they had worked with the Americans.

Many of the visas allocated for the Direct Access Program were never used. Between 2008 and 2022, the United States resettled just over 143,000 Iraqis. In 2018, more than one hundred thousand Iraqis were still in the process, waiting (Human Rights First 2018). And this was just the people who fit the program's narrow definition of eligibility. In 2023, two decades after the US-led invasion, more than 1.1 million Iraqis were still displaced within Iraq or outside its borders. The program was specifically and bureaucratically defined so as to exclude the majority of Iraqis. Karrar, who was eventually resettled to California based on family reunification with his brother, would not have qualified based on his informal support of the occupation forces. Neither would have Hassan or Entisar from chapter 1, whose relations with the occupation would not be counted as allyship by either them or the US, despite the fact that their perceived

176   CHAPTER 5

association came to threaten their lives. Even Iraqis like Ibrahim, who was directly employed by USAID, had many letters of commendation, and whose face had been featured on the USAID website, had a hard time proving their allyship.

But in addition to failing at its own ambitions, the Direct Access Program had larger impacts. Elevating and then enshrining in law the category of ally as a narrow version of moral responsibility for the violence of war was effective in motivating the US government to resettle certain Iraqis. However, the rhetoric that underpinned the law and the laws themselves reinforced the counterinsurgency military-security logics as well as the racialization of Iraqis as potential terrorists. Indeed, they did so explicitly. Johnson argues in the hearing: "If our moral fabric was so weak that it was torn by 9/11, that we now suddenly are incapable of seeing Iraqis who, by dint of their service to us—riding around in our Humvees with us, risking their lives to work for us—if we come to see these people as terrorists, *I don't know what left there is* [sic] *to protect against terrorists.* I think we risk losing the war on terror" (CSCE 2015, emphasis mine).

This argument does nothing to unsettle terrorism discourses but rather remains squarely inside it. Moreover, Johnson's arguments create the impression that the United States has clear and delineated obligations in the aftermath of war—and that Americans should be the ones to decide what those obligations are—and limit the terrain of conversation to the fulfillment (or not) of those specific obligations, closing off the possibility of broader discussions of obligation in the aftermath of imperial war.

Many of the US advocates for the Direct Access Program, such as Johnson, were themselves imbricated in the moral dilemmas implied by liberal war's reliance on the participation and assistance of civilian populations and the subsequent abandonment of those populations. Their accounts often draw on their own experiences of war in Iraq and the intimate relations that emerged. They describe the individual Iraqis with whom they work as fictive kin—as brothers-in-arms, as "one of us." The most thoughtful versions illuminate the shared conditions that color these relations that emerge in war, placing the military or aid workers themselves within categories of labor alongside the translators, drivers, support workers, and others on whom their work absolutely depended, while nonetheless reckoning with their greater protection, compensation, and recognition. The focus on the relations between individual soldiers, aid workers, and their sense of moral responsibility for the Iraqis they "left behind" is ultimately an imperial one, one that centers allyship from the point of view of soldiers and aid workers, thereby reproducing the ally/enemy dichotomy and reinforcing stereotypes about good and bad Muslims, good and bad Arabs. Johnson, for example, goes on to say: "Let's get our senses back here. There are allies, and there are enemies. And if we can't differentiate between them, we have lost our values."

RESETTLEMENT AS THREAT IN THE GWOT

At first glance, it might seem as though the creation of a resettlement program to resettle Afghans and Iraqis who collaborated with the United States, so-called Iraqi allies, is the opposite of this racialized construction of Iraqis as a threat. Indeed, these Iraqis often worked closely with Americans in Iraq, warning them, as Karrar did, of insurgent activity, providing essential cultural and linguistic information, and otherwise supporting and, in many ways, making possible the quotidian work of occupation. But Karrar's travails within the resettlement program provide a hint that the figure of the ally and enemy are co-constituted, an impossible binary within which Iraqis must navigate. Ally is not a stable category but one that is constantly in doubt and tested by the much more powerful empire with which one is aligned.

Karrar's concern that his resettlement was delayed because, as he put it, "They caught two Iraqis who were terrorists in Kentucky" was not unjustified. In 2011, two Iraqi men, Mohanad Shareef Hammadi and Waad Ramadan Alwan, were arrested in Bowling Green, Kentucky, and charged with attempting to provide "material support" to the insurgency and the "use, threats, or attempts to use weapons of mass destruction," (Johnson 2011). Hammadi and Alwan were ensnared in a sting operation—the FBI used an informant to draw the two men into a plan to ship explosives and weapons to insurgents back in Iraq. Hammadi was caught on surveillance tape bragging about having attacked US forces in Iraq. The FBI later claimed that his fingerprints were found on an IED that had been retrieved in Iraq. The two men had not been resettled through the Direct Access

178   CHAPTER 5

Program but through the humanitarian resettlement program. In the wake of their arrest, resettlement came under tremendous scrutiny. How, US government officials and media representatives asked, had the system failed in this way? How had these dangerous men been allowed to enter the country?[17]

However, things were not quite as clear cut as they seemed. The FBI's use of an informant certainly raises questions about the threat that these men posed. The informant came up with the idea to ship weapons to Iraq and supplied Alwan and Hammadi with weapons and explosives. Despite the representation that the men, and by extension the entire refugee resettlement program, constituted a threat to Americans on US soil, the men had not participated in a plot to carry out violence within the US. The slippage between insurgency against US troops in Iraq and threat to Americans "at home" reflects how, despite efforts to distance the wars in the Middle East from US populations, the militarization of US society renders armed opposition against an invading force abroad equivalent to threats against Americans in the United States. These slippages continue to power anti-immigrant and Islamophobic rhetoric and policy today. The 2011 arrests in Kentucky were understood to be one of the primary stated justifications for President Trump's Muslim ban, which included a wholesale halt on refugee resettlement. In 2017, Kellyanne Conway spuriously evoked the "Bowling Green massacre" as a justification for the Muslim ban. Of course, there were no deaths in Bowling Green and the plot, such as it was, was not directed at Americans in the United States.

The effects of the 2011 arrests were immediate, wide-ranging, and enduring. In response, Secretary of Homeland Security Janet Napolitano announced that the government would be reviewing the security clearances of fifty-eight thousand Iraqis who were already in the US. The US State Department instituted a complete pause on Iraqi resettlement while more stringent security clearances were implemented. Families who were ready to travel for resettlement found their flights suddenly canceled with no explanation. But news of the arrests spread rapidly to Iraqis in the diaspora. For those like Karrar who were already in the resettlement process, the arrests created fear and consternation. If these two men could be arrested as terrorists, it raised the specter that they too might be vulnerable to such charges. These fears were not irrational; in temporarily banning all Iraqis because of the arrest of two men, the US government was essentially reminding Iraqis of the conditionality of their relationship with the United States. Iraqis in Egypt experienced the security checks as an opaque, arbitrary form of collective punishment more than as a genuine attempt to uncover dangers to the US. Item seven on Karrar's petition reflects this incredulity: "It is not reasonable that a country like the United States of America, which owns the largest security and intelligence services, etc, finds it difficult to finish the security checking for more than four years."

When I first learned of the arrests, I felt a pervasive and familiar sense of foreboding. I knew right away what the arrests would mean for friends like Karrar, who had already been waiting for months and years in the resettlement process. When I read about the indictments, especially the charge of "material support for terrorism," I was brought back to my early legal aid work on resettlement with Dr. Barbara in 2007. At that time, refugees could be barred from the resettlement program because of so-called material support, a charge that particularly exemplifies the GWOT. Under international law, people are ineligible for refugee status if they are deemed to have persecuted others. Under US law, this includes providing or engaging in "material support" for terrorist activity (Micinski 2018). Yousef, kidnapped because of his brother's work with the Americans and then freed when his family paid a massive ransom that essentially bankrupted them, faced exactly this issue. During the conflict in Iraq, kidnapping was common and, while some kidnappers were exclusively politically motivated, many also extorted ransoms from families. These ransoms, which often amounted to tens of thousands of dollars, did not always secure a captive's release, but they were often a family's best chance at seeing their loved one again. If in the resettlement process refugees admitted to having paid a ransom to kidnappers, they would be accused of having provided material support to terrorists and excluded from resettlement, regardless of the fact that they had paid a ransom under extreme duress. In order to prove he had been threatened as a result of his association with the Americans, Yousef had to tell the resettlement interviewers about his kidnapping. But when he told them about the ransom he had paid, he was subsequently rejected for resettlement. To the resettlement adjudicators and in US law, Yousef's actions brought him under the capacious and

180   CHAPTER 5

shifting definition of terrorism in the GWOT, rendering him an enemy, not an ally. It was an impossible situation. We worked on many such cases at RLAP before the rule was eventually changed in response to advocacy from NGOs. However, even after the change, payment of a ransom would still trigger a high-level check in Washington if concerns about material support came up in resettlement proceedings.

Accusations of terrorism were not the only ways that Iraqis could be barred from refugee status and resettlement. In interviews with IOM staff and US refugee adjudicators, Iraqis learned which parts of their biographies would identify them as possible threats. In addition to the trap of material support, middle-aged and older Iraqis faced challenges because of work or military service in Saddam Hussein's Baath Party government. Interviewers would ask about party rank and military service, including years of service and locations of deployment. Service during the Iran-Iraq War was especially suspicious as were certain military positions, such as pilot. Interviewers of course did not note the US support for Saddam Hussein's government in the Iran-Iraq War. Civilian Baath Party members were also suspect. Ahlam, for example, was proud of her work as a teacher. She openly talked about her Baath Party membership, which was required for all teachers. This openness and defiance extended to her resettlement interview, which may have been the reason she was repeatedly denied resettlement despite many attempts. She told me that she had thought about lying in her interview but didn't see why she should. As she said, "If you don't tell about it, it will be a problem. If you do tell about it, it will be a problem." Plus there was the oath they had made her take.

The arrest and convictions of Hammadi and Alwan—and the way their arrests were used to temporarily halt the resettlement of all Iraqis and then reinvoked years later as justification for the Muslim ban—shows the geographically malleable and temporally enduring power of the War on Terror as a racializing project of empire.[18] Cainkar and Selod (2018) argue that the War on Terror predates the attacks of September 11; the attacks were so easily mobilized because Arabs and Muslims were already racialized in particular ways, as opposed to the attacks being the starting point for their racialization (see also Naber 2000). Islamophobia as a racial project is inextricable from empire (Mamdani 2002; Kumar 2021) and follows Iraqis across space and time. Deepa Kumar defines two forms of Islamophobia—liberal Islamophobia, which takes the form of selective inclusion into the projects of empire, and conservative Islamophobia, which is characterized by exclusion from empire. Resettlement, to the extent that it emerges from the GWOT, oscillates between the two forms but does not transcend them.

DIASPORAS OF EMPIRE

Resettlement programs such as the Direct Access Program attempt to use the tools of empire to solve the problems of empire. This is materially, infrastructurally, so; in the aftermath of the Vietnam War, refugees were airlifted to military bases where they awaited processing. The List Project and other advocates for Iraqi resettlement, including Dr. Barbara, explicitly advocated for Iraqis to be evacuated and temporarily housed in the archipelago of US military bases. When the US finally pulled out of Afghanistan in 2021, some Afghans who worked with the US were airlifted and housed on military bases. To the extent that refugees who collaborate with empire are prioritized for resettlement, and to the extent that resettlement is reliant on the support and endorsement of military personnel and imperial infrastructure, programs like the Direct Access Program militarize resettlement, creating what Espiritu (2014) has called "militarized refuge(e)," a term that highlights the effects on both refugees and the place of "refuge."

The labor of collaboration engendered diverse and complex relationships within the context of war. Iraqis' actual experiences working with the Americans break down and confound simple categorizations of allyship. Indeed, collaboration should not be confused with support for the war; nor were these uncomplicated, straightforward relationships. At the same time as it created new relations, interpretation and other forms of collaboration often strained, altered, or severed relations with kin and community (see also Campbell 2016, 130). At times, this work drew on and traversed Iraqis' kin relations, as with Karrar, who came to collaborate because of his brother's work with the Americans. And this work could likewise put kin at risk, just as Yousef was ultimately kidnapped and forced into exile when militias discovered that his brother was working

CHAPTER 5

with the American forces. This mobilization of the language of kin relationships while denying Iraqis' existing attachments illustrates the violence of the relations that emerge in imperial war. And yet both sets of relations—those forged in wars and those that preexist it but are nonetheless shaped by it—endure beyond war itself.

Nadine Naber, drawing on the work of Kobena Mercer, theorizes the idea of "diasporas of empire" as emerging "against the highly invasive and shifting relations of power central to *contemporary* US neocolonialism and imperial formations." (Naber 2014, 193). The framework of diaspora of empire helps to illuminate the spatial and temporal breadth of Iraqis' relationships with US empire. These relationships were structured by the impossible binaries of Islamophobia and the Global War on Terror. In both war and resettlement, Iraqis had to navigate the unstable and constantly shifting categories of ally and enemy. Karrar's experiences with resettlement illustrate how the ally and enemy are co-constituted. The Direct Access Program, as a process of state recognition, sought to apply bureaucratic reason to the complex and messy relationships that actually existed in war. It did this by defining the category of the ally as the sum repository for the United States' responsibility for the Iraq War. The petition that Karrar cowrote and shared with me illustrates how Iraqis were both constrained by these state logics and how they resisted and pushed against them. Despite resisting these categories, Iraqis constantly had to prove that they were not a danger; in work, in exile, and even in the United States. Allyship is conditional and unstable; the US government has at various points, including after the 2011 arrests and more recently, reviewed and/or revoked the refugee status, permanent residency, or citizenship of Iraqis already living in the United States.[19]

Ultimately, the Direct Access Program resettled many Iraqis whose lives were at risk. Some of these Iraqis have become US citizens, while others have left the United States and returned to Iraq or gone elsewhere. Some Iraqis were killed while they waited in the interminable bureaucratic process. Others gave up, unwilling or unable to wait. From 2008 to 2020, the US admitted 47,331 Iraqis under the Direct Access Program. In 2019, an estimated 110,000 Iraqis were still eligible and awaiting interviews (Jakes 2019). The program was suspended for ninety days in 2021 after the FBI reported they had uncovered a scheme to falsify information and documents. It was restarted in 2023. By its own metrics then, the Direct Access Program can at best be considered a very partial success.

But I am less interested in understanding the Direct Access Program through its own metrics than I am in understanding Iraqis' own articulations of accountability. Karrar lives in California now. His daughters attend college; one is studying to be a pharmacist and the other just graduated as a physician assistant. When I visit their Southern California apartment, Karrar shares photos of the family together at her graduation, his face beaming with paternal pride. The walls of their carefully decorated home are painted a terracotta hue and, over the din of us chatting over tea, yellow and blue songbirds sing out from a cage on the balcony. He lives in a community with many other Iraqis and Arabs; he and his family have a thriving social life. His life has changed immeasurably since he cowrote the petition and protested outside the IOM with fellow Iraqis. But is this change accountability or redress? The protest and its accompanying petition were partly constrained by the strictures of the Direct Access Program and the IOM, but it nonetheless is a reminder of forms of obligation and accountability that extend beyond those imagined by the architects of the Direct Access Program. The Direct Access Program represents efforts to limit and circumscribe the United States' obligation in the aftermath of war while nonetheless appearing to have met its moral responsibilities. This is achieved by limiting obligation to those who collaborated or supported empire, then limiting the definition of collaboration, making it extremely difficult to meet that standard, and finally, by making one's allyship, if granted, conditional. Iraqis' experiences with war and resettlement show us that that the relations forged and broken in war and displacement cannot be constrained by the ally/enemy binary. They also show us that obligation and redress in the wake of imperial war demand much more capacious thinking and action.

Conclusion

ARRIVAL

Two different days in the Resettlement Legal Aid Project (RLAP) office, a month apart:

On the first day, appointments were over and clients had gone home. Only staff and volunteers were left in the office, working quietly together. I sat in a corner trying to piece together the chronology for a testimony I was working on and drinking too strong Nescafé too late in the day. The door of the office burst open and Um Muhammad rushed in, crossing the room to where Shams was seated working. Suddenly the whole office was filled with sound and motion. I looked up to the sounds of jubilant shouting, happy crying, and congratulations. I soon learned that Um Muhammad had just come from the IOM, where she was volunteering in a women's outreach program, and had heard from an employee that Shams would be traveling soon, in a month. We surrounded Shams, hugging. An American volunteer legal advocate wiped tears from his eyes and said, "This is what we do." Shams, who had previously told me how "time had stopped" for her in Egypt, stood on a chair, stuck her arms out like airplane wings, and joyfully mimicked flying through the air.

On the second day, another rare quiet moment in the office was punctured. Shams had traveled the day before. We had held a goodbye party for

184

her and even though I was so happy for her, my heart ached a bit to see her go. I knew how much she had wanted to leave Egypt and how excited she was to go to Virginia, where she had relatives, a friend, and the promise of a job at the same women's rights organization she had worked at in Baghdad. But the office already felt empty without her there. A phone rang. Several minutes later, the legal director, a newly graduated American lawyer, came and found me. She looked distraught. Shams had just called her, panicked, from Tampa, Florida. Apparently, she had been resettled to Florida, not Virginia, a fact that she had not been aware of until the plane landed in Tampa and she realized that there would be no connecting flight. It seems hard to imagine that someone could get on a plane and not know where they were bound, but information about travel was rarely offered in clear and transparent ways to resettling refugees. Shams had worked at RLAP and so was well-versed in the uncertainties of the resettlement process, but this was a form of instability for which she had not been prepared. She had been communicating with a resettlement agency in Virginia until a few days before her departure. Her friends and relatives had been waiting for her. She was inconsolable. She had waited so long for this and here she was, alone, in a totally different place than she'd expected, far away from the people she knew and her planned-for future.

From Cairo, we tried to reach out to the IOM, the US Office of Refugee Resettlement, and to US-based resettlement agencies to see if we could help. From what we could gather, Shams' case had been switched at the last minute because of a housing shortage. Now that she was in the US, Shams could choose to leave Florida for Virginia, but if she did, she would give up the three months of housing and financial assistance that she would receive as a resettled refugee. That money had already been disbursed to the resettlement agency in Florida in her name and could not be transferred. Stay, we reluctantly advised her on the phone, at least for a little while.

Years later, I viscerally remember Shams's distress in that moment, as strong or stronger than I remember her joy at finding out that she would finally travel. When humanitarian agencies such as the United Nations High Commissioner for Refugees and states describe resettlement as a process of "selection and transfer," they mean it literally. Immersed in the quotidian work of writing testimonies and advocating for resettlement, I

186   CONCLUSION

had not yet understood how fully resettlement denies the relations that make up Iraqis' lives, privileging some relations over others but often disregarding the relationships and attachments—both damaging and sustaining—that are most significant for Iraqis themselves. Although Shams had friends, relatives, and a job waiting for her in the US, the resettlement program treated her as though she had no attachments, no preferences, and no claims. And worse, when she expressed a preference, she risked losing the already meager benefits to which she was entitled. Shams was not alone in this. I had other friends whose relations were altered, ignored, or undone by the resettlement process. In one family, for example, the nineteen-year-old daughter left first, on her own, for Massachusetts. Having no military or work history, her security clearance came through the quickest, and so she had to travel, despite her family's trepidation about sending their unaccompanied teenage daughter, who had never lived away from her family, to live alone in a strange country. According to the resettlement process, she was an adult, so could travel alone. A year later, her mother's security clearance came in and so she traveled to meet her daughter, leaving her husband behind. Finally, his security clearance came through and he was able to join them. Ahlam, the retired teacher who insisted on telling the truth about her Baath Party membership in her resettlement interviews, was never approved for resettlement. Her only daughter, twenty at the time, was approved but refused to leave her mother behind and so never traveled. They still live in Egypt. These may seem like temporary dislocations or isolated instances, but they reveal something fundamental about how resettlement views refugees as atomized cases and not as full social beings living in webs of relation.

Shams's experience of being treated as though she were without attachments, without relationships, and without claims to assert sharpened my attention for how Iraqis' accounts and experiences surfaced other forms of mutuality and relatedness that empire denied. By that point in my fieldwork, I was imbricated in new quotidian and affective relations of my own. In addition to legal and psychosocial work, I had been generously and graciously folded into the lives in exile of the Iraqis I knew. There were new babies, weddings, deaths, near deaths, graduations, birthdays, and holidays. Time had stopped—it was, after all, a station—yet time kept going, and so did life. Living and working in proximity to Iraqis and others whom I came to know in Cairo and listening to their stories changed me indelibly. Having followed Shams's experiences in the resettlement program as well as the experiences of many other people, I viscerally felt how awful and disorienting the experience must have been for her. This moment and others inspired me to tell a different story of the Iraq War and the humanitarian response to the so-called refugee crisis it created, one that foregrounds the relational dimensions of empire and, not least, how war and humanitarianism are sutured together.

Imperial war and humanitarianism not only deny some relationships and recognize others, they also create new relations, often violent ones. The framework of diasporas of empire developed by Mercer (1994) and Naber (2014) helps to illuminate the spatial and temporal breadth of Iraqis' relationships with US empire. These relationships were structured by the impossible binaries—good/bad Muslim, ally/enemy, good/bad refugee—of imperial war in the context of the Global War on Terror. Such imperial relations, or collateral damages, are enduring forms of unequal encounter brought about through imperial violence, and the effects they have on Iraqis' lives raise ethical and political questions of reparation and restitution. Given the collateral damages described within these pages and all the many that are, of course, not included, what would redress and repair in the aftermath of the Iraq War look like?

This question is not simply a question about the past. As Dina Khoury (2013, 245) writes in her book *Iraq in Wartime,* war in Iraq is a "perpetually present past" shaping the politics of Iraq, the United States, and indeed the world. In Iraq, as Khoury notes, the experience of war has not led to transformational politics that would disrupt the damages from decades of authoritarianism, conflict, and imperial war. But perhaps transformational politics emerge in opposition to war. Recent uprisings in Iraq in 2019 suggest that young Iraqis, many of whom were not yet born in 2003, seek new politics free from sectarian and undemocratic forms of rule.

The US also continues to be changed by the war, even if these changes are sometimes denied as part of ongoing imperial unknowing. In the United States, politicians on both the left and the right have drawn on Americans' frustrations with seemingly never-ending imperial wars. In January 2017, as one of his first acts after assuming the US presidency,

188   CONCLUSION

Donald Trump used executive power to enact the so-called Muslim ban—building on and exacerbating racism toward Muslims and people from the Middle East. The ban, which explicitly barred travel to the United States from seven Muslim-majority countries, also included a radical diminishment of refugee resettlement.[1] In response, protestors descended on US airports to rally against the order, and lawyers immediately began to challenge it through the courts. Many of the Americans with whom I had worked at RLAP were among some of the loudest US voices challenging the ban. They drew on their experiences working with and alongside refugees and how those relationships had changed them to argue against the racialized closure of borders and the ending of refugee resettlement.

Although the ban finally ended in 2021, its pause on resettlement unraveled many of the institutions and processes of the US refugee resettlement program, already weakened by a lack of support under neoliberal policies that emphasized self-sufficiency and limited reliance on state funding and support (Bonet 2022; Gowayed 2022). Building on earlier histories of anti-Arab and anti-Muslim racism, it further entrenched and emboldened these structures in the United States and specifically strengthened the racist link between immigrants and refugees, especially those of Arab or Muslim identity, with terrorism. The ban lowered the cap on the number of resettled refugees that could be admitted to the US from 110,000 in 2016 to only eighteen thousand in 2021, diminishing the role of the US in global refugee resettlement.[2] The use of sudden and seemingly capricious executive power to make these changes as opposed to moving them through the institutions of government created chaos that rippled well beyond the United States' borders: People from the affected countries living in the US were suddenly unable—or, even if not technically unable, afraid—to travel out of the US for fear of not being allowed back in. Long-awaited family reunifications were instantly upended, refugees who already had their cases approved and travel dates set were suddenly denied travel, and some people even found their ability to enter the United States changed while they were literally in the air en route to the US (Sacchetti 2022). The ban thus exacerbated the uncertainties described in this book—holding refugees waiting in the resettlement process even longer in suspension, further dividing and separating families, and impacting people and places far beyond those explicitly targeted by the order.

Then in December 2020, near the end of his term, President Trump used his presidential powers to pardon four military contractors who had been involved in one of the most egregious episodes of violence during the US-led invasion and occupation of Iraq. On September 16, 2007, contractors working for Blackwater Security Consulting (rebranded after the scandal as Xe and then Academi), founded by Trump supporter Erik Prince, engaged in the indiscriminate and unprovoked killing of fourteen Iraqi civilians and the wounding of seventeen others in Nisour Square in Baghdad. In their contract, the US State Department had offered Blackwater both civil and criminal immunity in Iraq, meaning that legal accountability for any crimes committed could only happen in the United States (Dickinson 2020). Critics noted how the pardons exculpate and set free war criminals who needlessly killed Iraqi civilians and had finally been brought to justice after a years-long battle in US courts. This is true. What is also true, however, is that the attention focused on the Nisour Square massacre and the legal consequences faced by its perpetrators were anomalous in the history of a war where the vast majority of crimes have gone unpunished and undiscussed in the United States. Trump's pardon undid the work of that lengthy legal fight and erases a rare instance in which the value of Iraqi lives was recognized and crimes associated with the war adjudicated in the United States. The pardons illustrate the long life of imperial unknowing: of imperial impunity, of the differential valuation of Iraqi and American lives, and the intentional, violent forgetting that allows Americans to ignore the long-standing and ongoing costs of the war.

On August 30, 2021, the US formally ended the nearly two-decade-long military occupation of Afghanistan. During the month of August, as the Taliban took over the Afghan government, thousands of Afghans fled the country every day, adding to the already nearly six million people displaced within and outside of Afghanistan since 2001 (Vine et al. 2020). Some 124,000 people, many of whom had worked for NATO or the Afghan government, were evacuated in the last days of the war (Fox 2021). During the last days and hours before the ground war ended, tens of thousands of civilians struggled to get space on overfull airplanes to leave the country. The US government's description of the withdrawal as orderly was belied by scenes of Afghan civilians trying desperately to cling to airplane wings as evacuation flights took off from Kabul airport (Daulatzai and Ghumkhor 2023). The evacuations, and especially the troubling scenes of Afghans left behind, reignited public conversations about the responsibility of the United States in the aftermath of its wars. While this conversation included US responsibility to Afghans in general, one group of people received significant attention in media and also in policy: those characterized as "allies." The scenes evoked iconic images of the fall of Saigon, when the US military infamously evacuated, leaving behind the Vietnamese who had worked for them. These images had recirculated in the aftermath of the Iraq War, when advocates used them to argue for the resettlement of Iraqi allies (Johnson 2013). And now they were being used again. The withdrawal illustrated once again how dependent US imperial occupation is on the labor and assistance of local people and how, despite how essential their labor is to the functioning of imperial occupation, these people are so easily discarded. US advocates draw on images of the US withdrawal from Vietnam to argue for US responsibility in the aftermath of war, but the repeated motif across imperial contexts suggests the connections between histories of militarism and racism and their relationships to displacement. These imperial resonances and repetitions suggest that restitution might not be found in the aftermath of imperial war—where empire can posit humanitarian rescue as a solution to its problems but not to refugees'—but in a rejection of imperial war and counterinsurgency altogether.

The year 2023 marked the twentieth anniversary of the invasion of Iraq. In the US, responses were muted, reflecting and reproducing empire's refusal to know. Imperial innocence precludes and renders impossible imaginations of what collective justice might look like in the aftermath of war. At the same time, there is a liberal impulse that airing or making visible harms somehow undoes the damage. Not only is making damage visible insufficient, but it can sometimes cause damage in itself (Tuck 2009). It is not enough simply to know. And yet, my exploration of war on Iraq and the humanitarian responses to displacement brought me into confrontation with the tremendous lengths to which empire goes in order to refuse to know. The investments that empire makes in unknowing, disavowal, denial, and innocence illuminate how imperial unknowing maintains and supports empire's continuation and allows it to avoid accounting for its damages.

Imperial unknowing has violent effects on the lives of the people exposed to it both within and beyond war. The use of humanitarianism to solve the problems of empire enacts epistemological violence on refugees, who are forced to adopt positions of gratefulness and denied an audience for accounts of imperial violence. Empire also blocks refugees' ability to know by plunging them into the uncertainty of indefinite life in transit and the unaccountable temporality of the resettlement process. Abu Nasim reminds us that living in an enforced condition of uncertainty has significant effects for well-being and survival. Part of imperial unknowing lies in the way the US maintains separate regimes of war-making and humanitarian response, obscuring how entangled these processes are. It is not surprising, then, that Latif refused the category of refugee altogether and Mazen rejected the confinements of the humanitarian process to move toward his own impulse for justice.

These processes of obscuring sever relations of complicity and solidarity across time and place that imperial violence has forged. While I am conscious of the perils of focusing too much on loss and harm in the context of the Global War on Terror, as Anila Daulatzai and Sahar Ghumkhor (2023, 209) write: "There is a far greater risk posed by an invitation to recuperate something positive from destruction—a consciously making unconscious of the conditions that allow for the bypassing altogether of the damages inflicted." The stories of the Iraqis in this book, whether Shams, Um Muhammad, Mazen, Faisal, or others, resist and refute imperial efforts to deny, silo, or ignore the enduring collateral damages of imperial war and displacement. Their voices and those of other Iraqis across the generations belong at the center of discussions of redress or restitution in the aftermath of war. It is important to listen to the voices of those most affected by imperial war not only for their sake; to the extent that histories deny or obscure the collateral damages of war, all of us—tied together in relation—are more impoverished for it. The conversations required by the deep relationships forged by war are long overdue.

Notes

INTRODUCTION: DEPARTURE

1. All names in this book, with the exception of public figures, are pseudonyms. Here, for Abu and Um Muhammad, I follow the Iraqi convention of addressing parents by the prefix father of (*Abu*) or mother of (*Um*), followed by the name of their eldest son. I do this only for interlocutors for whom this was their most typical form of address. In Cairo, where families were often separated, eldest sons were not always present and parents were sometimes referred to by the name of their eldest daughter or eldest present son. In general, I have attempted to choose a pseudonym that most closely resembles the forms of address used by my interlocutors and so these vary throughout the text.

2. While the entire population of Iraq was affected by the sanctions, which might less euphemistically be understood as a form of siege warfare, Nadje Al-Ali (2005, 746–48) has documented how Iraqi women were particularly impacted, mediated, of course, by other forms of difference such as class. Some 60 percent of the Iraqi population was dependent on food aid procured through the UN's Oil-for-Food program, which resulted in women having to bake bread at home with flour rations because they could not afford to purchase it. Along with the inability to access the means for basic survival, the breakdown of the welfare state under the sanctions regime pushed women out of employment and education and into the home.

193

194   NOTES TO INTRODUCTION

3. To say that Iraqi voices are underrepresented is not to say that they have not been present at all in scholarship. In recent years, a growing body of literature, some produced by Iraqi scholars, has centered Iraqis' experiences of imperial violence, war, and displacement (Al-Ali 2007, 2005; Al-Ali and Al-Najjar 2013; Al-Ali and Pratt 2009; A. Ali 2012; Dewachi 2017, 2015; Rubaii 2019; Saleh 2020; Al-Mohammad 2012, 2010) while, after a period in which research in Iraq has been difficult to carry out because of safety concerns, new and exciting scholarship on Iraq and Iraqis that does not focus predominantly on war is also being produced (Z. Ali 2018; Pursley 2019). Such work is urgently needed and I draw inspiration from and engage with its contributions throughout the book to come.

4. The Costs of War Project (2023) estimates that more than 4,500 US military were killed and more than 3,600 US contractors. Although this book focuses mostly on the effects of the war on Iraqis, many Americans also lost their lives and many who survived continue to live and struggle with the aftermaths of the war (Wool 2015).

5. On the United States' post-9/11 wars in the Middle East, see Inhorn (2020). On Vietnam, see Espiritu (2014) and M. T. Nguyen (2012). On Hmong resettlement to the US, see Vang (2021).

6. Neta Crawford (2013), writing about the post-9/11 wars, points out that although accidental killing and injury of civilians does happen in war, militaries either foresaw or could have foreseen much collateral damage but deemed the military advantage justified it. The argument about what military advantage or necessity justifies is reminiscent of US secretary of state Madeleine Albright's infamous *60 Minutes* interview in which she was asked about the approximately five hundred thousand Iraqi children who were killed by US sanctions. Albright responded that "I think this is a very hard choice, but the price—we think the price is worth it" ("Madeleine Albright" 2022).

7. One military definition: "Collateral damage—A form of collateral effect that causes unintentional or incidental injury or damage to persons or objects that would not be lawful military targets in the circumstances ruling at the time. collateral effect—Unintentional or incidental effect to objects that would not be lawful military targets in the circumstances ruling at the time" (Office of the Chairman of the Joint Chiefs of Staff 2020, 36).

8. Although my focus in this book is on Iraqis, especially Iraqi civilians, I would be remiss not to mention the harmful effects of the Global War on Terror and the Iraq War more specifically on American lives, including the thousands of US soldiers who lost their lives and the many more injured during the war. Their lives too have been impacted by imperial unknowing as, for example, the military tried to hide the first US casualties from the public. However it is also important to note that their lives are not valued equally in war and that this is indeed part of the military logic of collateral damage. Writing about the inequality of lives of US military and humanitarian workers as opposed to those who are

the objects of military intervention, Fassin (2007, 512) argues: "The corollary of the 'zero death' doctrine, however is the rhetoric of 'collateral damage.' Reducing the risks on one's own side implies increasing them on the enemy's side, including—in conflicts officially launched to 'liberate' or 'protect' populations—among civilians." The effects of the war for US publics have also been profound and far reaching, although Abu El-Haj (2022) has argued that here, too, focusing on military injury limits which violence and whose losses can be acknowledged in the aftermath of war.

9. Zainab Saleh (2020) uses the term "imperial entanglements" to describe the ways that Iraq, Britain, and the United States are co-constituted through their imperial relationships over time. Central to Saleh's intervention is the ways in which these relations, though they are of course violent, asymmetric, and exploitative, are mutually co-constitutive and shape the national identities and experiences of imperial subjects in both center and periphery. In Saleh's formulation, Iraqis are not only victims of imperial violence but also agents in larger national and imperial histories.

10. See Daulatzai and Ghumkhor (2023) for a related argument about the losses and damages of the war on Afghanistan and the War on Terror more generally.

11. Yến Lê Espiritu (2014) especially has written about a critical refugee studies approach—which, among other things, aims to offer research by, with, and for refugees as an alternative to damage-centered research on displaced people.

12. For an ethnographic account of the antiwar movement and especially the World Tribunal on Iraq, an initiative led by activists and scholars to document atrocities committed by the US, Britain, and other allies in the war, see Çubukçu (2018).

13. In both the US and the UK, a small but significant number of journalists, media personalities, academics, and government employees who spoke out against the war faced censure, censorship, and in some cases the loss of their jobs. As I discuss in chapter 2, journalists who covered the war, especially Iraqi journalists, faced significant threats to their lives and safety.

14. These include a range of different initiatives in a number of forms, including the work of activist and academic groups such as the Costs of War Project, Iraq Body Count, the Wikileaks revelations, official reports such as the Chilcot report, Freedom of Information Act requests by organizations like the ACLU and media outlets, as well as films, television shows, memoirs, and novels. The Costs of War Project, based at Brown University, is notable for both the expansive way they define "cost" to include not just monetary costs but also the human, political, and social toll of the War on Terror as well as for their long-standing documentation of the effects of War on Terror which, like the war itself, transcends state boundaries.

196 NOTES TO INTRODUCTION

15. Colonial or imperial amnesia is a set of related concepts that have been theorized differently over the years. Stuart Hall has written about how the violence and extraction of British colonization and imperialism have constituted an "absent/present centre" (Hall 2021, 58). Through a politics of what he calls collective amnesia, colonial relations are disavowed despite being materially and symbolically at the core of British society, both in the past and contemporary. For Hall, this collective amnesia is a central element of contemporary anti-Black and anti-migrant racism. More recently, scholars have noted how this process of amnesia enables the divorcing of humanitarian "crises" from the interconnected histories of colonization and exploitation that are their causes (Danewid 2017, 1681), allowing former colonizers to express surprise and dismay that people from countries they previously colonized are seeking asylum. Amnesia need not exclude veneration of colonial histories; forgetting or looking away from some aspects of imperial or colonial history may be necessary for the celebration of or feeling of nostalgia for imperial pasts (Fletcher 2012). Ann Stoler (2011, 125) has argued that amnesia is an insufficient term for describing the complex and contradictory processes of remembering and forgetting engaged in by modern colonial states, proposing instead the term *colonial aphasia*. Aphasia, Stoler argues, highlights not ignorance or forgetting but rather a process of loss and retrieval—"an occlusion of knowledge."

16. Many Iraqi exiles who had fled Saddam Hussein's regime were unable to return safely for many years and saw "regime change" as one avenue by which they might be able to return to Iraq (Saleh 2020). Many of the Iraqi exiles in London with whom Zainab Saleh worked were able to travel back to Iraq for the first time in the years after the 2003 invasion. Many, however, were dismayed by what they found when they returned.

17. The border between refugee camp and city can, at times, be blurry—take for example some of the Palestinian refugee camps in Lebanon or Jordan, which after more than fifty years of existence, have been engulfed by growing cities or self-organized camps in cities, like those that have sprung up in Calais, Belgrade, and Athens in recent years.

18. For a discussion of how rationales for resettlement have changed over time, see Garnier et al (2018).

1. "BAD HISTORY"

1. In this context, "academia becomes a poisoned chalice—both a means to speak truth to power and a means to tether scholars to particular dominant structures of power" (Deeb and Winegar 2016, 5).

2. In *Ethnographies of US Empire,* McGranahan and Collier (2018, 7) note that thinking of the US as an empire allows anthropologists to see the connections

NOTES TO CHAPTER 1   197

between different colonial and imperial formations and practices. As an example, they note how Indigenous scholar and activist Vine Deloria connected President Johnson's broken promises to Southeast Asian allies in the Vietnam War with the broken treaties the US government made with Indigenous nations (see also Deloria [1969]). Recent scholarship has taken up Deloria's approach, noting the resonances across imperial time and space as well as how imperial practices travel.

3. Agnotology, or the study of ignorance, has grown as a field of study in recent years, with a particular emphasis on how ignorance often represents social and political struggles (Proctor and Schiebinger 2008). Proctor and Schiebinger especially focus on how ignorance is often deliberately produced through, for example, the intentional suppression and distortion of scientific knowledge.

4. See Browne (2015) for an exploration of the long history of the surveillance of Blackness and its relationships to contemporary forms of surveillance and policing. For the freedom and political possibility of being "illegible," see Scott (1998).

5. In the War on Terror, public secrecy has been marshalled in moments where the use of torture has been revealed publicly, such as the revelations of torture in Abu Ghraib, at the detention center at Bagram Air Force Base in Afghanistan, and by police departments in the United States. In all cases, the selective relationship between secrecy and revelation has been deployed to represent such acts of violence as exceptional and rare as opposed to a routinized tactic associated with the War on Terror (Ralph 2020; Linnemann and Medley 2019; Puar 2004)

6. Secrecy can be an incisive concept for understanding social relations because of the ways it is predicated on the interplay between concealment and revelation, inclusion and exclusion (Simmel 1906; G. M. Jones 2014). Secrecy, then, is a technology of power, one that carries tremendous affective and performative charge. This is perhaps especially apparent in studies of governmental secrecy. In the United States, Masco (2006, 2014) has argued that the post-2001 antiterror security state has been built on the infrastructure of national security discourses and practices—in which secrecy played a crucial role—associated with early American nuclear weapons production.

7. For a short history of the term "neoconservative" in US politics and the movement's relevance to the Iraq War in particular, see Packer (2005, 15–24).

8. On the face of it, Rumsfeld's unknown unknowns and the "reality-based community" quip—two of the most infamous utterances made by an administration notorious for its infamous utterances—appear to contradict one another. Rumsfeld seems to imply that knowledge *is* central to imperial power; he does not explicitly deny the importance of evidence but suggests that its absence signals not-yet-imagined presence. But Rumsfeld's comments are perhaps not so different from those of the unnamed aide, especially when considered in context. Rumsfeld was known for finding ways to subvert and evade knowledge. He used the technologies of audit against audit itself; for example, instead of hiding

198   NOTES TO CHAPTER 1

evidence, which had proven disastrous in the Watergate scandal, Rumsfeld was famous for producing an overabundance of contradictory evidence through the production of so many memos—which came to be called "snowflakes" because they formed a blizzard of contradictory memos—such that no clear conclusions could be drawn from the archive.

9. Although the commencement of the bombardment was shocking, Iraqis had been living in a state of uncertainty for months as the threat of war loomed. Ali Ali (2020) describes how the city of Baghdad changed in the long lead-up to the war, as residents anticipated the coming bombardments and took precautions to protect themselves, particularly by leaving the city for the countryside in advance of the invasion (A. Ali 2020).

10. A certain military mythology seems to have emerged around the danger of "Route Irish." Nearly twenty years after the invasion, it is still possible to purchase "Route Irish" T-shirts on Amazon. These shirts feature text that says "Route Irish" over the classic US highway sign icon, riddled with bullet holes.

11. The US military also relied heavily on the Iraqi diaspora in the United States both as advisors and role-players in military simulations in the archipelago of fake "local villages" located on military bases around the United States (Stone 2017, 2018). Iraqi Americans and other Americans with Middle Eastern and/or Arab origins also fought in the war in Iraq and worked with contractors or with humanitarian or media organizations.

12. See Stone (2022) for a rich analysis of anthropology's complicity in and opposition to counterinsurgency. As part of anthropological resistance to the Human Terrain System, a group of scholars called the Network of Concerned Anthropologists produced a *Counter-Counterinsurgency Manual*, which critiqued and resisted the folding of anthropologists into imperial war. For an important discussion of the Human Terrain System, the Pentagon's Minerva project, and other government efforts to recruit anthropologists into the GWOT, especially in the Middle East and North Africa, see Deeb and Winegar (2016, 160–69). Deeb and Winegar note both how the participation of anthropologists and anthropology in the GWOT was opposed by the American Anthropological Association and also how scholars of the Middle East and North Africa were marginalized in these discussions and subject to recruitment and harassment. They also note that the Human Terrain System received the vast amount of attention to the exclusion of non-Human Terrain System military action. The debates within the discipline about the Human Terrain System echoed an earlier controversy when, during the US war on Vietnam, student activists uncovered information about social scientists, including prominent anthropologists, using their field research to collaborate with counterinsurgency operations (Wakin 1998).

13. The tremendous risk borne by Iraqi interpreters and the ways in which the occupying forces failed to see or act upon the danger they were in led many of them to be kidnapped or murdered (Johnson 2013).

NOTES TO CHAPTER 2   199

14. As Sally Engle Merry (2006, 40) notes, "Translators are both powerful and vulnerable. They work in a field of conflict and contradiction, able to manipulate others who have less knowledge than they do but still subject to exploitation by those who installed them." In occupied Iraq, the vulnerability associated with translation was even more pronounced, as interpreters were much more clearly perceived as double agents or collaborators with the occupation and were also not protected by their employers.

15. The United Kingdom presence in Iraq included the occupation from 1914 through 1920 and the Mandate period from 1920 through 1932. Created in the aftermath of the First World War, the mandate system was an international regime created for the purpose of governing the territories and peoples that had been colonized by the defeated German and Ottoman empires. Unlike previous forms of colonization, the League of Nations imagined the mandate system as a system of "tutelage" in which the ultimate goal, especially for the mandate territories of the Middle East, was for peoples to develop the capacities, as determined by the mandatory powers, to become a sovereign state. Sarah Pursley (2019, 31) writes about how biopsychological concepts were conscripted and crystallized into the discourse used to justify the mandate system. Building on colonial narratives that represented non-European peoples as "childlike," League of Nations documents and rhetoric described mandate states as "adolescent" and expressed hopes that they would reach "maturity" or "manhood." The racialized, gendered, and ableist dimensions of the mandate ideology were used by Britian, Pursley argues, not to encourage Iraqi self-rule or for biopolitical governance but to defer Iraqi sovereignty and to extract resources and retain control through necropolitics. For a discussion of the League of Nations Mandate System and its imbrication in the colonial encounter, see Anghie (2007, 2005).

16. Kali Rubaii (2018) has written eloquently about how sectarian categories were written across the landscape as part of an imperial effort to divide and conquer. In Anbar province, where Rubaii conducted fieldwork, she describes how her interlocutors argued that the imposition of sectarian categories of citizenship effectively eroded preexisting relationships of social trust between Sunni, Shia, and minorities that had previously allowed a collective opposition to US occupation. Hassan would likely agree.

2. WAR ARCHIVE

1. When she passed away in 2018, commemorations poured in from the many people whose lives she had affected, many of whom were former refugees. Yet working with Barbara was not uncomplicated; in a beautiful remembrance, Negar Azimi (2018) pointedly called Barbara a "human bulldozer" and a "fierce

advocate" for refugees. For those who came into her orbit, Barbara was fierce and an advocate in equal measure.

2. This change should not be understood only, or even primarily, as an effort to be more inclusive or not to discriminate on the basis of nationality. Rather, I see it as an illustration of how humanitarian temporalities based on crisis and the differential valuing of human lives based on national and racial identity (among other forms of difference) intersect. For example, the Iraqi Information Office was founded in response to the "Iraqi refugee crisis," a simultaneous sense of lack of support and services for the relatively large population of Iraqi refugees at that time, the opportunities enabled by the passage of the Kennedy Act in the United States, and to a lesser extent resettlement programs offered by other states to Iraqis. The Iraqi Information Office became the Resettlement Legal Aid Project and then opened to refugees and asylum-seekers of other nationalities partly because of a recognition that the "Iraqi refugee crisis" and its associated resettlement streams would not last forever: If the organization wanted to continue, it would eventually have to broaden its focus.

3. For an analysis of the militarization of Iraqi society from 1980 onwards and especially the effects of long-term war on society, the environment, and everyday life, see Khoury (2013).

4. Journalists in Iraq, not all of whom are Iraqi, have suffered the most casualties of any other country targeted in the War on Terror (Crawford and Lutz 2021).

5. While this argument carries significant force, it is also important to note that embedding is both a continuation of US military efforts to control and govern press access to a warzone and an innovation, in that controlling the press went from limiting their access to the battlefield (as was done in the war in Grenada in 1983, "pre-censorship") to one where journalists were controlled in a very different way by having unprecedented access to the battlefield and, in a sense, becoming part of the occupying forces (Kumar 2006).

6. Analyses of news media during the war have relatively uniformly found that among all major US news programs, coverage of the war generally privileged information and sources from the US government, and dissent was largely absent. At times, commentators or views critical of the war were actively suppressed as shows were canceled and reporters fired.

7. This same rationale was offered for the US military attack on the Al Jazeera bureau in Kabul, Afghanistan.

8. About what is revealed by the leaked recordings, Joanna Tidy (2017, 102) writes: "Wikileaks presented an unsettling alternative account of the experience of viewing and waging war from above, 'writing' the Apache crew not as the all-seeing paragons of American military power that Western populations are typically expected to respect and endorse, but as paradoxically blinkered by the visual modes they operated within."

NOTES TO CHAPTER 3   201

9. For a more detailed description of the aftereffects of the attack, how the military attempted to avoid responsibility or accountability for what are likely war crimes, and some of the aftereffects on Chmagh and Eldeen's colleagues at Reuters, see Daley (2020). It is notable too that despite drawing the most worldwide media attention of any of Wikileaks' leaks, "Collateral Murder" is never mentioned in US prosecutors' charges against Assange.

10. The Iraqi Governing Council (13 July 2003–1 June 2004) was a council of Iraqis set up by and under the authority of the Coalition Provisional Authority.

11. The imperial plunder of archives extends into the more recent past. In 2018, The New York Times was accused of pilfering archives of more than fifteen thousand pages from the Islamic State in Iraq (SAA 2018).

3. LIVING IN THE TRANSIT CITY

1. I conceptualize this stance as one of ambivalent refusal because, unlike resistance, refusal involves the assertion of a relation of equality, even if enacted on unequal terrain (McGranahan 2016; Simpson 2014).

2. Two-thirds of the Egyptians who reside abroad have traveled to work in Arab states, especially Saudi Arabia, Jordan, and the United Arab Emirates, although there are also large Egyptian diasporas in Europe and North America. Short- or long-term labor migration has increasingly become a gendered social fact in Egypt, with young men, especially from more rural areas, aspiring and feeling pressured to migrate to urban areas and internationally (Schielke 2020).

3. With so much attention focused on contemporary displacement from and within the Middle East, the histories of European refugees in Egypt as well as in the wider Middle East are often forgotten. In the twentieth century, diverse groups of European refugees sought refuge in Egypt. When the Armenian genocide began in 1915, Armenians fled to Egypt where they joined an already existing Armenian population and settled predominantly in Cairo and Alexandria. Following the Bolshevik revolution in 1917, the British evacuated White Russian refugees to Egypt, which was by then a British protectorate (Konn-Roberts 2021). Between 1944 and 1946, some thirty thousand Croats, many of them women and children, fled the Nazi occupation of the Dalmatian coast and, after fleeing to southern Italy with the help of the British Navy and Yugoslav partisans, found their way to a former British Army post transformed into a makeshift camp in the Egyptian desert (Bieber 2020). The role of imperial violence in these displacements as well as how imperial infrastructure was conscripted into both moving displaced populations and then providing aid to them in Egypt would be echoed in the experiences of Iraqi displacement and exile in Egypt, even if the material conditions and empires in question are different.

202 NOTES TO CHAPTER 3

4. The 1951 Convention is one part of the larger post-World War II human rights framework. Signed in the immediate aftermath of the mass population displacements of those who fled the Nazi regime, the Convention initially restricted the right to asylum to European refugees who had fled prior to 1951. As Abuya et al. (2021) note, this geographic and temporal restriction was neither reflective of the empirical reality of displacement at the time nor the majority position of states at the then newly formed United Nations. A tendency to focus on the role of Western states, and European states especially, in the post-World War II human rights system obscures the role of decolonizing states in the development of international law. Several Arab states—Egypt, Iraq, Lebanon, and Saudi Arabia—participated in drafting the 1951 Convention but ultimately refused to sign when it became clear that other states were unwilling to seriously address the issue of Palestinian refugees. Over the objections of primarily newly independent or postcolonial states, colonial empires rejected a more global definition of a refugee. In the years following 1951, newly decolonized states pressured the UN to adopt what would become the 1967 Protocol to the Convention, which dropped the geographic and temporal restrictions on who could become a refugee—thereby creating a global refugee protection regime instead of one confined to Europe—but otherwise left the definition of a refugee intact.

5. The *Nakba* refers to the expulsion and ethnic cleansing of some 750,000 Palestinians, many to neighboring Arab-majority countries, during the founding of the State of Israel. Scholars have noted that the Nakba is not a singular event but an ongoing process (Abu Hatoum 2021), which is reflected by the ongoing importance of Palestinian displacement in the refugee politics of the region.

6. However, because Palestinian refugees fall under the mandate of the United Nations Relief and Works Agency (UNRWA)—the UN Agency set up to support and manage displaced Palestinians in the aftermath of the Nakba—the memorandum of understanding did not apply to Palestinians in Egypt. Because UNRWA has not had a presence in Egypt, and because UNHCR does not offer services to Palestinians, Palestinians in the country have historically lacked international protection.

7. Such border policies have been deadly for refugees on a number of occasions. Egypt entered into an agreement with Israel to stop African refugees (labeled "infiltrators" by the Israeli government) who were trying to cross through Egypt into Israel. The resulting "shoot-to-stop" policy claimed many lives. In 2009, Egyptian border guards shot dead thirty-three refugees who were trying to leave Egypt for Israel through the Sinai border (Abdelaaty 2021). The Mediterranean route has also been deadly for people, including Egyptians, who seek to travel to Europe. In 2016, a boat carrying six hundred people attempting to make the crossing to Italy sank off the coast of the Beheira Governorate in northern Egypt in what came to be called the Rashid tragedy. Some two hundred people drowned or went missing. The Egyptian government, like other North

African states, has received significant encouragement and incentivization by Europe to implement antismuggling laws in an effort to slow migration from Africa to Europe (Rollins 2017). See Heck and Habersky (2024) for discussion of more recent European border externalization efforts in Egypt.

8. Darryl Li (2019, 198) writes about this transnational carceral circuit as a "sovereign underground: a network of sites, practices, technologies, and discourses that is transnational in nature." Within the context of US empire, this network allows the US to go after those it deems enemies by enlisting other sovereign states, and sometimes nonstate actors, to participate in its goals, thus rendering some practices invisible and minimizing US responsibility.

9. Chatty and Mansour (2011, 100) note that Jordan and Syria both classified Iraqis as guests to avoid giving them the legal status and potential longevity that both states associate with Palestinian refugees. They also document how some Iraqis in Jordan and Syria do not self-identify as refugees.

10. The Egyptian revolution of 2011 briefly changed how Cairo felt for many Iraqis. After more than a year of fieldwork, I reluctantly left Egypt in the summer of 2010. A few months after I returned to the United States, a twenty-six-year-old fruit seller, Mohamed Bouazizi, set himself alight in Ben Arous, Tunisia. When Bouazizi did not have the money to pay a bribe, police refused to allow him to operate his cart, violently seizing his wares and equipment and effectively denying him the means to support himself and his family. Bouazizi's gesture resonated with other young people who also saw their life possibilities constrained by rising social, political, and economic inequality as well as police violence and autocratic rule. They turned out for massive protests, and by January 2011, Tunisian president Ben Ali had stepped down and fled the country, inspiring a wave of protests around the region and, eventually, around the world. Protests followed in Egypt, Bahrain, Iraq, Jordan, Libya, Saudi Arabia, Syria, and Yemen, among others. On January 25, 2011, hundreds of thousands of people occupied Cairo's Tahrir Square, which became both the epicenter and symbol of the revolution.

I had been caught up in the hope, emotion, and drama of the revolution, watching as Egyptians came together in Tahrir Square and across the country to demand something better. When I returned to Egypt in 2012, those of my Iraqi friends who remained had many stories to tell about their time living in Egypt during the revolution. I was initially dismayed by the more cautious and pessimistic tenor of their reflections on the revolution. But as the years have passed, I realize that in many ways, they were more prepared for the counterrevolutionary moment than I was. They reminded me that they had lived through an authoritarian government and they had lived through regime change, even if by very different means, and while some of my younger Iraqi friends were excited by the events in Egypt, similar but much smaller protests in Iraq, and other developments in the region, many were wary if not afraid of what they experienced as increased instability and lawlessness.

204   NOTES TO CHAPTER 3

11. The metaphor of the camp evokes the subjugation, confinement, and "outsideness" of displacement for theorists like Arendt and Agamben, leading them to deplore the condition of "bare life"—the human stripped of the political, of the "right to have rights." Actual camps are much messier places that shape refugee lives (Feldman 2015) and politics, creating space for refugees to develop alternative political subjectivities that exceed the space of the camp (Malkki 1995a). More recently, scholars have noted how the camp can be a generative site for refugee politics or for reconceiving politics more generally (Allan 2013; Abourahme 2020). But urban displacement, which varies from place to place, of course, gives rise to a different kind of politics. In particular it creates an opportunity for refugees to relate differently to the refugee concept and perhaps to refuse it and choose different kinds of identifications. But urban Cairo as a site of displacement does not offer these same easy demarcations.

12. Analytically, studying urban displacement offers a possibility for recognizing the complexity of refugee experiences without focusing either exclusively on state sovereignty or on extraterritorial forms of border control, such as islands, offshore detention sites, and other forms of exceptional, if increasingly common, border enforcement.

13. Usually known just as *Seta Oktober* or simply *Oktober*, 6th of October City is a satellite town some thirty-two kilometers (twenty miles) to the west of downtown Cairo, established in 1979 by then Egyptian president Anwar al-Sadat. It is named for the October War, which began on the 6th of October 1973. Home to an industrial zone and seven private universities, 6th of October's population includes many Egyptian and international students. The UNHCR compound is also located in 6th of October. Much quieter than downtown Cairo, 6th of October seems perpetually under construction, with half-finished apartment buildings throughout its landscape. The air is cooler there, and cleaner. There is more space between apartment blocks and it's quieter than the city.

Nasr City is a residential and commercial district of Cairo located to the east of the city, dominated by towering condo blocks. Nasr City was established in the 1960s as part of efforts to modernize Cairo after the Egyptian revolution of 1952. Its name means "victory" in Arabic. Divided into ten neighborhoods, the sprawling district has significant socioeconomic diversity. The tenth neighborhood (Hay el-Asher) is home to many refugees and migrants, including a large population of Sudanese and Somalis.

Giza, southwest of Cairo, is technically a separate governorate, although it blends seamlessly into Cairo. Although it is most famous for the Great Pyramids of Giza and the Great Sphinx, the archeological and tourist industry is only one part of the larger agglomeration of neighborhoods that make up Giza, including working-class neighborhoods like Bulaq and Imbaba as well as prosperous areas like Mohandisin, the former site of the Cairo UNHCR office.

14. Published sources indicate a range from 1.5 to 7 or more million Egyptian migrant workers, depending on the time and the source. See Carroll (2013) and Feiler (1991). During fieldwork, the number I heard repeatedly was seven million, so I include it here as an upper limit with the recognition that precise numbers are unlikely to be available.

The relationship between Iraq and Egypt was, of course, complicated. At the end of the 1970s, Iraq was extremely critical of Egypt for entering into the 1978 Camp David Accords with Israel. At the same time, Egyptian migrant labor was growing and Egypt was selling weapons to Iraq and training Iraqi students and advisors.

15. Egypt governed Gaza until 1967, although the Egyptian state did not formally seek sovereignty over the territory but rather imagined itself as caretaking a space for Palestinians (Feldman 2007). Two-thirds of Gaza's population are Palestinian refugees.

4. NEGOTIATING HUMANITARIAN "SOLUTIONS" TO DISPLACEMENT

1. By *resettlement*, I mean the process of seeking or applying for resettlement.

2. Ambivalence has been variously theorized as psychological or dispositional, that is, the coupling of competing desires or feelings (Jovanović 2016); as intersubjective, arising from the emotional and material valences of human relationships (Segal 2016); and as sociological, emerging from contradictions within social roles and positions (Merton 1976). Here, I instead use ambivalence as a hermeneutic to read how the structural contours of war, displacement, and humanitarian bureaucracies are entangled in personal projects and aspirations, engendering the copresence and lived experience of contradiction. While the psychological definition tends to view ambivalence as disordered, I pursue a different valence to consider how ambivalence foregrounds a thinking, feeling, acting, and desiring subject as they navigate an impossible situation.

3. Resettlement is not one policy but rather a complex transnational assemblage of laws, practices, and guidelines that vary across time, place, and population.

4. In 2018, the UNHCR referred resettlement cases to twenty-nine countries (UNHCR 2019). Many states take few cases, while others have larger, well-established programs. For an overview of contemporary programs, see Cellini (2018).

5. It is difficult to say with any accuracy what percentage of refugees seek resettlement. This is so because the process—perhaps it would be more accurate to say processes—is so heterogenous across time and place. Even in Cairo at the

time of my fieldwork, it was challenging to know how many refugees sought resettlement. Except in the case of the Direct Access Program, the authorities discouraged people from "seeking resettlement" and did not count those who did. I observed, however, that Iraqis and other refugee populations in Cairo did pursue resettlement in ways that were sometimes officially acknowledged. Despite the absence of information that centers refugees' own pursuits of or interest in resettlement, we can see a discrepancy between the UNHCR's assessment of how many refugees need resettlement, how many they refer to resettlement countries, and how many people are actually resettled in a given year (for a recent example, see UNHCR [2021]).

6. By contrast, Retika Adhikari (2021) shows how Bhutanese refugees in Nepal who were awaiting resettlement in the United States did not anticipate hopeful futures but, after having learned about resettlement from friends who had preceded them, rather used their time in the camps to prepare to enter marginal positions in US labor hierarchies. The situation of Bhutanese refugees in Nepal is different from Iraqis but interesting to consider alongside them because both populations were being resettled to the US in relatively large numbers at about the same time. Nepali-speaking Bhutanese, who had been rendered stateless and expelled by Bhutan, did not have the same experiences of imperial intervention that Iraqis did and were not securitized in the same ways. Indeed, I heard from at least one resettlement worker that the US resettled Bhutanese in such numbers because, as a non-Muslim, non-Arab population unconnected to the Global War on Terror, they were seen to be much less of a security concern than Iraqis. Bhutanese also differed from Iraqis in that they lived in refugee camps for many years before being subject to a large-scale resettlement program.

7. From 2007 to 2021, 1,004,023 refugees of all nationalities were resettled. Of these, 131,652 were Iraqis, 89,405 of whom were resettled to the US (UNHCR n.d.).

8. The act also authorized the resettlement of some religious minorities and five thousand annual special immigrant visas for translators or contractors who provided "faithful service" to the US government (Congress.gov 2007).

9. Advocates for resettlement, notably The List Project to Resettle Iraqi Allies, invoked imagery of the fall of Saigon—when Vietnamese employees were left behind on rooftops as helicopters whisked American staff to safety—to argue that the occupying forces had a moral responsibility to resettle Iraqis who worked with them (Johnson 2010).

10. See Malkki (1992) for a critical discussion of how the figure of the refugee, through their exclusion, shores up the category of the nation-state.

11. The revised 2011 version of the resettlement handbook contains a similar sentiment: "UNHCR identifies refugees for resettlement based on a refugee's objective *need* for resettlement and not on their subjective *desire* for it" (UNHCR 2011, 216).

12. Omar Dewachi (2011, 2017) has written extensively about how Iraq's effective medical and public health systems were decimated by US-led sanctions and wars. Prior to the embargo, Iraq's health and education systems reached the majority of the population, and robust infrastructure also contributed to improvements in indicators of population health, such as infant and under-five mortality rates.

13. The inequalities between participants in humanitarianism, including givers and receivers as well as international staff and local or national staff, reproduce what Didier Fassin (2012, 233) has described as the "asymmetry of lives" at the center of humanitarianism. Didier Fassin (2011, 2010), Ilana Feldman and Miriam Ticktin (2010), Peter Redfield (2013), and Rania Sweis (2019) have all written about how humanitarian power structures mirror global inequities in terms of rights, resources, and access to mobility. Sweis has described what she calls a "hierarchy of humanitarians" in which national staff or humanitarians from the diaspora are precariously positioned as less deserving of protection, remuneration, and mobility than expatriate staff. Adia Benton (2016) has shown how structural racism permeates all aspects of the daily practice of humanitarianism, not only between humanitarian aid workers and recipients but also among humanitarian workers themselves. Humanitarian structures in Cairo reflected these hierarchies to a certain extent. On the one hand, some humanitarians (and here I use the term *humanitarian* very broadly to mean anyone engaged in work in the humanitarian realm) were able to travel easily between Egypt and the West without visas while others, including many Egyptian staff, did not have the same mobility. Egyptian staff of organizations such as the UNHCR or the IOM had significant power over refugees, yet refugees did not always respect their authority, as when Iraqis accused Egyptian interpreters of making translation mistakes in interviews, or of Egyptian staff making errors in files, et cetera. Also within the humanitarian workforce in Egypt are many refugees, such as Um Muhammad, Shams, and Haydar, some of whom are paid and others of whom labor as volunteers. Iraqis who worked at RLAP and in other organizations offered different reasons for doing so: The limited number of paid humanitarian positions offered some of the only remunerated work available to Iraqis. Some were able to use skills such as medical training, office management and logistics, organizing, language abilities, and other skills that they wanted to practice, given that they were otherwise denied the opportunity in Egypt. Some wanted to understand the humanitarian system better to increase their chances of resettlement or their ability to access aid. Some, like Um Muhammad, wanted to help their community. Some told me that they just wanted something to do to fill the long days, and this work gave them the opportunity to spend time with people.

14. The handbook specifies that the medical condition must be life threatening or impair function or limit a refugee's ability to live "a normal life and achieve

208   NOTES TO CHAPTER 4

self sufficiency" and that treatment must be available in the resettlement country that is not available or accessible in the country of asylum (UNHCR 2004, 70). The handbook notes that the UNHCR draws on qualified medical personnel to make such determinations, and this was the case in Cairo, where physicians would refer resettlement cases to the UNHCR for consideration.

15. On the gratefulness imposed on refugees, see Nayeri (2019).

16. According to such critics, who justify objections in the name of security, the solution is to limit or end refugee resettlement or to put it on hold until more stringent security procedures can be implemented. That these concerns have no basis in fact—no resettled refugees have been convicted of terrorism-related offenses in the US—has not limited their exclusionary force.

17. It was precisely on these grounds that women, those without land, religious minorities, et cetera were denied full political rights of participation in the West until relatively recently.

5. ALLIES AND ENEMIES

1. The displacement associated with the Arab Spring also led to the first refugee camp in Egypt's recent history, the Salloum camp, set up on the border with Libya in 2011.

2. Syrians' treatment by the Morsi government was not only a result of humanitarian sentiment but also represented the government's desire to support the Syrian opposition. After a military coup overthrew Morsi's government in 2013, the new military government launched a media campaign to portray Syrian refugees as "terrorists" and supporters of Morsi and the Muslim brotherhood (Norman 2017). The increasingly hostile treatment of Syrian refugees, alongside the difficulty of leaving Egypt in other ways, is one reason why more Syrians began to attempt dangerous boat journeys from Egyptian coastal cities to Europe in the aftermath of the 2013 coup.

3. The petition claimed to represent Iraqis who had been referred for resettlement to the US by the UNHCR as well as those who had applied directly for resettlement to the US through the IOM because of their association with the US.

4. At the time of my fieldwork, the IOM was not yet part of the UN system. It became a UN agency in 2016.

5. See Johnson (2013) for a thorough account of the campaign to pass the Refugee Crisis in Iraq Act.

6. Not all Iraqi refugees, including the ones that I worked with, were Muslim. However despite not all being Muslim or Arab, Iraqis as a whole were subject to Islamophobic and anti-Arab discrimination within the war and in resettlement programs. The targets of Islamophobia are a heterogeneous group of people,

NOTES TO CHAPTER 5   209

many of whom are neither Muslims nor Arabs. What characterizes them is their designation as either terrorists or potential terrorists (Cainkar and Selod 2018).

7. This is consistent with an understanding of Islamophobia and anti-Arab racism as both US and global structures and processes (Rana 2011).

8. See Saleh (2020) for a nuanced and historicized discussion of the role of Iraqi exiles in imperial politics.

9. The graphic images of US military personnel and private contractors torturing Iraqi detainees in Abu Ghraib prison outraged the world when they were released in 2004. In November 2024, a US court ordered CACI Premier Technology Inc., a private contractor that had been Involved in the torture of Iraqi prisoners in Abu Ghraib, to pay forty-two million dollars in damages. The Center for Constitutional Rights worked with the men to bring the case in 2008. The verdict, twenty years after the abuses took place and nearly fifteen since the case was filed, represents the first time a defense contractor has been held responsible for the torture and mistreatment at Abu Ghraib. Although eleven soldiers were convicted in US military courts for their conduct in the prison, the US government has not offered any compensation or redress to detainees (Sanbar 2024).

10. In 2014, after a lengthy and challenging investigation and legal process, four former Blackwater guards were convicted of crimes including murder and manslaughter for their role in the massacre. In 2020, President Trump pardoned the guards as one of his last acts in office. Even before the pardons, some Iraqi observers noted that the men had been held responsible not for committing war crimes and for the harm they caused Iraqi civilians but for violating the rules of engagement (Hassan and Arraf 2020).

11. Campbell (2016) describes the differential experiences of work, risk, and prestige of Iraqis who interpreted "on base" as opposed to those who went out "on mission," that is, those who worked on military bases in a variety of capacities (e.g., as personal interpreters to officials, in interrogations, at high level meetings) and those who traveled off military bases. Interpreters who worked on base were more often women; the occupiers imagined Iraqi women as more vulnerable than men and therefore tended to choose them for the nominally safer work "on base." Such work involved more technical interpretation and had greater prestige but was described as challenging and boring by Campbell's interlocutors. Interpreters "on mission" reported the work as much more dangerous and challenging in different ways, as they had to accompany their bosses, often combat units, on military patrols that involved going out into communities and could occur unpredictably at all hours of the day or night.

12. See Al-Ali and Pratt (2009) for a larger discussion of how gendered discourse of "liberating" Iraqi women (from Iraqi men) was used to justify the war. Al-Ali and Pratt show how, contrary to this rhetoric, the war in fact had the opposite effect of eroding and limiting women's roles and status. See also Abu-Lughod (2002).

210 NOTES TO CHAPTER 5

13. See, for example, National Public Radio (2014). For a scholarly discussion of the experience and idiom of militarized brotherhood in the context of the War on Terror (albeit in Afghanistan), see Jong (2022) and Campbell (2016). Jong argues that despite the fact that locally employed Afghan interpreters often spoke of relationships of brotherhood with the Western soldiers with whom they worked, these relations were always conditional, hierarchal, and uneven, what she calls "segregated brotherhood." In Iraq, Campbell argues that idioms of brotherhood were one way of coping with and pushing back against the constant suspicion that locally-employed Iraqi interpreters faced.

14. Titan Corp was acquired by L-3 Communications, a New York–based defense contractor, in 2005.

15. For the sake of simplicity, I do not discuss the special immigrant visa (SIV) program in detail here. The SIV program preceded the refugee crisis in Iraq, had more stringent application processes, focused exclusively on interpreters, and was always a much smaller program. Section 1059 of the National Defense Authorization Act for Fiscal Year 2006 initially allowed for only a maximum of fifty SIVs for Iraqi or Afghan translators/interpreters who worked with the US forces in Iraq or Afghanistan and their spouses and children. In 2007, President George W. Bush extended the law to authorize five hundred visas for fiscal years 2007 and 2008. SIV holders are classified not as refugees but as permanent employment-based immigrants under the Immigration and Nationality Act. While a separate category from refugees, the SIV holders would receive the same benefits as resettled refugees on admission to the United States. However, unlike refugees, who must wait a year before they can apply for permanent residence, SIV holders are granted permanent-resident status immediately upon admission to the United States. The program expired in 2013, although the application process was extended into 2014. From 2007 through the end of 2015, 17,561 Iraqi individuals, including principal applicants and dependents, had been granted SIVs. The Refugee Crisis in Iraq Act and the Afghan Allies Protection Act established SIV programs to prioritize resettlement of Iraqis and Afghans who worked for the US government (Abramson 2015). Both acts have failed to achieve their goals and targets.

16. This definition applies to P2 processing, one of three forms of resettlement processing (P1, P2, P3). These designations are the priority categories set by the US government for refugee resettlement each year. Priority 1 refers to resettlement cases identified by an intermediary such as the UNHCR, a US embassy, or certain recognized NGOs. The Iraqis whose experiences of resettlement I described in chapter 4 would have been considered under Priority 1. Priority 2 are for groups identified for special concern by the US refugee program. This would include Iraqis who were associated with the United States. Priority 3 is designated for family reunification for refugees or asylum seekers already in the country. It applies only to immediate family members and is

available to designated nationalities only (Bureau of Population, Relations, and Migration 2020).

17. For example, the Bowling Green chief of police asked in a story for *ABC News:* "How do you have somebody that we now know was a known actor in terrorism overseas, how does that person get into the United States? How do they get into our community?" (Meek et al. 2013).

18. Indeed, the US government's decision to review the cases of Iraqis already in the United States and presumably with refugee status, permanent residency, or citizenship, illustrates how legal status is not sufficient protection against the suspicion that one is a threat and also that solutions to displacement are contingent. This enduring threat evokes Ghassan Hage's (2016) formulation of reverse colonialism, which he articulates as the way that colonizers come to imagine that the people whom they are besieging are actually the ones committing violence against them.

19. A particularly upsetting example is the experience of Jimmy Aldaoud, documented by *The New York Times* in 2019. Aldaoud was born in a refugee camp in Greece to Iraqi parents and moved to the United States at six months old. He struggled with serious mental health issues and had received at least twenty criminal convictions. In 2019, Immigrations and Customs Enforcement deported Aldaoud to Iraq, a country where he had never been, did not speak the language, knew no one, and did not have access to his medications. He died alone in a Baghdad apartment two months after being deported (Rubin and Bogel-Burroughs 2019).

CONCLUSION: ARRIVAL

1. The ban was actually a series of bans as the initial executive order was challenged in court and the Trump administration revised it in response to each subsequent court challenge. The first iteration, executive order 13769, Protecting the Nation from Foreign Terrorist Entry into the United States, banned travel from Iraq, Iran, Libya, Somalia, Sudan, Syria, and Yemen for ninety days, suspended the refugee resettlement program for 120 days, and suspended the entry of Syrian refugees indefinitely.

2. For the first time since the passage of the Refugee Act in 1980, the US was no longer the country that resettled the most refugees in the world (Gowayed 2022).

References

Abdelaaty, Lamis Elmy. 2021. *Discrimination and Delegation: Explaining State Responses to Refugees*. Oxford: Oxford University Press.

Abdullah, Kifah N. 2008. "When Egyptians Lived in Iraq." *Iraqis in Egypt, Voices* (blog). August 5. http://www.iraqisinegypt.org/whenegyptians.html.

Abourahme, Nasser. 2020. "The Camp." *Comparative Studies of South Asia, Africa and the Middle East* 40 (1): 35–42. https://doi.org/10.1215/1089201X-8186016.

Abramson, Nadia. 2015. "Wasting My Time in the Waiting Line: Solutions for Improving the Afghanistan and Iraq Special Immigrant Visa Programs." *Virginia Journal of International Law* 55 (2): 483–519.

Abu El-Haj, Nadia. 2022. *Combat Trama: Imaginaries of War and Citizenship in post-9/11 America*. New York: Verso

Abu Hatoum, Nayrouz. 2021. "Decolonizing [in the] Future: Scenes of Palestinian Temporality." *Geografiska Annaler: Series B, Human Geography* 103 (4): 397–412. https://doi.org/10.1080/04353684.2021.1963806.

Abu-Lughod, Lila. 2002. "Do Muslim Women Really Need Saving? Anthropological Reflections on Cultural Relativism and Its Others." *American Anthropologist* 104 (3): 783–90.

Abuya, Edwin O., Ulrike Krause, and Lucy Mayblin. 2021. "The Neglected Colonial Legacy of the 1951 Refugee Convention." *International Migration* 59 (4): 265–67.

REFERENCES

Adhikari, Retika. 2021. "Temporalities of Resettlement: Date-Waiting for an American Future in a Bhutanese Refugee Camp in Nepal." *American Anthropologist* 123 (2): 237–49.

Agamben, Giorgio. 1998. *Homo Sacer: Sovereign Power and Bare Life*. Stanford, CA: Stanford University Press.

———. 2005. *State Of Exception*. Chicago: University of Chicago Press.

Agier, Michel. 2011. *Managing the Undesirables: Refugee Camps and Humanitarian Government*. Malden, MA: Polity Press.

Al-Ali, Nadje. 2005. "Reconstructing Gender: Iraqi Women between Dictatorship, War, Sanctions and Occupation." *Third World Quarterly* 26 (4–5): 739–58.

———. 2007. *Iraqi Women: Untold Stories from 1948 to the Present*. London; New York: Zed Books.

Al-Ali, Nadje Sadig, and Deborah Al-Najjar, eds. 2013. *We Are Iraqis: Aesthetics and Politics in a Time of War*. First Edition. Contemporary Issues in the Middle East. Syracuse: Syracuse University Press.

Al-Ali, Nadje Sadig, and Nicola Christine Pratt. 2009. *What Kind of Liberation? Women and the Occupation of Iraq*. Berkeley, CA: University of California Press.

Ali, Ali. 2012. "Displacement in Iraq after 2003: Coerced Decisions in a Time of Crisis." PhD Thesis, University of East London.

———. 2020. "3. Baghdad: War and Insecurity in the City." In *Cities at War*, edited by Mary Kaldor and Saskia Sassen, 78–102. New York: Columbia University Press.

Ali, Zahra. 2018. *Women and Gender in Iraq: Between Nation-Building and Fragmentation*. Cambridge, UK: Cambridge University Press.

———. 2020. "The Civic and the Popular: Reflections on the Iraqi Uprising." *Immanent Frame* (blog), Social Science Research Council, April 29. https://tif.ssrc.org/2020/04/29/the-civic-and-the-popular/.

Allan, Diana. 2013. *Refugees of the Revolution: Experiences of Palestinian Exile*. 1st edition. Stanford, CA: Stanford University Press.

Al-Mohammad, Hayder. 2010. "Relying on One's Tribe: A Snippet of Life in Basra since the 2003 Invasion." *Anthropology Today* 26 (6): 23–26. https://doi.org/10.1111/j.1467-8322.2010.00772.x.

———. 2010. "Towards an Ethics of Being-With: Intertwinements of Life in Post-Invasion Basra." *Ethnos: Journal of Anthropology* 75 (4): 425. https://doi.org/10.1080/00141844.2010.544394.

———. 2012. "A Kidnapping in Basra: The Struggles and Precariousness of Life in Postinvasion Iraq." *Cultural Anthropology* 27 (4): 597–614.

Alshaibi, Wisam H. 2019. "Weaponizing Iraq's Archives." *MERIP* 291 (Summer). https://merip.org/2019/09/weaponizing-iraqs-archives/.

REFERENCES

Al-Tikriti, Nabil. 2007. "'Stuff Happens': A Brief Overview of the 2003 Destruction of Iraqi Manuscript Collections, Archives, and Libraries." *Library Trends* 55 (3): 730–45. https://doi.org/10.1353/lib.2007.0000.

Andersson, Ruben. 2014. *Illegality, Inc.: Clandestine Migration and the Business of Bordering Europe*. Berkeley, CA: University of California Press.

Anghie, Antony. 2005. *Imperialism, Sovereignty and the Making of International Law*. Cambridge, UK: Cambridge University Press.

———. 2007. "The Evolution of International Law: Colonial and Postcolonial Realities." *Third World Quarterly*, January. https://doi.org/10.1080/01436590600780011.

Antoon, Sinan. 2019. *The Book of Collateral Damage*. Translated by Jonathan Wright. New Haven, CT: Yale University Press.

Arango, Tim. 2011. "Visa Delays Put Iraqis Who Aided U.S. in Fear." *The New York Times*, July 12, sec. World. https://www.nytimes.com/2011/07/13/world/middleeast/13baghdad.html.

Arendt, Hannah. 2008. *The Jewish Writings*. New York: Schocken Books.

Asad, Talal. 1986. "The Concept of Cultural Translation in British Social Anthropology." In *Writing Culture: The Poetics and Politics of Ethnography*, edited by James Clifford and George Marcus. Berkeley, CA: University of California Press.

Azimi, Negar. 2018. "Remembering Barbara Harrell-Bond, A Fierce Advocate for Refugees." *The Nation*. November 12. https://www.thenation.com/article/archive/remembering-barbara-harrell-bond-a-fierce-advocate-for-refugees/.

Azoulay, Ariella. 2016. "Photography Consists of Collaboration: Susan Meiselas, Wendy Ewald, and Ariella Azoulay." *Camera Obscura: Feminism, Culture, and Media Studies* 31 (1): 187–201.

Badawy, Tarek. 2010. "The Memorandum of Understanding between Egypt and the Office of the United Nations High Commissioner for Refugees: Problems and Recommendations." CARIM AS 2010/07, Robert Schuman Centre for Advanced Studies. San Domenico di Fiesole, Italy: European University Institute.

Baker, Mona. 2010. "Interpreters and Translators in the War Zone: Narrated and Narrators." *The Translator* 16 (2): 197–222.

Baker, Yousef K. 2020. "Iraqi Protesters Thwarted by Trump's Iran Policy." *MERIP*, February. https://merip.org/2020/02/iraqi-protesters-thwarted-by-trumps-iran-policy/.

Baldor, Lolita C. 2020. "US General Sees Smaller but Enduring Troop Presence in Iraq." *Washington Post,* July 8. https://www.washingtonpost.com/world/national-security/us-general-sees-smaller-but-enduring-troop-presence-in-iraq/2020/07/08/7bf9d6c6-c0d1-11ea-8908-68a2b9eae9e0_story.html.

REFERENCES

Becker, Gay. 1997. *Disrupted Lives: How People Create Meaning in a Chaotic World*. Berkeley: University of California Press.

Benton, Adia. 2016. African Expatriates and Race in the Anthropology of Humanitarianism." *Critical African Studies* 8 (3): 266–77.

Berman, Chantal. 2011. "Bordering on Conventional: Politics of Iraqi Resettlement to the US and Europe, 2003–2011." *Refuge* 28, no. 1 (Spring): 123–36.

Besteman, Catherine. 2016. *Making Refuge: Somali Bantu Refugees and Lewiston, Maine*. Durham, NC: Duke University Press.

———. 2019. "Militarized Global Apartheid." *Current Anthropology* 60 (S19): S26–38. https://doi.org/10.1086/699280.

Betts, Alexander. 2015. "The Normative Terrain of the Global Refugee Regime." *Ethics & International Affairs*, October. https://www.ethicsandinternationalaffairs.org/journal/the-normative-terrain-of-the-global-refugee-regime.

Bieber, Florian. 2020. "Building Yugoslavia in the Sand? Dalmatian Refugees in Egypt, 1944–1946." *Slavic Review* 79 (2): 298–322.

Biehl, Kristen Sarah. 2015. "Governing through Uncertainty: Experiences of Being a Refugee in Turkey as a Country for Temporary Asylum." *Social Analysis* 59 (1): 57–75.

Bohmer, Carol, and Amy Shuman. 2007. *Rejecting Refugees: Political Asylum in the 21st Century*. London: Routledge.

Bonet, Sally Wesley. 2022. *Meaningless Citizenship: Iraqi Refugees and the Welfare State*. Minneapolis, MN: University of Minnesota Press.

Bourdieu, Pierre. 1997. *Pascalian Meditations*. Stanford, CA: Stanford University Press.

Browne, Simone. 2015. *Dark Matters: On the Surveillance of Blackness*. Illustrated edition. Durham, NC: Duke University Press Books.

Brun, Cathrine. 2015. "Active Waiting and Changing Hopes: Toward a Time Perspective on Protracted Displacement." *Social Analysis* 59 (1): 19–37.

Bureau of Population, Refugees, and Migration. 2020. U.S. Refugee Admissions Program Access Categories. US Department of State. https://2017-2021.state.gov/refugee-admissions/u-s-refugee-admissions-program-access-categories/

Butler, Judith. 2016. *Frames of War: When Is Life Grievable?* London: Verso Books.

Cabot, Heath. 2012. "The Governance of Things: Documenting Limbo in the Greek Asylum Procedure." *PoLAR: Political and Legal Anthropology Review* 35 (1): 11–29. https://doi.org/10.1111/j.1555-2934.2012.01177.x.

———. 2013. "The Social Aesthetics of Eligibility: NGO Aid and Indeterminacy in the Greek Asylum Process." *American Ethnologist* 40 (3): 452–66.

Cainkar, Louise, and Saher Selod. 2018. "Review of Race Scholarship and the War on Terror." *Sociology of Race and Ethnicity* 4 (2): 165–77. https://doi.org/10.1177/2332649218762808.

REFERENCES 217

Campbell, Madeline Otis. 2016. *Interpreters of Occupation: Gender and the Politics of Belonging in an Iraqi Refugee Network*. Reprint edition. Syracuse, NY: Syracuse University Press.

Carroll, Lindsay. 2013. "There and Back Again: Egyptian Workers Remember Their Time in Iraq." *Egypt Independent*, March 21. https://egyptindependent.com/there-and-back-again-egyptian-workers-remember-their-time-iraq/.

Caswell, Michelle. 2011. "'Thank You Very Much, Now Give Them Back': Cultural Property and the Fight over the Iraqi Baath Party Records." *The American Archivist* 74 (1): 211–40.

Cellini, Amanda. 2018. "Current Refugee Resettlement Program Profiles." In *Refugee Resettlement: Power, Politics, and Humanitarian Governance*, edited by Adèle Garnier, Liliana Lyra Jubilut, and Kristin Bergtora Sandvik, 253–305. Oxford: Berghahn.

Chandrasekaran, Rajiv. 2006. *Imperial Life in the Emerald City: Inside Iraq's Green Zone*. New York: Vintage.

Chatty, Dawn. 2013. "Guests and Hosts." *The Cairo Review of Global Affairs* 9 (spring): 76–85.

Chatty, Dawn, and Nisrine Mansour. 2011. "Displaced Iraqis: Predicaments and Perceptions in Exile in the Middle East." *Refuge: Canada's Journal on Refugees* 28 (1): 97–108.

Chua, Jocelyn. 2014. *In Pursuit of the Good Life: Aspiration and Suicide in Globalizing South India*. Berkeley, CA: University of California Press.

Coburn, Noah. 2018a. "The Guards, Cooks, and Cleaners of the Afghan War: Migrant Contractors and the Cost of War." *Geopolitics, History and International Relations* 10 (2): 17–29. https://doi.org/10.22381/GHIR10220182.

———. 2018b. *Under Contract: The Invisible Workers of America's Global War*. Stanford, CA: Stanford University Press.

Coker, Elizabeth Marie. "'Traveling Pains': Embodied Metaphors of Suffering among Southern Sudanese Refugees in Cairo." *Culture, Medicine and Psychiatry* 28 (2004): 15–39.

Collins, John F., and Carole McGranahan. 2018. "Introduction: Ethnography and US Empire." In *Ethnographies of US Empire*, 1–24. Durham, NC: Duke University Press.

Congress.gov. 2007. "Text - S.1651 - 110th Congress (2007–2008): Refugee Crisis in Iraq Act." July 23. https://www.congress.gov/bill/110th-congress /senate-bill/1651/text.

Costs of War Project. 2023. Human Costs of Post 9/11 Wars. Providence, Rhode Island: Watson Institute for International and Public Affairs, Brown University. https://watson.brown.edu/costsofwar/figures/2021/WarDeathToll

Cowell, Alan. 1989. "Egyptian Laborers Are Fleeing Iraq." *The New York Times*, November 15, sec. World. https://www.nytimes.com/1989/11/15/world /egyptian-laborers-are-fleeing-iraq.html.

CPJ (Committee to Protect Journalists). n.d. "283 Journalists and Media Workers Killed in Iraq Between 1992 and 2022." Committee to Protect Journalists. https://cpj.org/data/killed/mideast/iraq/?status=Killed&motive Confirmed%5B%5D=Confirmed&motiveUnconfirmed%5B%5D=Unconfirm ed&type%5B%5D=Journalist&type%5B%5D=Media%20Worker&cc_ fips%5B%5D=IZ&start_year=1992&end_year=2022&group_by=location

———. 2006. "Iraq Report: Killed by U.S. Forces." Committee to Protect Journalists. https://cpj.org/reports/2006/01/js-killed-by-us-13sept05/

———. 2008. "Five Years after Deadly Palestine Hotel and Al-Jazeera Strikes, Unanswered Questions Linger." *Committee to Protect Journalists* (blog). April 7. https://cpj.org/2008/04/five-years-after-deadly-palestine-hotel-and-aljaze/

Crawford, Neta. 2013. *Accountability for Killing: Moral Responsibility for Collateral Damage in America's Post-9/11 Wars.* New York: Oxford University Press.

———. 2019. "Appendix: The Body Count." In *War and Health: The Medical Consequences of the Wars in Iraq and Afghanistan,* edited by Catherine Lutz and Andrea Mazzarino, 255–58. New York: New York University Press.

Crawford, Neta C., and Catherine Lutz. 2021. "Human Cost of Post-9/11 Wars: Direct War Deaths in Major War Zones, Afghanistan & Pakistan (Oct. 2001–Aug. 2021); Iraq (March 2003–Aug. 2021); Syria (Sept. 2014–May 2021); Yemen (Oct. 2002-Aug. 2021) and Other Post-9/11 War Zones. September 1, 2021. Published by the Costs of War Project." *Watson Institute for International and Public Affairs, Brown University.* https://watson.brown.edu/Costsofwar/Figures/2021/WarDeathToll.

CSCE (Commission on Security and Cooperation in Europe). 2015. *The Forgotten: Iraqi Allies Failed by the U.S.* Washington, DC: Commission on Security and Cooperation in Europe.

Çubukçu, Ayça. 2018. *For the Love of Humanity: The World Tribunal on Iraq.* Philadelphia: University of Pennsylvania Press.

Daley, Paul. 2020. "'All Lies': How the US Military Covered up Gunning down Two Journalists in Iraq." *The Guardian,* June 14, sec. US news. https://www.theguardian.com/us-news/2020/jun/15/all-lies-how-the-us-military-covered-up-gunning-down-two-journalists-in-iraq.

Damluji, Mona. 2015. "Introduction. Roundtable: Perspectives on Researching Iraq Today." *The Arab Studies Journal* 23 (1): 236–65.

Danewid, Ida. 2017. "White Innocence in the Black Mediterranean: Hospitality and the Erasure of History." *Third World Quarterly* 38 (7): 1674–89. https://doi.org/10.1080/01436597.2017.1331123.

Daniel, E. Valentine, and John Chr. Knudsen, eds. 1995. *Mistrusting Refugees.* Berkeley, CA: University of California Press.

Das, Veena. 2006. *Life and Words: Violence and the Descent into the Ordinary.* Berkeley, CA: University of California Press.

Das, Veena, Arthur Kleinman, Margaret Lock, Mamphela Ramphele, and Pamela Reynolds. 2001. *Remaking a World: Violence, Social Suffering, and Recovery.* 1st ed. Berkeley, CA: University of California Press.

Das, Veena, Arthur Kleinman, Mamphela Ramphele, and Pamela Reynolds. 2000. *Violence and Subjectivity.* 1st ed. Berkeley, CA: University of California Press.

Daulatzai, Anila. 2021. "Afghanistan: Serial Wat and the Cunning of Imperial Time." In *The Terror Trap: The Impact of the War on Terror on Muslim Communities since 9/11*, 105–11. Washington, DC: The Bridge Initiative. https://bridge.georgetown.edu/research/ the-terror-trap-the-impact-of-the-war-on-terror-on-muslim-communities- since-9-11/.

Daulatzai, Anila, and Sahar Ghumkhor. 2023. "Afghanistan, Racial Melancholia, and Loss That Exceeds Loss." *Critical Times* 6 (2): 202–11. https://doi .org/10.1215/26410478-10437138.

Davidson, Mark. 2009. "Displacement, Space and Dwelling: Placing Gentrification Debate." *Ethics, Place & Environment* 12 (2): 219–34. https://doi. org/10.1080/13668790902863465.

De Genova, Nicholas, ed. 2017. *The Borders of "Europe": Autonomy of Migration, Tactics of Bordering.* Durham, NC: Duke University Press.

De León, Jason. 2015. *The Land of Open Graves: Living and Dying on the Migrant Trail.* Oakland, CA: University of California Press.

Deloria, Vine. 1969. *Custer Died for Your Sins: An Indian Manifesto.* New York: Macmillan.

Deeb, Lara and Jessica Winegar. 2016. *Anthropology's Politics: Disciplining the Middle East.* Stanford, CA: Stanford University Press.

Dewachi, Omar. 2015. "When Wounds Travel." *Medicine Anthropology Theory* 2 (3): 61–82.

———. 2017. *Ungovernable Life: Mandatory Medicine and Statecraft in Iraq.* Stanford, CA: Stanford University Press.

Dickinson, Paul. 2020. "I Sued Blackwater for the Massacre of Iraqi Civilians. Trump Just Pardoned Those Convicted Killers." *The Intercept.* December 23. https://theintercept.com/2020/12/23/blackwater-massacre-iraq-pardons/.

Doraï, Kamel. 2024. "Refugees and the Urban Fabric: Palestinian and Syrian Settlement Patterns in Jordan." In *Urban Displacement*, edited by Are John Knudsen and Sarah A. Tobin, 189–209. Oxford: Berghahn.

Edwards, Elizabeth. 2016. "The Colonial Archival Imaginaire at Home." *Social Anthropology* 24 (1): 52–66. https://doi.org/10.1111/1469-8676.12283.

El-Abed, Oroub. 2005. "Palestinian Refugees of Egypt: What Exit Options Are Left for Them?" *Refuge: Canada's Periodical on Refugees* 22 (2): 15–30.

———. 2009. *Unprotected: Palestinians in Egypt Since 1948*. Edited by Linda Butler. Beirut, Lebanon, Washington, DC: Institute for Palestine Studies; Ottawa Ont.: International Development Research Centre.

El Dardiry, Giulia. 2020. *'At Home in the World': Iraqi Refugees in Jordan and the Search for Comfort*. PhD thesis, McGill University.

El-Haj, Nadia Abu. 2022. *Combat Trauma: Imaginaries of War and Citizenship in Post-9/11 America*. London: Verso Books.

El-Shaarawi, Nadia. 2015. "Living an Uncertain Future: Temporality, Uncertainty and Well-Being among Iraqi Refugees in Egypt." *Social Analysis* 59 (1): 38–56.

———. 2021. "A Transit State: The Ambivalences of the Refugee Resettlement Process for Iraqis in Cairo." *American Ethnologist* 48 (4): 404–17.

El Shakry, Omnia. 2015. "'History without documents': The Vexed Archives of Decolonization in the Middle East." *The American Historical Review* 120 (3): 920–34.

Espiritu, Yến Lê. 2014. *Body Counts: The Vietnam War and Militarized Refugees*. Oakland, CA: University of California Press.

Espiritu, Yến Lê, Lan Duong, Ma Vang, Victor Bascara, Khatharya Um, Lila Sharif, and Nigel Hatton. 2022. *Departures: An Introduction to Critical Refugee Studies*. Oakland, CA: University of California Press.

Fagan, Patricia Weiss. 2007. "Iraqi Refugees: Seeking Stability in Syria and Jordan." Qatar: Institute for the Study of International Migration, Georgetown University and Center for International and Regional Studies, Georgetown University School of Foreign Service.

Fanon, Frantz. 2008. *Black Skin, White Masks*. Translated by Richard Philcox. Revised edition. New York: Grove Press.

Fargues, Philippe, Saeed El-Masry, Sara Sadek, and Azza Shaban. 2008. "Iraqis in Egypt: A Statistical Survey in 2008." Cairo: Center for Migration and Refugee Studies, The American University in Cairo. http://www.aucegypt .edu/GAPP/cmrs/Documents/Iraqis%20in%20Egypt%20Provisional%20 Copy.pdf.

Fassin, Didier. 2005. "Compassion and Repression: Moral Economy of Immigration Policies in France." *Cultural Anthropology* 20 (3): 362–87.

———. 2007. "Humanitarianism as a Politics of Life." *Public Culture* 19 (3): 499–520.

———. 2008. "The Humanitarian Politics of Testimony: Subjectification through Trauma in the Israeli-Palestinian Conflict." *Cultural Anthropology* 23 (3): 531–58.

———. 2010. "Inequality of Lives, Hierarchies of Humanity: Moral Commitments and Ethical Dilemmas of Humanitarianism." In *In the Name of Humanity: The Government of Threat and Care*, edited by Ilana Feldman and Miriam Ticktin, 238–56. Durham, NC: Duke University Press.

———. 2011. "Policing Borders, Producing Boundaries. The Governmentality of Immigration in Dark Times." *Annual Review of Anthropology* 40 (1): 213–26.

———. 2012. *Humanitarian Reason: A Moral History of the Present.* Berkeley, CA: University of California Press.

Feiler, Gil. 1991. "Migration and Recession: Arab Labor Mobility in the Middle East, 1982–89." *The Population and Development Review* 17 (1): 134–55.

Feldman, Ilana. 2007. "Difficult Distinctions: Refugee Law, Humanitarian Practice, and Political Identification in Gaza." *Cultural Anthropology* 22 (1): 129–69. https://doi.org/10.1525/can.2007.22.1.129.

———. 2015. "What Is a Camp? Legitimate Refugee Lives in Spaces of Long-Term Displacement." *Geoforum* 66 (November): 244–52. https://doi.org/10.1016/j.geoforum.2014.11.014.

———. 2018. *Life Lived in Relief: Humanitarian Predicaments and Palestinian Refugee Politics.* Berkeley, CA: University of California Press.

Feldman, Ilana, and Miriam Ticktin, eds. 2010. *In the Name of Humanity: The Government of Threat and Care.* Durham, NC: Duke University Press.

Ferguson, James. 1999. *Expectations of Modernity: Myths and Meanings of Urban Life on the Zambian Copperbelt.* Berkeley, CA: University of California Press.

Fiddian-Qasmiyeh, Elena. 2020. "Introduction: Recentering the South in Studies of Migration." *Migration and Society* 3 (1): 1–18.

Fletcher, Robert. 2012. "The Art of Forgetting: Imperialist Amnesia and Public Secrecy." *Third World Quarterly* 33 (3): 423–39. https://doi.org/10.1080/01436597.2012.657476.

FMRS (Forced Migration and Refugee Studies Program). 2006. *A Tragedy of Failures and False Expectations: Report on the Events Surrounding the Three-Month Sit-In and Forced Removal of Sudanese Refugees in Cairo, September–December 2005.* Cairo: FMRS, American University in Cairo. https://documents.aucegypt.edu/Docs/GAPP/Report_Edited_v.pdf.

Fox, Ben. 2021. "What Happened to the Afghanistan Evacuation?" *AP News,* November 26. https://apnews.com/article/afghanistan-immigration-travel-lifestyle-kim-kardashian-west-346e0959989079e5fba109247967573c.

Fujibayashi, Hirotaka. 2022. "When an Arab State Entered into International Refugee Instruments: Behind the Scenes of Egypt's Accession to the 1951 Refugee Convention." *Journal of Refugee Studies* 35 (1): 220–41. https://doi.org/10.1093/jrs/feab086.

Gabiam, Nell. 2006. "Social Thought and Commentary: Negotiating Rights: Palestinian Refugees and the Protection Gap." *Anthropological Quarterly* 79 (4): 717–30.

Garnier, Adèle, Liliana Lyra Jubilut, and Kristin Bergtora Sandvik. 2018. *Refugee Resettlement: Power, Politics, and Humanitarian Governance.* Oxford: Berghahn.

222   REFERENCES

Geissler, P. Wenzel. 2013. "Public Secrets in Public Health: Knowing Not to Know While Making Scientific Knowledge." *American Ethnologist* 40 (1): 13–34.

Gibney, Matthew J. 2004. *The Ethics and Politics of Asylum: Liberal Democracy and the Response to Refugees*. Cambridge, UK: Cambridge University Press.

Gilbert, Emily. 2015. "The Gift of War: Cash, Counterinsurgency, and 'Collateral Damage'." *Security Dialogue* 46 (5): 403–21.

Giordano, Cristiana. 2014. *Migrants in Translation: Caring and the Logics of Difference in Contemporary Italy*. Berkeley, CA: University of California Press. http://onlinelibrary.wiley.com/doi/10.1111/maq.12201/abstract.

Githuku, Nicholas. 2018. "'Collaborators' or 'Resistors,' 'Loyalists' versus 'Rebels': Problematizing Colonial Binary Nomenclatures through the Prism of Dedan Kimathi's Career." *Groundings: Development, Pan-Africanism and Critical Theory* 3 (1): 50–67.

Gordon, Joy. 2010. *Invisible War: The United States and the Iraq Sanctions*. Cambridge, MA: Harvard University Press.

———. 2020. "The Enduring Lessons of the Iraq Sanctions." *Middle East Report* 294. https://merip.org/2020/06/ the-enduring-lessons-of-the-iraq-sanctions/.

Govindrajan, Radhika. 2018. *Animal Intimacies: Interspecies Relatedness in India's Central Himalayas*. 1st edition. Chicago: University of Chicago Press.

Gowayed, Heba. 2020. "Resettled and Unsettled: Syrian Refugees and the Intersection of Race and Legal Status in the United States." *Ethnic and Racial Studies* 43 (2): 275–93.

———. 2022. *Refuge: How the State Shapes Human Potential*. Princeton, NJ: University Press.

Grabska, Katarzyna. 2006. "Who Asked Them Anyway? Rights, Policies and Wellbeing of Refugees in Egypt." Falmer, UK: Development Research Centre on Migration, Globalisation and Poverty, University of Sussex.

Gregory, Derek. 2008a. "The Biopolitics of Baghdad: Counterinsurgency and the Counter-City." *Human Geography* 1 (1): 1–21.

———. 2008b. "The Rush to the Intimate: Counterinsurgency and the Cultural Turn in Late Modern War." *Radical Philosophy* 150: 8–23.

———. 2010. "Seeing Red: Baghdad and the Event-Ful City." *Political Geography* 29 (5): 266–79. https://doi.org/10.1016/j.polgeo.2010.04.003.

Gregory, Thomas. 2020. "The Costs of War: Condolence Payments and the Politics of Killing Civilians." *Review of International Studies* 46 (1): 156–76.

Griffiths, Melanie. 2014. "Out of Time: Temporal Uncertainties of Refused Asylum Seekers and Immigration Detainees." *Journal of Ethnic and Migration Studies* 40 (12): 1991–2009.

REFERENCES 223

Haas, Bridget. 2017. "Citizens-in-Waiting, Deportees-in-Waiting: Power, Temporality, and Suffering in the U.S. Asylum System." *Ethos* 45 (1): 75–97.

Haas, Bridget and Amy Shuman, Eds. 2019. *Technologies of Suspicion and the Ethics of Obligation in Political Asylum*. Athens, OH: Ohio University Press.

Hafez, Sherine. 2019. *Women of the Midan: The Untold Stories of Egypt's Revolutionaries*. Bloomington, IN: Indiana University Press.

Hage, Ghassan. 2009. "Waiting out the Crisis: On Stuckedness and Governmentality." In *Waiting*, edited by Ghassan Hage, 97–106. Melbourne: Melbourne University Press.

———. 2016. "État de Siège: A Dying Domesticating Colonialism?" *American Ethnologist* 43 (1): 38–49. https://doi.org/10.1111/amet.12261.

Hall, Stuart. 2021. *Selected Writings on Race and Difference*. Durham, NC: Duke University Press. https://doi.org/10.1215/9781478021223.

Hardt, Michael and Antonio Negri, 2001. *Empire*. Cambridge, MA: Harvard University Press.

Harrell-Bond, Barbara. 1986. *Imposing Aid: Emergency Assistance to Refugees*. Oxford: Oxford University Press.

Harrell-Bond, Barbara, Eftihia Voutira, and Mark Leopold. 1992. "Counting the Refugees: Gifts, Givers, Patrons and Clients." *Journal of Refugee Studies* 5 (3–4): 205–25.

Hartman, Saidiya. 2008. "Venus in Two Acts." *Small Axe* 12 (2): 1–14.

Harvey, David. 2003. *The New Imperialism*. Oxford: Oxford University Press.

Hassan, Falih, and Jane Arraf. 2020. "Blackwater, Iraq, and Trump's Pardon." *The New York Times*, December 23, sec. World. https://www.nytimes.com/2020/12/23/world/middleeast/blackwater-trump-pardon.html

Heck, Gerda, and Elena Habersky. 2024. "Externalising Migration Controls through Development Programs in Egypt." *Geopolitics* (February): 1–24. https://doi.org/10.1080/14650045.2024.2316659.

Horst, Cindy. 2006. "Buufis amongst Somalis in Dadaab: Transnational and Historical Logics behind Resettlement Dreams." *Journal of Refugee Studies* 19 (2): 143–57.

Horst, Cindy, and Katarzyna Grabska. 2015. "Introduction: Flight and Exile— Uncertainty in the Context of Conflict-Induced Displacement." *Social Analysis* 59 (1): 1–18.

Human Rights First. 2018. *How the Trump Administration's Executive Orders on Refugees Harm our Wartime Allies*. https://humanrightsfirst.org/library/how-the-trump-administrations-executive-orders-on-refugees-harm-our-iraqi-wartime-allies/

Immerwahr, Daniel. 2019. *How to Hide an Empire: A History of the Greater United States*. First Edition. New York: Farrar, Straus and Giroux.

Inhorn, Marcia C. 2020. "America's Arab Refugees." In *America's Arab Refugees*. Stanford, CA: Stanford University Press.

Isikoff, Michael. 2008. "Senate Report's New Findings on Pre-War Deception." *Newsweek*. June 10. https://www.newsweek.com/ senate-reports-new-findings-pre-war-deception-90891.

Isikoff, Michael, and David Corn. 2007. *Hubris: The Inside Story of Spin, Scandal, and the Selling of the Iraq War*. Reprint edition. New York: Crown.

Jadallah, Dina. 2015. "Economic Aid to Egypt: Promoting Progress or Subordination." *Class, Race and Corporate Power* 3 (2). https://digitalcommons.fiu .edu/classracecorporatepower/vol3/iss2/1.

Jakes, Lara. 2019. "Under Trump, Iraqis Who Helped U.S. in War Are Stalled in Refugee System." *The New York Times*, November 2, sec. World. https://www. nytimes.com/2019/11/02/world/middleeast/trump-refugees-iraq.html.

James, Erica Caple. 2010. *Democratic Insecurities: Violence, Trauma, and Intervention in Haiti*. Berkeley, CA: University of California Press.

Jansen, Bram. 2008. "Between Vulnerability and Assertiveness: Negotiating Resettlement in Kakuma Refugee Camp, Kenya." *African Affairs* 107 (429): 569–87.

Jenkins, Janis Hunter. "The State Construction of Affect: Political Ethos and Mental Health among Salvadoran Refugees." *Culture, Medicine and Psychiatry* 15, no. 2 (1991): 139–65.

Johnson, Carrie. 2011. Terrorism Case Exposes Gaps in Refugee Screening. *National Public Radio*, June 8. https://www.npr. org/2011/06/08/137033910/ terrorism-case-exposes-gaps-in-refugee-screening

Johnson, Kirk. 2010. "Left behind in Iraq." *Foreign Policy*, May 18. https:// foreignpolicy.com/2010/05/18/left-behind-in-iraq-2/.

———. 2013. *To Be a Friend Is Fatal: The Fight to Save the Iraqis America Left Behind*. New York: Scribner.

Jones, Graham M. 2014. "Secrecy*." *Annual Reviews*. World. October 21. https://doi.org/10.1146/annurev-anthro-102313-030058.

Jones, Toby Craig. 2012. "America, Oil, and War in the Middle East." *The Journal of American History* 99 (1): 208–18.

Jong, Sara de. 2022. "Segregated Brotherhood: The Military Masculinities of Afghan Interpreters and Other Locally Employed Civilians." *International Feminist Journal of Politics* 24 (2): 243–63. https://doi.org/10.1080/146167 42.2022.2053296.

Jovanović, Deana. 2016. "Ambivalence and the Work of Hope: Anticipating Futures in a Serbian Industrial Town." PhD diss., University of Manchester. http://rifdt.instifdt.bg.ac.rs/handle/123456789/1734.

Kagan, Michael. 2011. "'We Live in a Country of UNHCR': The UN Surrogate State and Refugee Policy in the Middle East." The UN Refugee Agency: Policy Development & Evaluation Service Research Paper No. 201. http:// papers.ssrn.com/sol3/papers.cfm?abstract_id=1957371.

Kaufman, Michael T. 2003. "The World: Film Studies; What Does the Pentagon See in 'Battle of Algiers'?" *The New York Times*, September 7. https://www.nytimes.com/2003/09/07/weekinreview/the-world-film-studies-what-does-the-pentagon-see-in-battle-of-algiers.html

Khalili, Laleh. 2012. *Time in the Shadows: Confinement in Counterinsurgencies*. Stanford, CA: Stanford University Press.

Khosravi, Shahram. 2010. *"Illegal" Traveller: An Auto-Ethnography of Borders*. New York: Springer.

———, ed. 2021. *Waiting—A Project in Conversation*. Bielefeld, Germany: Transcript.

Khoury, Dina Rizk. 2013. *Iraq in Wartime: Soldiering, Martyrdom, and Remembrance*. New York: Cambridge University Press.

Klein, Naomi. 2010. *The Shock Doctrine: The Rise of Disaster Capitalism*. New York: Henry Holt and Company.

Konn-Roberts, Tania. 2021. "'Guests of the British Crown': White Russian Refugee Camps in Egypt, 1920–1922." *Slavonica* 26 (1): 37–57.

Kumar, Deepa. 2006. "Media, War, and Propaganda: Strategies of Information Management during the 2003 Iraq War." *Communication and Critical /Cultural Studies* 3 (1): 48–69.

———. 2021. *Islamophobia and the Politics of Empire: Twenty Years after 9/11*. London: Verso Books.

LaTowsky, Robert J. 1984. "Egyptian Labor Abroad: Mass Participation and Modest Returns." *MERIP Reports*, no. 123, 11–18.

Li, Darryl. 2015a. "Migrant Workers and the US Military in the Middle East." *Middle East Report* 275. https://merip.org/2015/06/migrant-workers-and-the-us-military-in-the-middle-east/

———. 2015b. "Offshoring the Army: Migrant Workers and the US Military." *UCLA L. Rev.* 62: 123.

———. 2019. *The Universal Enemy: Jihad, Empire, and the Challenge of Solidarity*. Stanford, CA: Stanford University Press.

Libal, Kathryn, and Scott Harding. 2007. "The Politics of Refugee Advocacy and Humanitarian Assistance." *Middle East Report* 37 (244): 18.

Lindquist, Johan, Biao Xiang, and Brenda SA Yeoh. 2012. "Opening the Black Box of Migration: Brokers, the Organization of Transnational Mobility and the Changing Political Economy in Asia." *Pacific Affairs* 85 (1): 7–19.

Linnemann, Travis, and Corina Medley. 2019. "Black Sites, 'Dark Sides': War Power, Police Power, and the Violence of the (Un)Known." *Crime, Media, Culture* 15 (2): 341–58. https://doi.org/10.1177/1741659018777779.

Lutz, Catherine. 2006. "Empire Is in the Details." *American Ethnologist* 33 (4): 593–611.

———. 2019. "Bureaucratic Weaponry and the Production of Ignorance in Military Operations on Guam." *Current Anthropology* 60 (S19): S108–21.

226   REFERENCES

Lynch, Emily. 2013. "Mudende: Trauma and Massacre in a Refugee Camp." *Oral History Forum d'histoire orale* 33 (August). http://www.oralhistory-forum.ca/index.php/ohf/article/view/537/615.

"Madeleine Albright Dies at 84; Once Defended U.S. Sanctions Despite Deaths of 500K+ Iraqi Children." 2022 *Democracy Now!* March 24. https://www.democracynow.org/2022/3/24/former_secretary_state_madeleine_albright_dies.

Malkki, Liisa. 1992. "National Geographic: The Rooting of Peoples and the Territorialization of National Identity among Scholars and Refugees." *Cultural Anthropology* 7(1): 24–44.

———. 1995a. *Purity and Exile: Violence, Memory, and National Cosmology among Hutu Refugees in Tanzania.* Chicago: University of Chicago Press.

———. 1995b. "Refugees and Exile: From 'Refugee Studies' to the National Order of Things." *Annual Review of Anthropology* 24: 495–523.

Mamdani, Mahmood. 2002. "Good Muslim, Bad Muslim: A Political Perspective on Culture and Terrorism." *American Anthropologist* 104 (3): 766–75. https://doi.org/10.1525/aa.2002.104.3.766.

Marfleet, Philip. 2007. "Refugees and History: Why We Must Address the Past." *Refugee Survey Quarterly* 26 (3): 136–48.

Masco, Joseph. 2006. *The Nuclear Borderlands: The Manhattan Project in Post-Cold War New Mexico.* Princeton, NJ: Princeton University Press.

———. 2014. *The Theater of Operations: National Security Affect from the Cold War to the War on Terror.* Durham, NC: Duke University Press Books.

Massey, Doreen B. 2005. *For Space: A Relational Politics of the Spatial.* London: Sage Publications.

Mayblin, Lucy. 2017. *Asylum after Empire: Colonial Legacies in the Politics of Asylum Seeking.* London: Rowman & Littlefield Publishers.

Mazzarino, Andrea, C. Inhorn, and Catherine Lutz. 2019. "Introduction: The Health Consequences of War." In *War and Health: The Medical Consequences of the Wars in Iraq and Afghanistan,* edited by Catherine Lutz and Andrea Mazzarino, 1–40. New York: New York University Press.

McGranahan, Carole. 2016. "Theorizing Refusal: An Introduction." *Cultural Anthropology* 31 (3): 319–25.

McGranahan, Carole, and John F. Collins. 2018. *Ethnographies of US Empire.* Durham, NC: Duke University Press

Meek, James Gordon, Cindi Galli, and Brian Ross. 2013. "Exclusive: US May Have Let 'Dozens' of Terrorists Into Country As Refugees." *ABC News.* November 19. https://abcnews.go.com/Blotter/al-qaeda-kentucky-us-dozens-terrorists-country-refugees/story?id=20931131.

Mercer, Kobena. 1994. *Welcome to the Jungle: New Positions in Black Cultural Studies.* New York, NY: Routledge.

Merry, Sally Engle. 2006. "Transnational Human Rights and Local Activism: Mapping the Middle." *American Anthropologist* 108 (1): 38–51.

Merton, Robert. 1976. *Sociological Ambivalence and Other Essays*. New York: Free Press.

Micinski, Nicholas R. 2018. "Refugee Policy as Foreign Policy: Iraqi and Afghan Refugee Resettlements to the United States." *Refugee Survey Quarterly* 37 (3): 253–78.

Mills, Charles W. 2007. "White Ignorance." In *Race and Epistemologies of Ignorance,* edited by Shannon Sullivan and Nancy Tuana, 13–38. Albany, NY.

Miller, T. Christian. 2009. "Foreign Interpreters Hurt in Battle Find U.S. Insurance Benefits Wanting." *ProPublica*. December 18. https://www.propublica.org/article/iraqi-translators-denied-promised-health-care-1218?token=uoYT3QQC93fqm0Bw2XM2uFPVTHBJBAML.

Milner, James, and Gil Loescher. 2011. "Responding to protracted refugee situations: Lessons from a decade of discussion." Oxford, UK: University of Oxford Refugee Studies Centre.

Mittermaier, Amira. 2019. *Giving to God: Islamic Charity in Revolutionary Times*. First edition. Oakland, CA: University of California Press.

Morefield, Jeanne. 2014. *Empires without Imperialism: Anglo-American Decline and the Politics of Deflection*. Electronic resource. Oxford: Oxford University Press.

Moulin, Carolina, and Peter Nyers. 2007. "'We Live in a Country of UNHCR'— Refugee Protests and Global Political Society." *International Political Sociology* 1 (4): 356–72.

Naber, Nadine. 2000. "Ambiguous Insiders: An Investigation of Arab American Invisibility." *Ethnic and Racial Studies* 23 (1): 37–61.

———. 2014. "Diasporas of Empire: Arab Americans and the Reverberations of War." In *At the Limits of Justice: Women of Colour on Terror,* edited by Suvendrini Perera and Sherene Razack, 191–214. Toronto: University of Toronto Press.

National Defense Authorization Act for Fiscal Year 2008. 2008.

National Public Radio. 2014. "American Soldier, Iraqi Interpreter: From Strangers To 'Brothers.'" *Weekend Edition Saturday,* October 18. https://www.npr.org/2014/10/18/357009194/american-soldier-iraqi-interpreter-from-strangers-to-brothers.

Nayeri, Dina. 2019. *The Ungrateful Refugee: What Immigrants Never Tell You*. New York: Catapult.

NBC News. 2004. "U.S. Contractors in Iraq Penalized." *NBC News*. April 26. https://www.nbcnews.com/id/wbna4838246.

Network of Concerned Anthropologists. 2009. *The Counter Counterinsurgency Manual: Or, Notes on Demilitarizing American Society*. Chicago: University of Chicago Press.

Nguyen, Mimi Thi. 2012. *The Gift of Freedom: War, Debt, and Other Refugee Passages*. Durham, NC: Duke University Press Books.

Nguyen, Vinh-Kim. 2010. *The Republic of Therapy: Triage and Sovereignty in West Africa's Time of AIDS*. Durham, NC: Duke University Press.

Nojan, Saugher. 2022. "Racialized Hauntings: Examining Afghan Americans' Hyper(in)Visibility amidst Anti-Muslim Ethnoracism." *Ethnic and Racial Studies* 45 (7): 1347–70. https://doi.org/10.1080/01419870.2021.1931391.

Nordstrom, Carolyn. 1997. *A Different Kind of War Story*. Philadelphia: University of Pennsylvania Press.

Norman, Kelsey P. 2017. "Ambivalence as Policy: Consequences for Refugees in Egypt." *Égypte/Monde arabe* 15 (1): 27–45. https://doi.org/10.4000/ema.3663.

Office of the Chairman of the Joint Chiefs of Staff. 2020. *DOD Dictionary of Military and Associated Terms*. Washington DC: The Joint Staff.

Ong, Aihwa. 2000. "Graduated Sovereignty in South-East Asia." *Theory, Culture and Society* 17 (4): 55–75.

———. 2003. *Buddha Is Hiding: Refugees, Citizenship, the New America*. Berkeley, CA: University of California Press.

Packer, George. 2005. *The Assassins' Gate: America in Iraq*. New York: Farrar, Straus and Giroux.

Patel, Hasan Salim. 2011. "Tareq Ayoub: A 'Martyr to the Truth.'" *Al Jazeera*. December 14. https://www.aljazeera.com/news/2011/12/14/tareq-ayoub-a-martyr-to-the-truth.

Peltier, Heidi. 2020. "The Growth of the 'Camo Economy' and the Commercialization of the Post-9/11 Wars." Costs of War Project. Watson Institute for International & Public Affairs, Brown University. https://watson.brown.edu/costsofwar/files/cow/imce/papers/2020/Peltier%202020%20-%20Growth%20of%20Camo%20Economy%20-%20June%2030%202020%20-%20FINAL.pdf

Peteet, Julie. 2010. "Cartographic Violence, Displacement and Refugee Camps: Palestine and Iraq." In *Palestinian Refugees: Identity, Space and Place in the Levant*, edited by Are Knudsen and Sari Hanafi, 27–42. London: Routledge.

Piot, Charles. 2010. *Nostalgia for the Future: West Africa after the Cold War*. Chicago: University of Chicago Press.

Proctor, Robert N., and Londa Schiebinger, eds. 2008. *Agnotology: The Making and Unmaking of Ignorance*. Stanford, CA: Stanford University Press.

Puar, J. K. 2004. "Abu Ghraib: Arguing against Exceptionalism." *Feminist Studies* 30 (2): 522–34. https://doi.org/10.2307/20458978.

Pursley, Sara. 2019. *Familiar Futures: Time, Selfhood, and Sovereignty in Iraq*. 1st edition. Stanford, CA: Stanford University Press.

Quadri, Zaynab. 2022. "War Is Still a Racket: Private Military Contracting, US Imperialism, and the Iraq War." *American Quarterly* 74 (3): 523–43. https://doi.org/10.1353/aq.2022.0033.

Ralph, Laurence. 2020. "The Making of Richard Zuley: The Ignored Linkages between the US Criminal In/Justice System and the International Security State." *American Anthropologist* 122 (1): 133–42.

Ramsay, Georgina. 2017. "Incommensurable Futures and Displaced Lives: Sovereignty as Control over Time." *Public Culture* 29 (3): 515–38.

———. 2017. *Impossible Refuge: The Control and Constraint of Refugee Futures.* London: Routledge.

———. 2020. "Time and the Other in Crisis: How Anthropology Makes Its Displaced Object." *Anthropological Theory* 20 (4): 385–413.

Rana, Junaid Akram. 2011. *Terrifying Muslims: Race and Labor in the South Asian Diaspora.* Durham, NC: Duke University Press.

Razsa, Maple, and Andrej Kurnik. 2014. "Occupy Slovenia: How Migrant Movements Contributed to New Forms of Direct Democracy." In *Border Politics,* edited by Nancy A. Naples and Jennifer Bickham Mendez, 206–29. New York: New York University Press.

Redfield, Peter. 2008. "Sacrifice, Triage, and Global Humanitarianism." In *Humanitarianism in Question: Politics, Power, Ethics,* edited by Michael Barnett and Thomas G. Weiss, 196–214. Ithaca, NY: Cornell University Press.

———. 2013. *Life in Crisis: The Ethical Journey of Doctors without Borders.* Berkeley, CA: University of California Press.

Ricoeur, Paul. 1977. *Freud and Philosophy.* New Haven, CT: Yale University Press.

Robinson, Piers. 2017. "Learning from the Chilcot report: Propaganda, deception and the 'war on terror'." *International Journal of Contemporary Iraqi Studies* 11, no. 1–2 (2017): 47–73.

Rollins, Tom. 2017. "Egypt's Rashid Tragedy Survivors: 'Justice Is Done.'" *Al Jazeera.* April 18. https://www.aljazeera.com/features/2017/4/18/remembering-the-victims-of-egypts-rashid-tragedy.

Rubaii, Kali J. 2018. "Counterinsurgency and the Ethical Life of Material Things in Iraq's Anbar Province." PhD diss., University of California, Santa Cruz. https://www.proquest.com/docview/2088897811/abstract/57153971BD364A1APQ/1.

———. 2019. "Tripartheid: How Sectarianism Became Internal to Being in Anbar, Iraq." *PoLAR: Political and Legal Anthropology Review* 42 (1): 125–41. https://doi.org/10.1111/plar.12278.

———. 2020. "Birth Defects and the Toxic Legacy of War in Iraq." *Middle East Report* 296 (September). https://merip.org/2020/09/birth-defects-and-the-toxic-legacy-of-war-in-iraq/.

Rubin, Alissa J., and Nicholas Bogel-Burroughs. 2019. "ICE Deported Him to a Country He'd Never Seen. He Died 2 Months Later." *The New York Times,* August 8, sec. U.S. https://www.nytimes.com/2019/08/08/us/iraq-jimmy-aldaoud-deport.html.

SAA (Society of American Archivists). 2018. "Statement on Removal of ISIS Records from Iraq by New York Times Reporter." Society of American Archivists. https://www2.archivists.org/statements/statement-on-removal-of-isis-records-from-iraq-by-new-york-times-reporter

Sacchetti, Maria. 2022. "Lawyers Say the Biden Administration Is Still Rejecting Some Refugees Once Banned by Trump." *Washington Post*, February 16. https://www.washingtonpost.com/national-security/2022/02/16/biden-trump-refugees/.

Sadek, Sara. 2010. "Iraqi 'Temporary Guests' in Neighbouring Countries." In *On the Move: Migration Challenges in the Indian Ocean Littoral*, edited by Ellen Laipsan and Amit Pandya, 43–55. Washington, DC: Henry L. Stimson Center.

Said, Edward W. 1994. *Culture and Imperialism*. New York: Vintage.

Saleh, Zainab. 2018. "'Toppling' Saddam Hussein in London: Media, Meaning, and the Construction of an Iraqi Diasporic Community." *American Anthropologist* 120 (3): 512–22.

———. 2020. *Return to Ruin: Iraqi Narratives of Exile and Nostalgia*. Stanford, CA: Stanford University Press.

Sanbar, Sarah. 2024. "US Jury Awards $42 Million to 3 Iraqis Abused at Abu Ghraib Prison." Human Rights Watch. https://www.hrw.org/news/2024/11/14/us-jury-awards-42-million-3-iraqis-abused-abu-ghraib-prison

Sandvik, Kristin Bergtora. 2011. "Blurring Boundaries: Refugee Resettlement in Kampala—between the Formal, the Informal, and the Illegal." *PoLAR* 34 (1): 11–32.

Savell, Stephanie. 2023. *How Death Outlives War: The Reverberating Impact of the Post-9/11 Wars on Human Health*. Costs of War Project, Watson Institute for International & Public Affairs, Brown University. https://watson.brown.edu/costsofwar/papers/2023/IndirectDeaths

Schielke, Joska Samuli. 2020. *Migrant Dreams: Egyptian Workers in the Gulf States*. Cairo: The American University in Cairo Press.

Schiltz, Julie, Sofie Vindevogel, Ilse Derluyn, and Wouter Vanderplasschen. 2019. "Uncertainty in Situations of Forced Displacement: A Critical Interpretative Synthesis of Refugee Literature." *Population, Space and Place* 25 (3): e2194.

Scott, James C. 1998. *Seeing like a State: How Certain Schemes to Improve the Human Condition Have Failed*. New Haven, CT: Yale University Press.

Sedgwick, Eve. 1988. "Privilege of Unknowing." *Genders*, no. 1, 102–24.

Segal, Lotte Buch. 2016. "Ambivalent Attachment—Melancholia and Political Activism in Contemporary Palestine." *Ethos* 44 (4): 464–84.

Simmel, Georg. 1906. "The Sociology of Secrecy and of Secret Societies." *American Journal of Sociology* 11 (4): 441–98.

Simpson, Audra. 2014. *Mohawk Interruptus: Political Life across the Borders of Settler States.* Durham, NC: Duke University Press.

Singh, Amrit, and David Berry. 2013. "Globalizing Torture: CIA Secret Detention and Extraordinary Rendition." New York: Open Society Justice Initiative.

Singh, Juliette. 2018. *Unthinking Mastery: Dehumanism and Decolonial Entanglements.* Durham, NC: Duke University Press.

Solh, Camillia Fawsi. 1985. "Egyptian Migrant Peasants in Iraq. A Case-Study of the Settlement Community in Khalsa." Ph.D. thesis, England: University of London, Bedford College. https://www.proquest.com/docview/1791541746/abstract/3C455E1374E643B4PQ/1.

Stevenson, Lisa. 2014. *Life beside Itself: Imagining Care in the Canadian Arctic.* Oakland, CA: University of California Press.

Stillman, Sarah. 2011. "The Invisible Army." *The New Yorker,* May 30. https://www.newyorker.com/magazine/2011/06/06/the-invisible-army.

Stoler, Ann Laura. 2011. "Colonial Aphasia: Race and Disabled Histories in France." *Public Culture* 23 (1): 121–56.

———. 2018. "On Archiving as Dissensus." *Comparative Studies of South Asia, Africa, and the Middle East* 38 (1) 43–56.

Stoler, Ann Laura, and Carole McGranahan. 2018. "Afterword: Disassemblage: Rethinking U.S. Imperial Formations." In *Ethnographies of US Empire,* edited by John F. Collins. Durham, NC: Duke University Press.

Stone, Nomi. 2017. "Living the Laughscream: Human Technology and Affective Maneuvers in the Iraq War." *Cultural Anthropology* 32 (1): 149–74. https://doi.org/10.14506/ca32.1.10.

———. 2018. "Imperial Mimesis." *American Ethnologist* 45 (4): 533–45. https://doi.org/10.1111/amet.12707.

———. 2022. *Pinelandia: An Anthropology and Field Poetics of War and Empire.* Oakland, CA: University of California Press.

Suskind, Ron. 2004. "Faith, Certainty and the Presidency of George W. Bush." *The New York Times,* October 17, sec. Politics. https://www.nytimes.com/2004/10/17/magazine/faith-certainty-and-the-presidency-of-george-w-bush.html.

Sweis, Rania Kassab. 2019. "Doctors with Borders: Hierarchies of Humanitarians and the Syrian Civil War." *International Journal of Middle East Studies* 51 (4): 587–601.

Tang, Eric. 2015. *Unsettled: Cambodian Refugees in the New York City Hyperghetto.* Philadelphia: Temple University Press.

Taussig, Michael T. 1999. *Defacement: Public Secrecy and the Labor of the Negative.* Stanford, CA: Stanford University Press.

Thomson, Marnie. 2012. "Black Boxes of Bureaucracy: Transparency and Opacity in the Resettlement Process of Congolese Refugees." *PoLAR* 35 (2): 186–205.

232   REFERENCES

———. 2018. "What Documents Do Not Do: Papering Persecution and Moments of Recognition in a Congolese Refugee Camp." *Anthropologica* 60 (1): 223–35.

Ticktin, Miriam. 2006. "Where Ethics and Politics Meet." *American Ethnologist* 33 (1): 33–49.

———. 2011. *Casualties of Care: Immigration and the Politics of Humanitarianism in France.* Berkeley, CA: University of California Press.

Tidy, Joanna. 2017. "Visual Regimes and the Politics of War Experience: Rewriting War 'from above' in WikiLeaks' 'Collateral Murder.'" *Review of International Studies* 43 (1): 95–111.

Tripp, Charles. 2007. *A History of Iraq.* Third edition. Cambridge: Cambridge University Press.

Trouillot, Michel-Rolph. 2015. *Silencing the Past: Power and the Production of History, 20th Anniversary Edition.* 2nd Revised edition. Boston, MA: Beacon Press.

Tuck, Eve. 2009. "Suspending Damage: A Letter to Communities." *Harvard Educational Review* 79 (3): 409–28.

Twu, Marianne. 2009. "A Sanctuary for Those Who Serve: United States Iraqi Special Immigrant Visa Programs." *NCJ Int'l L. & Com. Reg.* 35: 723.

UNHCR. n.d. "Resettlement Data Finder." UNHCR. Accessed August 22, 2021. https://rsq.unhcr.org/en/#v81G

———. 2004. *UNHCR Resettlement Handbook.* Geneva: UNHCR. https://www.unhcr.org/pages/4a2ccba76.html.

———. 2011. *UNHCR Resettlement Handbook.* Geneva: UNHCR. http://www.unhcr.org/refworld/docid/4ecb973c2.html.

———. 2012. "The State of the World's Refugees 2012: In Search of Solidarity." Geneva: UNHCR. https://www.unhcr.org/publications/sowr/4fc5ceca9/state-worlds-refugees-2012-search-solidarity.html.

———. 2018. "Global Trends 2018." Geneva: UNHCR. https://www.unhcr.org/statistics/unhcrstats/5d08d7ee7/unhcr-global-trends-2018.html.

———. 2019. "Projected Global Resettlement Needs 2020." Geneva: UNHCR. https://www.unhcr.org/protection/resettlement/5d1384047/projected-global-resettlement-needs-2020.html.

———. 2021. "Resettlement Fact Sheet 2020." https://www.unhcr.org/protection/resettlement/600e95094/resettlement-fact-sheet-2020.html.

———. 2024. "UNHCR—UNHCR Global Trends 2024." 2024. https://www.unhcr.org/global-trends.

UN News Service. 2010. "Iraqi Refugees Regret Returning Home, UN Agency Finds." October 19. http://www.unhcr.org/refworld/docid/4cc51ce41e.html.

———. 2012. "Violence in Syria Forces More Than 10,000 Iraqi Refugees to Leave Country." July 24. https://news.un.org/en/story/2012/07/416182-violence-syria-forces-more-10000-iraqi-refugees-leave-country-un.

van Selm, Joanne. 2018. "Strategic Use of Resettlement: Enhancing Solutions for Greater Protection?" In *Refugee Resettlement: Power, Politics, and Humanitarian Governance*, edited by Adèle Garnier, Liliana Lyra Jubilut, and Kristin Bergtora Sandvik, 31–45. Oxford: Berghahn.

Vang, Ma. 2021. *History on the Run: Secrecy, Fugitivity, and Hmong Refugee Epistemologies*. Durham, NC: Duke University Press.

Verdirame, Guglielmo, and Barbara Harrell-Bond. 2005. *Rights in Exile: Janus-Faced Humanitarianism*. Oxford: Berghahn.

Vimalassery, Manu, Juliana Hu Pegues, and Alyosha Goldstein. 2016. "Introduction: On Colonial Unknowing." *Theory & Event* 19 (4). https://muse.jhu.edu/pub/1/article/633283

Vine, David. 2015. *Base Nation: How America's Bases Abroad Harm the World*. New York: Henry Holt.

———. 2018. "Islands of Imperialism: Military Bases and the Ethnography of US Empire." In *Ethnographies of US Empire*, 249–69. Duke University Press.

Vine, David, Cala Coffman, Katalina Khoury, Madison Lovasz, Helen Bush, Rachel Leduc, and Jennifer Walkup. 2020. "Creating Refugees: Displacement Caused by the United States' Post-9/11 Wars." Costs of War Project, Watson Institute for International & Public Affairs, Brown University. https://watson.brown.edu/costsofwar/files/cow/imce/papers/2020/Displacement_Vine%20et%20al_Costs%20of%20War%202020%2009%2008.pdf.

Wakin, Eric. 1998. *Anthropology Goes to War: Professional Ethics and Counterinsurgency in Thailand*. Madison, WI: Center for Southeast Asian Studies. University of Wisconsin Press.

Walters, William. 2015. "Migration, Vehicles, and Politics: Three Theses on Viapolitics." *European Journal of Social Theory* 18 (4): 469–88.

Walzer, Michael. 1983. *Spheres of Justice: A Defense of Pluralism and Equality*. New York: Basic Books.

Watters, Charles. 2019. "Geographies of Aspiration and the Politics of Suspicion in the Context of Border Control." In *Technologies of Suspicion and the Ethics of Obligation in Political Asylum*, edited by Bridget Haas and Amy Shuman, 47–60. Athens, OH: Ohio University Press.

Whyte, Jessica. 2019. "Calculated Indifference: The Politics of Collateral Damage." *Journal of Genocide Research* 21 (2): 263–68. https://doi.org/10.1080/14623528.2019.1589928.

WikiLeaks. n.d. "Collateral Murder." Accessed October 7, 2024. https://collateralmurder.wikileaks.org/

Willen, Sarah. 2012. How is Health-related "Deservingness" Reckoned? Perspectives from Unauthorized Im/migrants in Tel Aviv. *Social Science & Medicine*, 74(6), 812–821.

Wool, Zoë H. 2015. *After War: The Weight of Life at Walter Reed*. Durham, NC: Duke University Press.

Yarris, Kristin, and Heide Castañeda. 2015. "Special Issue Discourses of Displacement and Deservingness: Interrogating Distinctions between 'Economic' and 'Forced' Migration: Introduction." *International Migration* 53 (3): 64–69. https://doi.org/10.1111/imig.12170.

Yoshikawa, Lynn. 2007. "Iraqi Refugees in Egypt." *Forced Migration Review* 29 (June): 54.

Zarowsky, Christina. 2004. "Writing Trauma: Emotion, Ethnography, and the Politics of Suffering among Somali Returnees in Ethiopia." *Culture, Medicine and Psychiatry* 28, no. 2 (June): 189–209.

Zohry, Ayman, and Barbara Harrell-Bond. 2003. "Contemporary Egyptian Migration: An Overview of Voluntary and Forced Migration." Working Paper C3. Cairo, Egypt: Forced Migration and Refugee Studies Program, The American University in Cairo. http://www.hic-mena.org/img/documents/DRC%20working%20paper%203-Egypt.pdf.

Index

Abdallah, 3–4
Abdullah, Kifah N., 113
Abu Ghraib prison, 163, 197n5, 209n9
Abu Muhammad, 3–4, 14
Abu Nasim, 133–35, 161, 191
Afghanistan, US war in, 31, 77, 93, 162, 181, 189–90
Ahlam, 180, 186
Ahmed, 137
Airport Road/Route Irish (*Tariiq al-maTaar*), 45–47
Al Arabiya, 74–75, 80–81
Albright, Madeleine, 194n6
Aldaoud, Jimmy, 211n19
Alexandria, 105, 115
Al Jazeera, 75, 78, 80, 104
al-Libi, Ibn al-Sheikh, 92–93
Al-Nadeem Centre, 138
al-Qaeda, 11, 31–32, 40, 78, 93
Al-Rubiae, Najim, 80
al-Sadat, Anwar, 92, 112
Alshaibi, Wisam, 85, 87
Alwan, Waad Ramadan, 177–78, 180
Amman, 18, 105, 107
Anfal campaign, 73
anthropology, 38, 49, 63–64, 125, 198n12
Antoon, Sinan, 9

Arab Spring, 104, 153, 203n10
archives, 62–63, 83–85, 85–87, 201n11
Arendt, Hannah, 89–90
Assange, Julian, 79
Australia, resettlement in, 22, 128, 141, 150–51
Ayyoub, Tareq, 78
Azoulay, Ariella, 159

Baath Party, 70, 86, 97–98, 100, 113, 116, 120, 180, 186
Baghdad, bombardment of, 4, 12, 44, 50, 198n9
Battle of Algiers, The (film), 37
Becker, Gay, 135
Beirut, 18, 105, 107
Blackwater Security Consulting, 163, 189, 209n10
Blair, Tony, 16, 34, 40, 130
Bonet, Sally Wesley, 129, 146
Bourdieu, Pierre, 148
Bremer, Paul, 54–55, 80
Bush, George W., 11–12, 16, 31–32, 34, 40–41, 86, 130
Butler, Judith, 78

Cabot, Heath, 68
Cainkar, Louise, 180

236 INDEX

Cairo, refugee presence in, 18–19, 28–29, 90, 105–11. *See also* Egypt
Campbell, Madeline, 166
Camp David Accords, 92, 116
Canada, resettlement in, 22, 50, 128, 139, 141, 148
Canal Hotel, 160–61
casualties, 7, 45, 73, 168, 194n4; hiding of, 45, 47, 167–68, 194n8
Chalabi, Ahmed, 159
Chandrasekaran, Rajiv, 164
Chmagh, Saeed, 79
civilians, murder of, 163, 189
Coalitional Provisional Authority (CPA), 43, 54–56, 73–74, 98, 160, 163
coalition of the willing, 11–12, 40, 58
Coker, Elizabeth, 135
collaboration, with US forces, 52, 131, 158–77, 181, 183. *See also* "Iraqi allies" (who assisted US forces)
collateral damage(s), 7–10, 79–80, 187, 191, 194n7, 194–95n8
Committee to Protect Journalists, 62, 76, 83. *See also* journalists, murder of in war
contractors, use of in Iraq War, 43, 45, 48, 161–64, 167–69, 189
Conway, Kellyanne, 178
Costs of War Project, 195n14
counterinsurgency, 8, 34, 43–49, 52, 58, 82, 164–66
counterterrorism, 52, 80, 157
Couso, José, 78
Crocker, Ryan, 171

Damascus, 18, 105, 107
Daulatzai, Anila, 191
death threats, 50, 58, 97, 131, 144, 167, 170–72
de-Baathification, 55
De Genova, Nicholas, 219
De León, Jason, 36
Department of Defense, 73, 86, 162, 169
Department of Homeland Security, 83, 139–41
Department of State, 175, 178, 189
Development Fund for Iraq, 163
Dewachi, Omar, 16, 54
Direct Access Program, 30, 101, 126, 131, 133, 146, 155–58, 160, 170–78, 181–83. *See also* Refugee Crisis in Iraq Act

Egypt: history of refugee reception in, 17–18, 91–95, 106, 115–17; life in, for Iraqi ref-

ugees, 2, 15, 19–20, 95–102, 106–11, 118–22, 133–34, 154. *See also* Cairo, refugee presence in
Egyptians, experiences of in Iraq, 111–14
El Shakry, Omnia, 84
empire, United States as, 35, 41–42, 53–54
Entisar, 39, 50–52, 57–59, 175
Eskander, Saad Bashir, 87
Espiritu, Yến Lê, 129, 181

Faisal, 160–61, 168, 170, 191
Fanon, Frantz, 167
Fatima, 45
Firdos Square, 12, 50
fog of war, 43
Free Officers' Movement, 92

Ghumkhor, Sahar, 191
Giza, 24, 106, 141, 204n13
Global North, 5, 29, 92, 146, 150–51
Global South, 22, 91, 96, 105, 151
Global War on Terror (GWOT), 6, 8–10, 31, 42, 92–93, 155, 166, 180–82
Gordon, Joy, 6
Green Zone, 44–45, 55, 86, 162, 164, 170–72
Gregory, Derek, 44
"guest" status, 18, 93, 130, 203n9
Gulf War of 1990–91, 5, 8, 13, 43, 73, 112

Haas, Bridget, 121
Hall, Stuart, 196n15
Halliburton, 162, 164
Hammadi, Mohanad Shareef, 177–78, 180
Harrell-Bond, Barbara, 25–26, 63–65, 179, 181
Hartman, Saidiya, 83–84
Hassan, 39, 44–48, 51–52, 56–58, 144–45, 150, 175
Hatem, 39, 52–53
Haydar, 1, 3–4, 107, 111, 118–21
Hoover Institution, 87
Horst, Cindy, 129
Human Terrain System, 49, 198n12
Hussein, Saddam, 43, 50, 72–73, 80, 86, 111–13, 116; atrocities committed by, 17–18, 73, 87; killing of, 51, 53; US opposition to, 11–12, 31–32, 40–41, 87, 110, 159; US support for, 73, 100, 180

imperial amnesia, 14, 196n15
imperial unknowing, 14–16, 27, 32–39, 43, 52–55, 58–59, 92, 162, 190–91

INDEX 237

International Organization for Migration (IOM), 3–4, 68–69, 139, 153–57, 175
interpreters. *See* translators/interpreters
Iran-Iraq War, 13, 50, 72–73, 112, 180
"Iraqi allies" (who assisted US forces), 21, 30, 131–32, 155–62, 170–77, 190. *See also* collaboration, with US forces
Iraqi National Library and Archives, 85, 87
Islamic State, 13, 18
Islamophobia, 12, 118, 157, 178, 180–82, 208n6. *See also* racism
Israel, 17, 91–92, 110, 116. *See also* refugees: Palestinian

James, Erica, 144
Janna, 108–9
Johnson, Kirk, 170, 174, 176–77
Jordan, 17–19, 93, 98–101, 115, 130
journalists, murder of in war, 27, 33, 45, 61–62, 74–82, 200n4. *See also* Committee to Protect Journalists

Karrar, 101, 121, 153–57, 160, 173, 175, 177–79, 181–83
Kennedy, Edward, 157
Khedoori, Rachel, 77
Khosravi, Shahram, 93
Khoury, Dina, 187
kidnapping, 58, 70, 82, 97, 131, 138, 140, 167, 169, 179
knowledge production, 25, 34, 49, 52, 62, 67, 71, 87. *See also* imperial unknowing
Kumar, Deepa, 180
Kurds, 55, 73, 86, 97
Kuwait, 12, 73

labor migration, 112–13, 201n2
Latif, 89–90, 106
Lawrence, T. E., 37
League of Nations mandate system, 11, 13, 40, 53–54, 199n15
Lebanon, 17–18, 93, 99, 115, 130
Li, Darryl, 93, 164
Lina, 143, 161
List Project to Resettle Iraqi Allies, 170–71, 173, 181
local integration, 22, 117, 126, 132

Makiya, Kanan, 86–87, 159
Malkki, Liisa, 88
Manning, Chelsea, 79
Mariam, 122, 137–38, 141–42, 144, 150–51

Massey, Doreen, 106
material support for terrorism, 70, 171, 179–180
Mazen, 27–28, 61–63, 67, 71–76, 79–82, 87–88, 191
McGranahan, Carole, 37
Mercer, Kobena, 182, 187
Merry, Sally, 166–67
Miklaszewski, Jim, 31
Mills, Charles, 35–36
Mohammed, 138–41, 148, 150–51
Morsi, Mohamed, 154, 208n2
Mubarak, Hosni, 104
Muslim ban (Trump administration executive order), 178, 180, 188, 211n1
Muslim Brotherhood Party, 154, 208n2

Naber, Nadine, 182, 187
Najla, 138–41, 148, 151
Nakba, 91, 115, 202n5. *See also* refugees: Palestinian
Napolitano, Janet, 178
Nasr City, 24, 106, 204n13
Nasser, Gamal, 92, 116
Naza, 97–98
Nguyen, Mimi Thi, 13
Nisour Square massacre, 163, 189, 209n10
Non-Aligned Movement, 92
Nour-Eldeen, Namir, 79
Nugent, Christopher, 170

Office of Refugee Resettlement, 185
O'Kane, Maggie, 77
Operation Iraqi Freedom, 11, 40
Organization of African Unity Convention (1969), 92

Palestine. *See* refugees: Palestinian
Palestine Hotel, 78
Pan-Arabism, 18, 112–13
Pentagon, 31, 55, 78, 87, 163
Petraeus, David, 49
pillaging, 85–87, 201n11
Powell, Colin, 40, 80, 93
Protsyuk, Taras, 78
Pursley, Sara, 54, 199n15

Quadri, Zaynab, 163

racialization, 20, 35–37, 47, 106, 136, 157–58, 167, 176–77, 180, 188
racism, 10, 20, 64, 106, 118, 157, 166, 188, 190. *See also* Islamophobia

238   INDEX

Ramsay, Georgina, 125, 151
refugee camps, 18–19, 104–7, 196n17, 204n11
Refugee Convention (1951), 18, 59, 91–93, 107, 127, 202n4
Refugee Crisis in Iraq Act, 65, 126, 131–32, 155, 157, 170–71. *See also* Direct Access Program
refugee legal aid, 25–26, 59, 63, 65–68, 81, 83
refugees: Afghan, 155, 177, 189–90, 210n15; characterizations of as "burdens," 7, 128, 136, 145–46, 156; European, 91, 92, 201n3; Palestinian, 17, 91–93, 95, 105, 108, 115–16, 202nn5,6; Sudanese, 117, 148; Syrian, 154. *See also* refugee status; resettlement; resettlement process
refugee status: determination of, 69, 90, 92–98, 117, 132, 142, 145; international law and, 69, 90, 95, 105, 136, 179; refusal of, 28, 89–90, 95, 106; role of testimonies and interviews in, 68–72, 83, 140–41, 144. *See also* refugees; resettlement; resettlement process
refugee studies, 9–10, 64
repatriation, 17, 20, 22, 29, 87, 117, 126, 128, 136
resettlement, 7, 22–23, 29–30, 126; ambivalence toward, 21–23, 125–26, 130, 142–44, 146–47, 149, 205n2; financial costs of, 3–4, 14; scarcity of, 22, 101, 119–20, 129, 143, 150–51; third-country, 21, 23, 29, 65, 69, 99, 102, 117, 119, 136. *See also* refugees; refugee status; resettlement process
Resettlement Legal Aid Project (RLAP), 26–27, 63–64, 69, 83, 89–90, 99, 127, 137, 139, 175, 184–85
resettlement process, 21–23, 70–72, 123–30, 132, 137–41; duration of, 23, 129, 134, 136, 140, 154, 156, 174; opacity of, 119, 125, 145, 147–48, 156; uncertainties of, 1–3, 125–27, 134–35, 140, 148, 156, 185–86. *See also* refugees; refugee status; resettlement
Reuters, 78–79
Rice, Condoleezza, 41, 171
Route Irish/Airport Road (*Tariiq al-maTaar*), 45–47
Rove, Karl, 42
Rumsfeld, Donald, 31–33, 40, 80, 197n8

Sadat, Anwar, 92, 112
Sadek, Sara, 19
Saif, 123–25, 127, 148, 151
Saleh, Zainab, 7, 37, 195n9
Salloum, 105
Samar, 100
sanctions, 5–6, 13, 50, 108, 112, 193n2, 194n6
Sara, 100–101
sectarian identities, 55–57, 118–19. *See also* Kurds; Shias; Sunnis
sectarian violence, 2, 6, 17, 56–58, 96, 101
Sedgwick, Eve, 15, 34–35
Selod, Saher, 180
September 11 attacks, 11–12, 31, 40–41, 131, 176, 180
Shams, 21, 99, 101–2, 104, 121, 134, 161, 184–87, 191
Shias, 2, 55–58, 72, 118
6th of October City, 24, 103, 106, 118, 123, 133, 204n13
Soleimani, Qasem, 13
special immigrant visa program, 210n15
State Department, 13, 55
Stevenson, Lisa, 59
Stillman, Sarah, 162
Stoler, Ann, 37, 196n15
Stone, Nomi, 48–49
Suad, 33, 39, 98–99
Sunnis, 2, 55–58
Suskind, Ron, 41–42
Syria, 17–19, 93, 97, 99–101, 115, 130
Syrian Civil War, 13, 18, 154

Tahrir Square, 103–4, 153, 203n10
Taussig, Michael, 36, 59
testimony, in refugee legal aid, 65, 68–72, 140; before US Congress, 171–173
Titan Corp, 168
torture, 15, 93, 138, 140, 173, 197n5
translators/interpreters, 48–51, 131, 139, 164–68, 199n14, 209n11, 210n15. *See also* collaboration, with US forces; "Iraqi allies" (who assisted US forces)
Trouillot, Michel-Rolph, 71, 84
Trump, Donald, 178, 188–89, 209n10
Tuck, Eve, 10

Um Muhammad, 1–7, 16, 19, 121, 184, 191
Um Nasim, 133–34

UNHCR Resettlement Handbook, 132, 138, 142, 145
United Kingdom, colonial rule of Iraq, 7, 13, 40, 53–54, 199n15
United Nations, 12
United Nations High Commissioner for Refugees (UNHCR), 16, 22, 29, 68–69, 92–94, 105, 126–27, 132, 136, 139; Cairo office of, 103, 117, 123–25; memorandum of understanding with Egypt, 92–93
United Nations Relief and Works Agency, 115–16, 136
United Nations Security Council, 11, 40, 93
United States, resettlement in, 21, 101, 128–29, 170–72, 175, 182, 188. *See also* Direct Access Program; Refugee Crisis in Iraq Act

United States Agency for International Development (USAID), 170–72, 174, 176

Vang, Ma, 36, 38, 84
Vietnam War, 8, 129, 132, 181, 190
visas, 94, 97–99, 101, 109, 112, 174–75, 210n15

weapons of mass destruction, 11, 32, 40, 54, 73, 93
WikiLeaks, 79
World War I, 53
World War II, 35, 37, 91

Yousef, 168–69, 179, 181

Zahra, 3–4

CALIFORNIA SERIES IN PUBLIC ANTHROPOLOGY

1. *Twice Dead: Organ Transplants and the Reinvention of Death*, by Margaret Lock

2. *Birthing the Nation: Strategies of Palestinian Women in Israel*, by Rhoda Ann Kanaaneh (with a foreword by Hanan Ashrawi)

3. *Annihilating Difference: The Anthropology of Genocide*, edited by Alexander Laban Hinton (with a foreword by Kenneth Roth)

4. *Pathologies of Power: Health, Human Rights, and the New War on the Poor*, by Paul Farmer (with a foreword by Amartya Sen)

5. *Buddha Is Hiding: Refugees, Citizenship, the New America*, by Aihwa Ong

6. *Chechnya: Life in a War-Torn Society*, by Valery Tishkov (with a foreword by Mikhail S. Gorbachev)

7. *Total Confinement: Madness and Reason in the Maximum Security Prison*, by Lorna A. Rhodes

8. *Paradise in Ashes: A Guatemalan Journey of Courage, Terror, and Hope*, by Beatriz Manz (with a foreword by Aryeh Neier)

9. *Laughter Out of Place: Race, Class, Violence, and Sexuality in a Rio Shantytown*, by Donna M. Goldstein

10. *Shadows of War: Violence, Power, and International Profiteering in the Twenty-First Century*, by Carolyn Nordstrom

11. *Why Did They Kill? Cambodia in the Shadow of Genocide*, by Alexander Laban Hinton (with a foreword by Robert Jay Lifton)

12. *Yanomami: The Fierce Controversy and What We Can Learn from It*, by Robert Borofsky

13. *Why America's Top Pundits Are Wrong: Anthropologists Talk Back*, edited by Catherine Besteman and Hugh Gusterson

14. *Prisoners of Freedom: Human Rights and the African Poor*, by Harri Englund

15. *When Bodies Remember: Experiences and Politics of AIDS in South Africa*, by Didier Fassin

16. *Global Outlaws: Crime, Money, and Power in the Contemporary World*, by Carolyn Nordstrom

17. *Archaeology as Political Action*, by Randall H. McGuire

18. *Counting the Dead: The Culture and Politics of Human Rights Activism in Colombia*, by Winifred Tate

19. *Transforming Cape Town*, by Catherine Besteman

20. *Unimagined Community: Sex, Networks, and AIDS in Uganda and South Africa*, by Robert J. Thornton

21. *Righteous Dopefiend*, by Philippe Bourgois and Jeff Schonberg

22. *Democratic Insecurities: Violence, Trauma, and Intervention in Haiti*, by Erica Caple James

23. *Partner to the Poor: A Paul Farmer Reader*, by Paul Farmer, edited by Haun Saussy (with a foreword by Tracy Kidder)

24. *I Did It to Save My Life: Love and Survival in Sierra Leone*, by Catherine E. Bolten

25. *My Name Is Jody Williams: A Vermont Girl's Winding Path to the Nobel Peace Prize*, by Jody Williams

26. *Reimagining Global Health: An Introduction*, by Paul Farmer, Jim Yong Kim, Arthur Kleinman, and Matthew Basilico

27. *Fresh Fruit, Broken Bodies: Migrant Farmworkers in the United States*, by Seth M. Holmes, PhD, MD

28. *Illegality, Inc.: Clandestine Migration and the Business of Bordering Europe*, by Ruben Andersson

29. *To Repair the World: Paul Farmer Speaks to the Next Generation*, by Paul Farmer

30. *Blind Spot: How Neoliberalism Infiltrated Global Health*, by Salmaan Keshavjee (with a foreword by Paul Farmer)

31. *Driving after Class: Anxious Times in an American Suburb*, by Rachel Heiman

32. *The Spectacular Favela: Violence in Modern Brazil*, by Erika Robb Larkins

33. *When I Wear My Alligator Boots: Narco-Culture in the U.S. Mexico Borderlands*, by Shaylih Muehlmann

34. *Jornalero: Being a Day Laborer in the USA*, by Juan Thomas Ordóñez

35. *A Passion for Society: How We Think about Human Suffering*, by Iain Wilkinson and Arthur Kleinman

36. *The Land of Open Graves: Living and Dying on the Migrant Trail*, by Jason De León (with photographs by Michael Wells)

37. *Living with Difference: How to Build Community in a Divided World,* by Adam Seligman, Rahel Wasserfall, and David Montgomery

38. *Scratching Out a Living: Latinos, Race, and Work in the Deep South,* by Angela Stuesse

39. *Returned: Going and Coming in an Age of Deportation,* by Deborah A. Boehm

40. *They Leave Their Kidneys in the Fields: Injury, Illness, and Illegality among U.S. Farmworkers,* by Sarah Bronwen Horton

41. *Threshold: Emergency Responders on the U.S.-Mexico Border,* by Ieva Jusionyte

42. *Lives in Transit: Violence and Intimacy on the Migrant Journey,* by Wendy A. Vogt

43. *The Myth of International Protection: War and Survival in Congo,* by Claudia Seymour

44. *Dispossessed: How Predatory Bureaucracy Foreclosed on the American Middle Class,* by Noelle Stout

45. *Deported to Death: How Drug Violence Is Changing Migration on the US–Mexico Border,* by Jeremy Slack

46. *Getting Wrecked: Women, Incarceration, and the American Opioid Crisis,* by Kimberly Sue

47. *Making Global MBAs: The Culture of Business and the Business of Culture,* by Andrew Orta

48. *The United States of War: A Global History of America's Endless Conflicts, from Columbus to the Islamic State,* by David Vine

49. *The Spirit Ambulance: Choreographing the End of Life in Thailand,* by Scott Stonington

50. *Scripting Death: Stories of Assisted Dying in America,* by Mara Buchbinder

51. *Worlds of Care: The Emotional Lives of Fathers Caring for Children with Disabilities,* by Aaron J. Jackson

52. *All I Eat Is Medicine: Going Hungry in Mozambique's AIDS Economy,* by Ippolytos Kalofonos

53. *The Succeeders: How Immigrant Youth Are Transforming What It Means to Belong in America,* by Andrea Flores

54. *Fighting to Breathe: Race, Toxicity, and the Rise of Youth Activism in Baltimore,* by Nicole Fabricant

55. *Textures of Terror: The Murder of Claudina Isabel Velásquez and Her Father's Quest for Justice,* by Victoria Sanford

56. *Nuclear Ghost: Atomic Livelihoods in Fukushima's Gray Zone,* by Ryo Morimoto

57. *Exit Wounds: How America's Guns Fuel Violence across the Border,* by Ieva Jusionyte

58. *Call the Mothers: Searching for Mexico's Disappeared in the War on Drugs,* by Shaylih Muehlmann

59. *Dawn Rose on a Dead Body: Armed Violence and Poppy Farming in Mexico,* by Adèle Blazquez, translated by H. W. Randolph

60. *Collateral Damages: Tracing the Debts and Displacements of the Iraq War,* by Nadia El-Shaarawi

Founded in 1893,
UNIVERSITY OF CALIFORNIA PRESS
publishes bold, progressive books and journals
on topics in the arts, humanities, social sciences,
and natural sciences—with a focus on social
justice issues—that inspire thought and action
among readers worldwide.

The UC PRESS FOUNDATION
raises funds to uphold the press's vital role
as an independent, nonprofit publisher, and
receives philanthropic support from a wide
range of individuals and institutions—and from
committed readers like you. To learn more, visit
ucpress.edu/supportus.

www.ingramcontent.com/pod-product-compliance
Ingram Content Group UK Ltd.
Pitfield, Milton Keynes, MK11 3LW, UK
UKHW041023250325
456687UK00001B/1